A Guide To Critical Reviews

Part II

The Musical From Rodgers-And-Hart to
Lerner-And-Loewe

by

James M. Salem

The Scarecrow Press, Inc.

Metuchen, N. J.   1967

Dedication

To Betsy

Foreword

This bibliography is the second part of a projected four volume series under the general title of A Guide to Critical Reviews. Part II varies somewhat in format from Part I, American Drama from O'Neill to Albee, in that the spectacle of the musical seemed to require that set designers, costume designers, choreographers, and directors be included with authors, lyricists, and composers. The format for Part III, Modern British and Continental Drama, and Part IV, The Screenplay, will be similar to that of Part I.

The purpose of Part II is to provide a bibliography of critical reviews of the Broadway musical from 1920-1921 to the 1964-1965 season. The beginning date was selected because 1920 was the year of Poor Little Ritz Girl, the first show in which Richard Rodgers and Lorenz Hart worked together. From 1920-1921 to 1927-1928 I have selected musicals by the following composers and lyricists: Irving Berlin, Rudolf Friml, George Gershwin, Oscar Hammerstein II, Lorenz Hart, Victor Herbert, Jerome Kern, Cole Porter, Richard Rodgers, Sigmund Romberg, and Vincent Youmans. Beginning with the 1920-1929 season, I have included all musicals which opened on Broadway. I have tried to avoid listing operettas, though some works considered operas (Porgy and Bess, The Consul, Regina) have consciously been included. The only revival of a play originally produced before 1920 that has been included is The Red Mill (1906), which ran for 531 performances during the 1945-1946 season.

Much of the statistical information has been taken from The Best Plays of the Year and the Yearbook of the Drama in America series (New York: Dodd, Mead and Company), edited by Burns Mantle and others. In addition, the following volumes are valuable for statistical, historical, or general reference information:

Baral, Robert. Revue: A Nostalgic Reprise of the Great Broadway Period. New York: Fleet Publishing Co., 1962.

Chapman, John, ed. Broadway's Best (series from 1957-1960). Garden City, New York: Doubleday and Co., 1957-1960.

_____. Theatre (series from 1953-1956). New York: Random House, 1953-1956.

Ewen, David. "American Musical Comedies and Plays," pp. 751-935 in Lubbock, Mark. The Complete Book of Light Opera. New York: Appleton-Century-Crofts, 1962.

_____. Complete Book of the American Musical Theater. New York: Henry Holt, 1958.

_____. The Story of America's Musical Theater. Philadelphia and New York: The Chilton Co., 1961.

Green, Stanley. The World of Musical Comedy. New York: Ziff-Davis Pub. Co., 1960.

Lewine, Richard and Alfred Simon. Encyclopedia of Theatre Music. New York: Random House, 1961.

Smith, Cecil. Musical Comedy in America. New York: Theatre Art Books, 1950.

The organization of Part II is by Broadway seasons, with musicals presented alphabetically for each season. A complete index of titles appears last; indexes of authors, composers, and lyricists; of directors, designers, and choreographers; and of original authors and works are also provided. It should be noted that the number of performances for plays from 1963-1964 and 1964-1965 was not always available.

The reviews cited in this volume are those which appeared in American or Canadian periodicals and in the New York Times, and which, therefore, should be available in most libraries. Reviews in other New York newspapers have not been indexed, but New York Theatre Critics' Reviews, which has reprinted reviews from the New York Journal-American, Daily News, Post, Mirror, World Telegram and Sun, Herald Tribune, and

<u>Times</u> since 1940, has been cited for plays produced after that date.

I should like to acknowledge a debt of gratitude to Professor Bernard Benstock, a colleague, for his valuable advice; Mr. Herbert Mansfield, Drama Librarian, Cleveland Public Library; Mrs. Linda Eisenhut, a member of the Kent State University Library staff; and Pat and Harlan Stone, my typist and proofreader. I am also indebted to my wife, Donna McLernon Salem, for her help and patience throughout the project.

James M. Salem

Kent, Ohio
June, 1966

Table of Contents

Season of 1920-1921 (Selected)

Follies (1920) (see Ziegfeld Follies)

The Girl in the Spotlight (56 performances)
book: Richard Bruce (Robert B. Smith)
music: Victor Herbert
lyrics: Richard Bruce (Robert B. Smith)
staging: George W. Lederer
opened: July 12, 1920
    Dramatic Mirror page 97, Jul 17, 1920
    Independent 103:97, Jul 24, 1920
    New York Clipper 68:23, Jul 21, 1920
    New York Times page 9, Jul 13, 1920
    Theatre Magazine 32:105, Sep 1920

Hitchy-Koo 1920 (71 performances)
book: Glen MacDonough and Anne Caldwell
music: Jerome Kern
lyrics: Glen MacDonough and Anne Caldwell
staging: Ned Wayburn
opened: October 19, 1920
    Dramatic Mirror page 777, Oct 23, 1920
    New York Clipper 68:28, Oct 27, 1920
    New York Times page 11, Oct 20, 1920
    Theatre Magazine 33:29, Jan 1921

June Love (50 performances)
book: Otto Harbach and W. H. Post, adapted
                from a story by Charlotte Thompson
music: Rudolph Friml
lyrics: Brian Hooker
staging: George Vivian
opened: April 25, 1921
    Dramatic Mirror 83:733, Apr 30, 1921
    Life (New York) 77:688, May 12, 1921
    New York Clipper 69:19, Apr 27, 1921
    New York Times page 20, Apr 26, 1921
    Theatre Magazine 34:30, Jul 1921

Love Birds (105 performances)
book: Edgar Allen Woolf
music: Sigmund Romberg
lyrics: Ballard McDonald
staging: Edgar MacGregor and Julian Alfred
opened: March 15, 1921
    Dramatic Mirror 83:505+, Mar 19, 1921
    Life (New York) 77:464, Mar 31, 1921
    New York Clipper 69:19, Mar 23, 1921
    New York Times page 12, Mar 16, 1921
    Theatre Magazine 33:342, May 1921

Poor Little Ritz Girl (119 performances)
book: Lew Fields and George Campbell
music: Richard Rodgers and Sigmund Romberg
lyrics: Lorenz Hart and Alex Gerber
staging: Ned Wayburn
opened: July 27, 1920
    Dramatic Mirror page 23, Aug 4, 1920
    New York Clipper 68:25, Jun 2, 1920
    New York Times page 7, Jul 29, 1920
    Theatre Magazine 32:187, Oct 1920

Sally (570 performances)
book: Guy Bolton
music: Jerome Kern and Victor Herbert
lyrics: Clifford Grey, additional lyrics by B.
                G. DeSylva
staging: Edward Royce
opened: December 21, 1920
    Catholic World 167:268, Jun 1948
    Dramatic Mirror page 1241, Dec 25, 1920
    New Republic 118:34, May 31, 1948
    New York Clipper 68:18, Dec 29, 1920
    New York Theatre Critics' Reviews 1948:271+
    New York Times page 16, Dec 22, 1920
                page 20, Sep 11, 1921
                page 20, Mar 30, 1922
                page 31, May 7, 1948
    New Yorker 24:48+, May 15, 1948
    Newsweek 31:90, May 17, 1948
    Theatre Arts 32:14, Jun 1948
    Theatre Magazine 33:178, Mar 1921

Time 51:88, May 17, 1948

Tickle Me (207 performances)
book: Otto Harbach, Oscar Hammerstein II,
                 Frank Mandel
music: Herbert Stothart
lyrics: Otto Harbach, Oscar Hammerstein II,
                 Frank Mandel
staging: William Collier
choreography: Bert French
opened: August 17, 1920
   Dramatic Mirror page 327, Aug 21, 1920
   New York Clipper 68:19, Aug 25, 1920
   New York Times page 12, Aug 19, 1920
   Theatre Magazine 32:240, Oct 1920

Two Little Girls in Blue (135 performances)
book: Fred Jackson
music: Vincent Youmans and Paul Lannin
lyrics: Arthur Francis (Ira Gershwin)
staging: Ned Wayburn
opened: May 3, 1921
   Dramatic Mirror 83:715, Apr 23, 1921
                  83:769, May 7, 1921
   New York Clipper 69:19, May 11, 1921
   New York Times page 10, May 4, 1921
   Theatre Magazine 34:30, Jul 1921

Ziegfeld Follies (123 performances)
sketches: W. C. Fields, George V. Hobart, James
                 Montgomery
music and   Irving Berlin, Dave Stamper, Gene Buck,
   lyrics: Joseph McCarthy, Harry Tierney,
                 Victor Herbert
staging: Edward Royce
opened: June 22, 1920
   New York Clipper 68:14, Mar 17, 1920
   New York Times page 14, Jun 23, 1920

                 Season of 1921-1922 (Selected)
Blossom Time (592 performances)
book: Dorothy Donnelly, adapted from the
                 German Das Dreimädlerhaus
music: Sigmund Romberg, derived from Franz
                      13

Schubert themes
lyrics: Dorothy Donnelly
opened: September, 29, 1921
   Dramatic Mirror 84:520, Oct 8, 1921
   Life (New York) 78:18, Oct 20, 1921
   New York Clipper 69:17, Oct 12, 1921
   New York Theatre Critics' Reviews 1943:286+
   New York Times page 10, Sep 30, 1921
                    VI, page 1, Oct 9, 1921
                    page 26, Aug 8, 1922
                    page 14, May 22, 1923
                    page 15, May 20, 1924
                    VIII, page 8, Mar 7, 1926
                    page 32, Mar 5, 1931
                    VIII, page 4, Mar 22, 1931
                    page 12, Dec 27, 1938
                    page 21, Sep 6, 1943
   Theatre Magazine 34:388, Dec 1921

The Blue Kitten (140 performances)
book: Otto Harbach and William Cary Duncan,
               adapted from Le Chassear de Chez
               Maxim's
music: Rudolf Friml
lyrics: Otto Harbach and William Cary Duncan
staging: Edgar Selwyn, Leon Errol, Julian
               Mitchell
opened: January 13, 1922
   Dramatic Mirror 95:63, Mar 1922
   Life (New York) 79:18, Feb 2, 1922
   New York Clipper 69:20, Jan 11, 1922
   New York Times page 9, Jan 14, 1922
   Theatre Magazine 35:264, Apr 1922

The Blushing Bride (144 performances)
book: Cyrus Wood, based on a play by Edward
               Clark
music: Sigmund Romberg
lyrics: Cyrus Wood
staging: Frank Smithson
opened: Feb 6, 1922
   New York Clipper 70:20, Feb 15, 1922
   New York Times page 12, Feb 7, 1922

14

Theatre Magazine 35:262, Apr 1922

Bombo (219 performances)
book: Harold Atteridge
music: Sigmund Romberg
lyrics: Harold Atteridge
staging: J. C. Huffman
opened: October 6, 1921
    Dramatic Mirror 84:556, Oct 15, 1921
    New York Clipper 69:26, Oct 12, 1921
    New York Times page 20, Oct 7, 1921
                VI, page 1, Oct 30, 1921
                page 22, May 15, 1923
    Theatre Magazine 34:424, Dec 1921

Follies (1921) (See Ziegfeld Follies)

George White's Scandals (97 performances)
book: "Bugs" Baer and George White
music: George Gershwin
lyrics: Arthur Jackson
staging: George White
opened: July 11, 1921
    Life (New York) 78:18, Jul 28, 1921
    New York Clipper 69:25, Jul 20, 1921
    New York Times page 14, Jul 12, 1921

Good Morning Dearie (265 performances)
book: Anne Caldwell
music: Jerome Kern
lyrics: Anne Caldwell
staging: Edward Royce
opened: November 1, 1921
    Dramatic Mirror 84:665, Nov 5, 1921
    Life (New York) 78:18, Nov 17, 1921
    New York Clipper 69:20, Nov 9, 1921
    New York Times page 20, Nov 2, 1921
                VI, page 1, Nov 27, 1921
    Theatre Magazine 35:32, Jan 1922

Music Box Revue (440 performances)
book: Irving Berlin
music: Irving Berlin
lyrics: Irving Berlin

15

staging: Hassard Short
choreography: I. Tarasoff
opened: September 22, 1921
  Independent 107:856, Dec 31, 1921
  Life (New York) 78:18, Oct 20, 1921
  New York Times page 18, Sep 23, 1921
  Theatre Magazine 34:387, Dec 1921

Scandals (1921) (see George White's Scandals)

Ziefeld Follies of 1921 (119 performances)
book: Willard Mack, Raymond Hitchcock,
                 Channing Pollock, Ralph Spence
music: Victor Herbert, Rudolf Friml, Dave
                 Stamper
lyrics: Gene Buck, B. G. DeSylva, Brian Hooker
staging: Edward Royce
opened: June 21, 1921
  Life (New York) 78:18, Jul 14, 1921
  New York Clipper 69:20, Jun 29, 1921
  New York Times page 8, Jun 17, 1921
                page 10, Jun 22, 1921
  Theatre Magazine 34:168, Sep 1921

           Season of 1922-1923 (Selected)

The Bunch and Judy (63 performances)
book: Anne Caldwell and Hugh Ford
music: Jerome Kern
lyrics: Anne Caldwell
staging: Fred G. Latham
opened: November 28, 1922
  New York Clipper 70:20, December 6, 1922
  New York Times VIII, page 6, Nov 12, 1922
                page 20, Nov 29, 1922
  Theatre Magazine 37:20, Feb 1923

Cinders (31 performances)
book: Edward Clark
music: Rudolf Friml
lyrics: Edward Clark
staging: Edward Royce
opened: April 3, 1923

New York Clipper 71:14, Apr 11, 1923
New York Times page 22, Apr 4, 1923

Daffy Dill (71 performances)
book: Guy Bolton and Oscar Hammerstein II
music: Herbert Stothart
lyrics: Oscar Hammerstein II
staging: Julian Mitchell
opened: August 22, 1922
    New York Clipper 70:20, Aug 30, 1922
    New York Times page 14, Aug 23, 1922
    Theatre Magazine 36:228, Oct 1922

The Dancing Girl (126 performances)
book: Harold Atteridge
music: Sigmund Romberg and Alfred Goodman
lyrics: Harold Atteridge
staging: J. C. Huffman
opened: January 24, 1923
    New York Clipper 71:14, Feb 7, 1923
    New York Times page 16, Jan 25, 1923

George White's Scandals of 1922 (88 performances)
book: George White, W C Fields, Andy Rice
music: George Gershwin
lyrics: B. G. DeSylva and Ray Goetz
staging: George White
opened: August 28, 1922
    New York Clipper 70:20, Sep 6, 1922
    New York Times page 10, Aug 29, 1922

Music Box Revue (273 performances)
book: Irving Berlin
music: Irving Berlin
lyrics: Irving Berlin
staging: Hassard Short
choreography: William Seabury
opened: October 23, 1922
    Forum 68:1037-8, Dec 1922
    New York Times page 18, Oct 24, 1922

Orange Blossoms (95 performances)
book: Fred deGresac, based on Fred deGresac

17

and Francis deCroisset's play The
Marriage of Kitty
music: Victor Herbert
lyrics: B. G. deSylva
staging: Edward Royce
opened: September 19, 1922
  New York Clipper 70:20, Oct 25, 1922
  New York Times page 18, Sep 20, 1922

Our Nell (40 performances)
book: A. E. Thomas and Brian Hooker
music: George Gershwin and William Daly
lyrics: Brian Hooker
staging: W. H. Gilmore, Edgar MacGregor,
              Julian Mason
opened: December 4, 1922
  New York Clipper 70:20, Dec 13, 1922
  New York Times page 24, Dec 5, 1922

Passing Show (118 performances)
book: Harold Atterdige
music: Jean Schwartz and Sigmund Romberg
lyrics: Harold Atteridge
staging: J. C. Huffman
opened: June 14, 1923   .
  Life (New York) 82:20, Jul 5, 1923
  New York Clipper 71:30, Jun 20, 1923
  New York Times page 24, Jun 15, 1923
  Theatre Magazine 38:15, Aug 1923

Queen of Hearts (39 performances)
book: Frank Mandel and Oscar Hammerstein II
music: Lewis Gensler and Dudley Wilkinson
lyrics: Oscar Hammerstein II and Sydney
              Mitchell
staging: Ira Hards
opened: October 10, 1922
  New York Clipper 70:20, Oct 18, 1922
  New York Times page 22, Oct 11, 1922
  Theatre Magazine 32:31, Midsummer 1920
                   36:377, Dec 1922

Scandals (1922) (see George White's Scandals)

18

Springtime of Youth (68 performances)
book: Based on the book by Bernhauser and
                Rudolph Schanzer
music: Sigmund Romberg and Walter Rollo
lyrics: Harry B. Smith, Cyrus Wood, Matthew
                Woodward
staging: John Harwood
opened: October 26, 1922
   New York Clipper 70:20, Nov 1, 1922
   New York Times page 15, Oct 27, 1922

Wildflower (477 performances)
book: Otto Harbach and Oscar Hammerstein II
music: Herbert Stothart and Vincent Youmans
lyrics: Otto Harbach and Oscar Hammerstein II
staging: Oscar Eagle
choreography: David Bennett
opened: February 7, 1923
   Life (New York) 81:18, Mar 1, 1923
   New York Clipper 71:14, Feb 14, 1923
   New York Times page 17, Feb 8, 1923
   Theatre Magazine 38:16, Aug 1923

Season of 1923-1924 (Selected)

Follies (1923) (see Ziegfeld Follies)

George White's Scandals (168 performances)
book: George White and W. K. Wells
music: George Gershwin
lyrics: B. G. DeSylva, Ray Goetz, Ballard
                McDonald
staging: George White
opened: June 18, 1923
   Life (New York) 82:20, Jul 12, 1923
   New York Clipper 71:14, Jun 27, 1923
   New York Times page 22, Jun 19, 1923
   Theatre Magazine 38:15, Aug 1923

Innocent Eyes (126 performances)
book: Harold Atteridge
music: Sigmund Romberg and Jean Schwartz
lyrics: Harold Atteridge and Tot Seymour

opened: May 20, 1924
   New York Times page 22, May 21, 1924
                  page 8, Aug 22, 1924
   Theatre Magazine 40:15, Aug 1924

Lollipop (152 performances)
book: Zelda Sears
music: Vincent Youmans
lyrics: Zelda Sears and Walter DeLeon
opened: January 21, 1924
   New York Times page 15, Jan 22, 1924
                 VIII, page 2, Apr 27, 1924
   Theatre Magazine 39:68, Mar 1924

Mary Jane McKane (151 performances)
book: William Cary Duncan and Oscar
                 Hammerstein II
music: Herbert Stothart and Vincent Youmans
lyrics: William Cary Duncan and Oscar
                 Hammerstein II
opened: December 25, 1923
   New York Times page 13, Dec 26, 1923
   Theatre Magazine 39:19, Mar 1924

Music Box Revue (273 performances)
book: Irving Berlin
music: Irving Berlin
lyrics: Irving Berlin
staging: Hassard Short
opened: September 22, 1923
   New York Times page 5, Sep 24, 1923
   Theatre Magazine 38:54, Nov 1923

Scandals (1923) (see George White's Scandals)

Sitting Pretty (95 performances)
book: Guy Bolton and P. G. Wodehouse
music: Jerome Kern
lyrics: P. G. Wodehouse
opened: April 8, 1924
   New York Times VIII, page 2, Mar 30, 1924
                 page 24, Apr 9, 1924
   Theatre Magazine 39:19, Jun 1924

Stepping Stones (241 performances)
book: Anne Caldwell and R. H. Burnside
music: Jerome Kern
lyrics: Anne Caldwell
staging: R. H. Burnside
opened: November 6, 1923
    New York Times page 14, Nov 7, 1923
                        VI, page 8, Dec 16, 1923
                        page 8, Aug 20, 1924
    Theatre Magazine 39:58, Jan 1924

Sweet Little Devil (120 performances)
book: Frank Mandel and Laurence Schwab
music: George Gershwin
lyrics: B. G. DeSylva
opened: January 21, 1924
    New York Times page 15, Jan 22, 1924
    Theatre Magazine 39:70, Mar 1924

Ziegfeld Follies (233 performances)
sketches: Eddie Cantor and Gene Buck
music: Victor Herbert, Rudolf Friml, Dave
                 Stamper
lyrics: Gene Buck
staging: Ned Wayburn
opened: October 20, 1923
    Dial 76:618, Dec 1923
    Life (New York) 82:18, Nov 8, 1923
    New York Times page 17, Oct 22, 1923
                        VIII, page 1, Oct 28, 1923
                        page 25, Mar 18, 1924
    Theatre Magazine 38:19, Dec 1923

                Season of 1924-1925 (Selected)

Annie Dear (103 performances)
book: Clare Kummer
music: Sigmund Romberg and Clare Kummer
lyrics: Clifford Grey and Clare Kummer
staging: Edward Royce
opened: November 4, 1924
    New York Times page 25, Nov 5, 1924
    Theatre Magazine 41:22, Jan 1925

Artists and Models (261 performances)
sketches: Harry Wagstaff Gribble
music: Sigmund Romberg and J. Fred Coots
lyrics: Clifford Grey and Sam Coslow
staging: J. J. Shubert
opened: October 15, 1924
    New York Times page 33, Oct 16, 1924
                  page 16, Jun 17, 1925
                  page 16, Jun 25, 1925
    Theatre Magazine 40:64, Dec 1924

Dear Sir (15 performances)
book: Edgar Selwyn
music: Jerome Kern
lyrics: Howard Dietz
opened: September 23, 1924
    New York Times page 21, Sep 24, 1924

The Dream Girl (117 performances)
book: Rida Johnson Young and Harold
                  Atteridge
music: Victor Herbert
lyrics: Rida Johnson Young and Harold
                  Atteridge
opened: August 20, 1924
    New York Times page 12, Aug 21, 1924
    Theatre Magazine 40:16, Oct 1924

Garrick Gaieties (211 performances)
sketches: Benjamin Kaye, Louis Sorin, Sam Jaffe,
                  Newman Levy, Morrie Ryskind
music: Richard Rodgers
lyrics: Lorenz Hart
additional
 lyrics: Benjamin Kaye, Louis Sorin, Sam
                  Jaffe, Newman Levy, Morrie Ryskind
staging: Philip Loeb
choreography: Herbert Fields
opened: June 8, 1925
    Nation 121:77, Jul 8, 1925
    New York Times page 12, May 18, 1925
                  page 16, Jun 9, 1925
    Theatre Magazine 44:15, Aug 1926

22

George White's Scandals (171 performances)
book: William K. Wells and George White
music: George Gershwin
lyrics: B. G. DeSylva
staging: George White
opened: June 30, 1924
   Life (New York) 84:18, Jul 31, 1924
   New York Times page 16, Jul 1, 1924
   Theatre Magazine 40:15, Sep 1924

Greenwich Village Follies (180 performances)
music: Cole Porter
lyrics: Cole Porter, Irving Caesar, John
                 Murray Anderson
staging: John Murray Anderson
opened: September 16, 1924
   Life (New York) 84:18, Oct 9, 1924
   New York Times page 19, Feb 11, 1924
                 page 16, Sep 17, 1924
                 VII, page 1, Sep 21, 1924
                 VIII, page 1, Sep 28, 1924
   Theatre Magazine 40:64, Nov 1924

Lady Be Good (330 performances)
book: Guy Bolton and Fred Thompson
music: George Gershwin
lyrics: Ira Gershwin
opened: December 1, 1924
   Canadian Magazine 64:164-6, Jul 1925
   New York Times page 23, Dec 2, 1924
                 VII, page 1, Dec 28, 1924
   Theatre Magazine 41:16, Feb 1925

Louie the 14th (319 performances)
book: Arthur Wimperis, adapted from the
                 German
music: Sigmund Romberg
lyrics: Arthur Wimperis
staging: Edward Royce
opened: . March 3, 1925
   Life (New York) 85:22, Apr 2, 1925
   New York Times page 17, Mar 4, 1925
   Theatre Magazine 41:32, May 1925

Music Box Revue (184 performances)
book: Irving Berlin
music: Irving Berlin
lyrics: Irving Berlin
staging: John Murray Anderson
opened: December 1, 1924
   New York Times page 23, Dec 2, 1924
   Theatre Magazine 41:19, Feb 1925

The Passing Show of 1924 (106 performances)
book: Harold Atteridge
music: Sigmund Romberg and Jean Schwartz
lyrics: Harold Atteridge and Alex Gerber
staging: J. C. Huffman
opened: September 3, 1924
   New York Times page 13, Sep 4, 1924
   Theatre Magazine 40:16, Nov 1924

Rose-Marie (311 performances)
book: Otto Harbach and Oscar Hammerstein II
music: Rudolf Friml and Herbert Stothart
lyrics: Otto Harbach and Oscar Hammerstein II
staging: Paul Dickey
choreography: David Bennett
opened: September 2, 1924
   Canadian Magazine 64:164-6, Jul 1925
   New York Times VII, page 1, Aug 24, 1924
                    page 12, Sep 3, 1924
                    page 16, Mar 21, 1925
                    page 26, Dec 4, 1925
                    page 17, Apr 1, 1926
                    page 1, Sep 14, 1926
                    page 16, Sep 16, 1926
                    page 19, Jan 25, 1927
                    II, page 8, Apr 17, 1927
                    VII, page 2, May 8, 1927
                    page 15, Jul 17, 1927
                    page 23, Mar 31, 1928
                    IX, page 2, Apr 29, 1928
   Theatre Magazine 40:16, Nov 1924

Scandals (1924) (see George White's Scandals)

Tell Me More (32 performances)
book: Fred Thompson and William K. Wells
music: George Gershwin
lyrics: B. G. DeSylva and Ira Gershwin
opened: April 13, 1925
    Life (New York) 85:18, May 28, 1925
    New York Times page 27, Apr 14, 1925
    Theatre Magazine 42:16, Jul 1925

Season of 1925-1926 (Selected)

The City Chap (72 performances)
book: James Montgomery, adapted from
                     Winchell Smith's The Fortune Hunter
music: Jerome Kern
lyrics: Anne Caldwell
staging: R. H. Burnside
opened: October 26, 1925
    New York Times page 21, Oct 27, 1925

The Cocoanuts (377 performances)
book: George S. Kaufman
music: Irving Berlin
lyrics: Irving Berlin
staging.   Sammy Lee and Oscar Eagle
opened: December 8, 1925
    Dial 80:166-7, Feb 1926
    New York Times page 30, Dec 9, 1925
                     IX, page 1, Dec 13, 1925
                     VIII, page 1, Apr 18, 1926
                     page 27, May 17, 1927
    Vogue 67:61+, Feb 1, 1926

Dearest Enemy (286 performances)
book: Herbert Fields
music: Richard Rodgers
lyrics: Lorenz Hart
staging: John Murray Anderson
opened: September 18, 1925
    Literary Digest 87:31-2, Oct 19, 1925
    New York Times page 9, Sep 19, 1925
    Theatre Magazine 42:44, Dec 1925

Garrick Gaieties (174 performances)
sketches: Benjamin Kaye, Newman Levy, Herbert
                  Fields, Philip Loeb
music: Richard Rodgers
lyrics: Lorenz Hart
staging: Philip Loeb
choreography: Herbert Fields
opened: May 10, 1926
   Bookman 63:588-9, Jul 1926
   New York Times page 25, May 11, 1926
                  VII, page 1, Jun 13, 1926
   Theatre Magazine 44:15, Aug 1926

George White's Scandals (424 performances)
sketches: George White and William K. Wells
music: Ray Henderson
lyrics: B. G. DeSylva and Lew Brown
staging: George White
opened: June 14, 1926
   Life (New York) 88:21, Jul 8, 1926
   New York Times page 23, Jun 15, 1926
                  VII, page 1, Jul 3, 1927
   Theatre Magazine 44:15, Aug 1926
   Vogue 68:71+, Sep 1, 1926

The Girl Friend (409 performances)
book: Herbert Fields
music: Richard Rodgers
lyrics: Lorenz Hart
staging: Lew Fields
opened: March 17, 1926
   New York Times page 26, Mar 18, 1926
                  page 8, Dec 14, 1927
   Theatre Magazine 43:50, Jun 1926

No! No! Nanette! (321 performances)
book: Otto Harbach and Frank Mandel
music: Vincent Youmans
lyrics: Otto Harbach and Irving Caesar
staging: H. H. Frazee
opened: September 16, 1925
   New York Times page 17, Mar 12, 1925
                  page 28, Nov 17, 1925

                    page 23, Mar 8, 1926
                    page 25, Oct 18, 1926
                    VIII, page 2, Feb 26, 1928
    Theatre Magazine 44:17, Aug 1926
    Time 47:90, Apr 15, 1946

Scandals (1926) (see George White's Scandals)

Sunny (517 performances)
book: Otto Harbach and Oscar Hammerstein II
music: Jerome Kern
lyrics: Otto Harbach and Oscar Hammerstein II
opened: September 22, 1925
    New Republic 44:303, Nov 11, 1925
    New York Times page 29, Sep 10, 1925
                    page 22, Sep 23, 1925
                    page 29, Dec 6, 1926
    Theatre Magazine 42:16, Dec 1925

Tip-Toes (194 performances)
book: Guy Bolton and Fred Thompson
music: George Gershwin
lyrics: Ira Gershwin
staging: John Harwood
opened: December 28, 1925
    New York Times page 20, Dec 29, 1925
                    page 27, Sep 1, 1926
    Vogue 67:102+, Feb 15, 1926

                Season of 1926-1927 (Selected)

Betsy (39 performances)
book: Irving Caesar and David Freedman
music: Richard Rodgers
lyrics: Lorenz Hart
staging: William Anthony McGuire and Sammy
                Lee
opened: December 28, 1926
    New York Times page 24, Dec 29, 1926

Cherry Blossoms (56 performances)
book: Harry B. Smith, adapted from
                Benrimo and Harrison Rhodes' The

27

                    Willow Tree
music: Sigmund Romberg
lyrics: Harry B. Smith
staging: Lew Morton
opened: March 28, 1927
    New York Times page 22, Mar 29, 1927

Criss Cross (206 performances)
book: Otto Harbach and Anne Caldwell
music: Jerome Kern
lyrics: Otto Harbach and Anne Caldwell
staging: R. H. Burnside
opened: October 12, 1926
    New York Times page 20, Oct 13, 1926

Hit the Deck (352 performances)
book: Herbert Fields, adapted from the play
                    Shore Leave
music: Vincent Youmans
lyrics: Leo Robin and Clifford Grey
staging: Lew Fields, Seymour Felix, Alexander
                    Leftwich
opened: April 25, 1927
    Life (New York) 89:23, May 19, 1927
    New York Times page 32, Apr 26, 1927
                    page 8, Dec 14, 1927
                    IX, page 4, Apr 1, 1928
                    IX, page 2, Apr 29, 1928
    Theatre Magazine 46:18, Jul 1927
    Vogue 69:75+, Jun 15, 1927

Lucky (71 performances)
book: Harry Ruby, Bert Kalmar, Otto
                    Harbach
music: Harry Ruby and Jerome Kern
lyrics: Harry Ruby, Bert Kalmar, Otto
                    Harbach
staging: Hassard Short
opened: March 22, 1927
    Life (New York) 89:31, Apr 7, 1927
    New Republic 50:196, Apr 6, 1927
    New York Times page 24, Mar 25, 1927
    Theatre Magazine 45:26, Jun 1927

Vogue 69:118+, May 15, 1927

No Foolin' (Ziegfeld's American Revue of 1926)
(Glorifying the American Girl) (108 performances)
sketches: J. P. McEvoy and James Barton
music: Rudolf Friml and James Hanley
lyrics: Gene Buck and Irving Caesar
staging: Florenz Ziegfeld and John Boyle
opened: June 24, 1926
    Bookman 64:86, Sep 1926
    New York Times page 25, June 25, 1926
    Theatre Magazine 44:23, Aug 1926

Oh, Kay (256 performances)
book: Guy Bolton and P. G. Wodehouse
music: George Gershwin
lyrics: Ira Gershwin
staging: John Harwood and Sammy Lee
opened: November 8, 1926
    New York Times page 31, Nov 9, 1926
                   page 33, Sep 22, 1927
                   page 29, Jan 3, 1928
                   page 37, Apr 18, 1960
                   page 28, Jun 29, 1960
    Vogue 69:100+, Jan 1, 1927

Oh, Please (75 performances)
book: Otto Harbach and Anne Caldwell, based
                   on a story by Maurice Hennequin
                   and Pierre Veber
music: Vincent Youmans
lyrics: Clifford Grey and Leo Robin
staging: Hassard Short
opened: December 17, 1926
    Life (New York) 89:21, Jan 13, 1927
    New York Times page 24, Dec 22, 1926

Peggy-Ann (333 performances)
book: Herbert Fields
music: Richard Rodgers
lyrics: Lorenz Hart
staging: Robert Milton
opened: December 27, 1926

New York Times page 16, Dec 28, 1926
                    VII, page 2, Mar 27, 1927
                    VII, page 1, Jul 3, 1927
                    VIII, page 4, Jan 29, 1928

The Wild Rose (61 performances)
book: Otto Harbach and Oscar Hammerstein II
music: Rudolf Friml
lyrics: Otto Harbach and Oscar Hammerstein II
staging: William J. Wilson
opened: October 20, 1926
   New York Times page 23, Oct 21, 1926
   Theatre Magazine 45:16, Jan 1927

              Season of 1927-1928 (Selected)

A Connecticut Yankee (418 performances)
book: Herbert Fields, adapted from Mark
                Twain's novel A Connecticut Yankee
                in King Arthur's Court
music: Richard Rodgers
lyrics: Lorenz Hart
staging: Alexander Leftwich
opened: November 3, 1927
   Catholic World 158:395, Jun 1944
   Life (New York) 90:23, Nov 24, 1927
   New York Theatre Critics' Reviews 1943:219+
   New York Times VIII, page 1, Oct 9, 1927
                    page 24, Nov 4, 1927
                    VIII, page 2, Jun 10, 1928
                    page 30, Nov 18, 1943
                    II, page 1, Nov 21, 1943
   Theatre Arts 28:17-18, Jan 1944
   Theatre Magazine 47:49, Feb 1928

Follies (1927) (see Ziegfeld Follies)

Funny Face (244 performances)
book: Fred Thompson and Paul Gerard Smith
music: George Gershwin
lyrics: Ira Gershwin
opened: November 22, 1927
   New York Times page 28, Nov 23, 1927

                        30

X, page 2, Dec 4, 1927
page 22, Nov 9, 1928
Theatre Magazine 47:58, Feb 1928
Vogue 71:118, Jan 15, 1928

Golden Dawn (184 performances)
book: Otto Harbach and Oscar Hammerstein II
music: Emmerich Kalman and Herbert Stothart
lyrics: Otto Harbach and Oscar Hammerstein II
staging: Dave Bennett and Reginald Hammer-
                  stein
opened: November 30, 1927
   New York Times VIII, page 4, Oct 2, 1927
                 page 32, Dec 1, 1927

The Love Call (88 performances)
book: Harry B. Smith and Edward Locke
music: Sigmund Romberg
lyrics: Harry B. Smith
staging: J. C. Huffman
opened: October 24, 1927
   New York Times page 33, Oct 25, 1927
                 IX, page 5, Nov 13, 1927

My Maryland (312 performances)
book: Dorothy Donnelly
music: Sigmund Romberg
lyrics: Dorothy Donnelly
staging: J. J. Shubert
opened: September 12, 1927
   New York Times page 37, Sep 13, 1927
   Time 49:40, Mar 17, 1947
   Vogue 70:126, Nov 1, 1927

Present Arms (155 performances)
book: Herbert Fields
music: Richard Rodgers
lyrics: Lorenz Hart
staging: Alexander Leftwich
opened: April 26, 1928
   New York Times page 16, Apr 27, 1928
   Outlook 149:185, May 30, 1928
   Theatre Magazine 47:65, Jun 1928

Vogue 71:74, Jun 15, 1928

Rosalie (335 performances)
book: William Anthony McGuire and Guy
                Bolton
music: George Gershwin and Sigmund Romberg
· lyrics: P. G. Wodehouse and Ira Gershwin
staging: Florenz Ziegfeld, Seymour Felix,
                William A. McGuire
opened: January 10, 1928
    New York Times IX, page 2, Dec 18, 1927
                    page 26, Jan 11, 1928
    Outlook 148:344, Feb 29, 1928
    Vogue 71:114, Mar 1, 1928

She's My Baby (71 performances)
book: Bert Kalmar and Harry Ruby
music: Richard Rodgers
lyrics: Lorenz Hart
staging: Edward Royce
opened: January 3, 1928
    Life (New York) 91:21, Jan 19, 1928
    New York Times page 22, Jan 4, 1928

Show Boat (572 performances)
book: Oscar Hammerstein II, adapted from
                Edna Ferber's novel
music: Jerome Kern
lyrics: Oscar Hammerstein II
staging: Florenz Ziegfeld and Zeke Cohan
sets: Joseph Urban
costumes: John Harkrider
choreography: Sammy Lee
opened: December 27, 1927
    America 91:227+, May 22, 1954
            95:351, Jul 7, 1956
            97:490, Aug 10, 1957
    Arts and Decoration 37:43+, Sep 1932
    Catholic World 162:456, Feb 1946
                   168:77, Oct 1948
                   179:308, Jul 1954
                   183:388, Aug 1956
                   185:469, Sep 1957

Commonweal 74:379, Jul 7, 1961
Cosmopolitan 120:32-3+, Apr 1946
Life (New York) 91:21, Jan 12, 1928
Life 20:71-2+, Jan 28, 1946
Musical America 74:10, May 1954
Nation 134:660, Jun 8, 1932
      162:138, Feb 2, 1946
      178:390, May 1, 1954
      192: 378, Apr 29, 1961
New Republic 119:38, Sep 27, 1948
New York Theatre Critics' Reviews 1946:496+
New York Times page 26, Dec 28, 1927
               VIII, page 1, Jan 8, 1928
               page 31, May 4, 1928
               page 9, May 5, 1928
               page 14, Dec 26, 1928
               VIII, page 4, Dec 30, 1928
               page 22, May 20, 1932
               VIII, page 5, May 29, 1932
               II, page 5, Jul 3, 1938
               page 17, Jan 7, 1946
               II, page 1, Jan 13, 1946
               II, page 1, Feb 24, 1946
               II, page 1, Jun 23, 1946
               VI, page 25, Sep 30, 1946
               VI, page 23, Dec 8, 1946
               page 33, Sep 9, 1948
               II, page 1, Sep 19, 1948
               page 19, Jun 6, 1952
               page 44, May 6, 1954
               page 28, Oct 29, 1954
               page 27, Nov 1, 1954
               page 16, Jun 22, 1956
               page 30, Jun 28, 1957
               page 32, Apr 13, 1961
New Yorker 21:40+, Jan 12, 1946
       30:116, Apr 17, 1954
Newsweek 27:77, Jan 14, 1946
      43:52-3, Apr 19, 1954
Outlook 148:265, Feb 15, 1928
Saturday Review 29:30-2, Jan 26, 1946
           37:27, Apr 24, 1954
Stage 9:4, Jul 1932

Theatre Arts 27:246, Apr 1943
                30:138, Mar 1946
Theatre Magazine 47:58, Feb 1928
                47:35, May 1928
Time 47:47, Jan 14, 1946
Vogue 71:122, Feb 15, 1928

White Eagle (48 performances)
book: Brian Hooker and W. H. Post, based
                   on Edwin Milton Royle's The Squaw
                   Man
music: Rudolf Friml
lyrics: Brian Hooker and W. H. Post
staging: Richard Boleslavsky
opened: December 26, 1927
    New York Times page 24, Dec 27, 1927
                VIII, page 4, Jan 1, 1928
    Theatre Magazine 47:62, Mar 1928

Ziegfeld Follies (167 performances)
sketches: Harold Atteridge and Eddie Cantor
music: Irving Berlin
lyrics: Irving Berlin
staging: Florenz Ziegfeld, Sammy Lee, Zeke
                   Colvan
opened: August 16, 1927
    Independent 119:362, Oct 8, 1927
    Life 90:21, Sep 1, 1927
    New York Times VII, page 1, Aug 7, 1927
                page 27, Aug 17, 1927
                VII, page 1, Aug 28, 1927
                VII, page 2, Sep 18, 1927
    Vogue 70:96, Oct 15, 1927

Season of 1928-1929

Americana (12 performances)
book: J. P. McEvoy
music: Roger Wolfe Kahn
lyrics: J. P. McEvoy and Irving Caesar
staging: J. P. McEvoy
opened: October 30, 1928
    New York Times X, page 1, Oct 14, 1928

page 28, Oct 31, 1928
page 34, Nov 6, 1928

Animal Crackers (191 performances)
book: George S. Kaufman and Morrie
                Ryskind
music: Harry Ruby
lyrics: Bert Kalmar
opened: October 23, 1928
  Life (New York) 92:14, Nov 16, 1928
  New Republic 56:351-2, Nov 14, 1928
  New York Times page 26, Oct 24, 1928
                page 26, Apr 7, 1929
  Theatre Magazine 52:47, Nov 1930

Billie (112 performances)
book: George M. Cohan, adapted from his
                play Broadway Jones
music: George M. Cohan
lyrics: George M. Cohan
staging: Edward Royce and Sam Forrest
opened: October 1, 1928
  New York Times page 34, Oct 2, 1928
  Theatre Magazine 49:60, Jan 1929

Boom Boom (72 performances)
book: Fanny Todd Mitchell, adapted from
                Louis Verneuil's Mlle. Ma Mere
music: Werner Janssen
lyrics: Mann Holiner and J. Keirn Brennan
staging: George Marion
opened: January 28, 1929
  New York Times page 26, Jan 29, 1929
  Theatre Magazine 49:47, May 1929

Chee-Chee (31 performances)
book: Lew Fields
music: Richard Rodgers
lyrics: Lorenz Hart
staging: Alexander Leftwich and Jack Haskell
opened: September 25, 1928
  Life (New York) 92:19, Oct 28, 1928
  New York Times page 25, Sep 26, 1928

Cross My Heart (64 performances)
book: Daniel Kusell
music: Harry Tierney
lyrics: Joseph McCarthy
staging: Sammy Lee
opened: September 17, 1928
   New York Times page 32, Sep 18, 1928
   Theatre Magazine 48:48, Nov 1928

Fioretta (111 performances)
book: Earl Carroll, adapted by Charlton
               Andrews
music: George Babgy and G. Romilli
lyrics: George Babgy and G. Romilli
staging: Earl Carroll
opened: February 5, 1929
   Life (New York) 93:24, Mar 15, 1929
   New York Times VIII, page 4, Jan 6, 1929
                 page 30, Feb 6, 1929
   Theatre Magazine 49:46, Apr 1929

Follow Thru (403 performances)
book: Laurence Schwab and B. G. DeSylva
music: Ray Henderson
lyrics: B. G. DeSylva and Lew Brown
staging: Edgar Mac Gregor and Donald
               Oenslager
opened: January 9, 1929
   Theatre Magazine 49:51, Mar 1929
   Vogue 73:72, Mar 2, 1929

Gambols (1929) (see Ned Wayburn's Gambols)

George White's Scandals (230 performances)
sketches: William K. Wells and George White
lyrics: William K. Wells and George White
music: Ray Henderson
lyrics: B. G. DeSylva and Lew Brown
staging: George White
opened: July 2, 1928
   Life (New York) 92:16, Jul 19, 1928
   New York Times page 19, Jul 3, 1928
   Outlook 149:467, Jul 18, 1928

Theatre Magazine 48:36, Sep 1928
                48:41, Oct 1928
Vogue 72:74-5, Sep 1, 1928

Good Boy (235 performances)
book: Otto Harbach, Oscar Hammerstein II,
                   Henry Myers
music: Herbert Stothart and Harry Ruby
lyrics: Bert Kalmar
staging: Reginald Hammerstein
choreography: Busby Berkeley
opened: September 5, 1928
   Life (New York) 92:17, Sep 28, 1928
   New York Times page 23, Sep 6, 1928
   Theatre Magazine 48: 78, Dec 1928

Grand Street Follies of 1929 (93 performances)
book: Agnes Morgan
music: Arthur Schwartz and Max Ewing,
                   additional numbers by William Irwin
                   and Serge Walter
lyrics: Agnes Morgan
staging: Agnes Morgan
choreography: Dave Gould
opened: May 1, 1929
   Bookman 64:85-6, Sep 1926
   Independent 117:133, Jul 31, 1926
   Life (New York) 88:21, Jul 8, 1926
                   93:20, May 31, 1929
   Nation 121:77, Jul 8, 1925
          124:616-17, Jun 1, 1927
          128:594-5, May 15, 1929
   New Republic 51:70, Jun 8, 1927
                59:24-5, May 22, 1929
   New York Times IX, page 2, Apr 18, 1929
                   page 20, May 2, 1929
                   IX, page 1, May 12, 1929
                   page 34, Jun 19, 1929
   Outlook 152:191, May 29, 1929
   Theatre Magazine 42:15+, Sep 1925
                    50:42, Jul 1929
   Vogue 70:98, Jul 15, 1927
         74:92+, Jul 6, 1929

Hello Daddy (198 performances)
book: Herbert Fields
music: Jimmy McHugh
lyrics: Dorothy Fields
staging: John Murray Anderson
opened: December 26, 1928
   Life (New York) 93:21, Jan 25, 1929
   New York Times page 26, Dec 27, 1928

Hello Yourself (87 performances)
book: Walter DeLeon
music: Richard Myers
lyrics: Leo Robin
staging: Clarke Silvernail
opened: October 30, 1928
   New York Times page 28, Oct 31, 1928
   Theatre Magazine 49:60, Jan 1929

Hold Everything (413 performances)
book: B. G. DeSylva and John McGowan
music: Ray Henderson
lyrics: B. G. DeSylva, Lew Brown
choreography: Jack Haskell and Sam Rose
opened: October 10, 1928
   Life (New York) 92:21, Nov 2, 1928
   New York Times page 24, Oct 11, 1928
   Theatre Magazine 49:60, Jan 1929

Just A Minute (80 performances)
book: H. C. Greene
music: Harry Archer
lyrics: Walter O'Keefe
staging: H. C. Greene
opened: October 8, 1928
   New York Times page 34, Oct 9, 1928

Lady Fingers (132 performances)
book: Eddie Buzzell, based on Owen Davis's
                 Easy Come, Easy Go
music: Joseph Meyer
lyrics: Edward Eliscu
staging: Lew Levenson
opened: January 31, 1929

New York Times VIII, page 2, Jan 13, 1929
                page 22, Feb 1, 1929

The Little Show (321 performances)
book: Howard Dietz
music: Arthur Schwartz; additional songs by
                 Kay Swift and Ralph Rainger
lyrics: Howard Dietz
staging: Dwight Deere Wiman
choreography: Danny Dare
opened: April 30, 1929
  Life (New York) 93:22, May 24, 1929
  Nation 131:331, Sep 24, 1930
  New Republic 59:25, May 22, 1929
  New York Times page 28, May 1, 1929
                  IX, page 1, May 12, 1929
                  IX, page 2, May 12, 1929
                  IX, page 7, Jul 14, 1929
  Theatre Magazine 50:42, Jul 1929
  Vogue 74:57+, Jul 6, 1929

Music In May (80 performances)
book: Fanny Todd Mitchell, adapted from the
                 original by Heinz Merley and Kurt
                 Breuer
music: Emile Berte and Maury Rubens
lyrics: J. Kiern Brennan
staging: Lew Morton and Stanley Logan
opened: April 1, 1929
  New York Times IX, page 1, Jan 7, 1929
                  page 29, Apr 2, 1929

Ned Wayburn's Gambols (31 performances)
book: Ned Wayburn
music: Walter G. Samuels
lyrics: Morrie Ryskind
staging: Ned Wayburn
opened: January 15, 1929
  New York Times page 22, Jan 16, 1929

The New Moon (509 performances)
book: Oscar Hammerstein II, Frank Mandel,
                 Laurence Schwab

music: Sigmund Romberg
lyrics: Oscar Hammerstein II
staging: Bobby Connelly
choreography: Bobby Connelly
opened: September 19, 1928
   Life (New York) 92:28, Oct 5, 1928
   New York Times VII, page 4, Sep 2, 1928
                    page 33, Sep 20, 1928
                    IX, page 2, Sep 20, 1928
                    IX, page 2, Sep 15, 1929
                    page 16, May 18, 1944
                    page 26, Jul 5, 1950
                    page 13, Jul 1, 1955
   New Yorker 20:40, May 27, 1944
   Theatre Magazine 48:80, Nov 1928
   Vogue 72:100, Nov 10, 1928

A Night in Venice (175 performances)
music: Lee Davis and Maury Rubens
lyrics: J. Keirn Brennan and Moe Jaffe
staging: Lew Morton and Thomas A. Hart
choreography: Busby Berkeley
opened: May 21, 1929
   Life (New York) 93:26, Jun 14, 1929
   New York Times IX, page 1, May 12, 1929
                    page 30, May 22, 1929
   Outlook 152:234, Jun 5, 1929
   Theatre Magazine 50:42, Sep 1929

Paris (195 performances)
book: Martin Brown
music: Cole Porter; additional words and
                    music by Ray Goetz and Walter Kollo
lyrics: Cole Porter; additional words and
                    music by Ray Goetz and Walter Kollo
staging: W. H. Gilmore
opened: October 8, 1928
   Life (New York) 92:17, Oct 28, 1928
   New York Times VIII, page 4, Apr 8, 1928
                    page 34, Oct 9, 1928
   Outlook 150:1124, Nov 7, 1928
   Theatre Magazine 48:81, Dec 1928

Pleasure Bound (136 performances)
book: Harold Atteridge, Max and Nathaniel
                Lief
music: Muriel Pollock
lyrics: Harold Atteridge, Max and Nathaniel
                Lief
staging: Lew Morton
choreography: Busby Berkeley
opened: February 18, 1929
    New York Times IX, page 2, Feb 10, 1929
                    page 22, Feb 19, 1929
                    X, page 4, Mar 17, 1929
        Theatre Magazine 49:47, Apr 1929

Polly (15 performances)
book: Guy Bolton and George Middleton,
                based on David Belasco's Polly with
                a Past
music: Herbert Stothart and Phillip Charig
lyrics: Irving Caeser
staging: Jack Haskell
opened: January 8, 1929
    Life (New York) 93:28, Jan 25, 1929
    New York Times X, page 2, Nov 11, 1028
                    page 28, Jan 9, 1929

Rainbow (29 performances)
book: Laurence Stallings and Oscar Hammer-
                stein II
music: Vincent Youmans
lyrics: Oscar Hammerstein II
staging: Oscar Hammerstein II
choreography: Busby Berkeley
opened: November 21, 1928
    New York Times page 1, Nov 4, 1928
                    page 25, Nov 22, 1928
                    IX, page 1, Dec 16, 1928
        Theatre Magazine 49:60, Jan 1929

Say When (24 performances)
book: Calvin Brown, based on Amelie Rives
                and Gilbert Emery's Love in a Mist
music: Jesse Greer

41

lyrics: Raymond Klages
staging: Bertram Harrison and Max Scheck
opened: June 26, 1928
  Golden Book Magazine 21:30a, Feb 1935
  New York Times page 29, Jun 27, 1928
  Outlook 149:425, Jul 11, 1928

Scandals (1928) (see George White's Scandals)

Spring is Here (104 performances)
book: Owen Davis
music: Richard Rodgers
lyrics: Lorenz Hart
staging: Alexander Leftwich
choreography: Bobby Connelly
opened: March 11, 1929
  Catholic World 129:205-6, May 1929
  Life (New York) 93:25, Apr 12, 1929
  New York Times page 26, Mar 12, 1929
  Outlook 151:508, Mar 27, 1929
  Theatre Magazine 49:47, May 1929
  Vogue 73:150, May 11, 1929

Three Cheers (210 performances)
book: Anne Caldwell and R. H. Burnside
music: Raymond Hubbell
lyrics: Anne Caldwell
staging: R. H. Burnside
choreography: Dave Bennett
opened: October 15, 1928
  New York Times page 28, Oct 16, 1928
                  IX, page 1, Oct 21, 1928
  Outlook 150:1086, Oct 31, 1928
  Theatre Magazine 48:46, Dec 1928
  Vogue 72:146, Dec 8, 1928

Treasure Girl (68 performances)
book: Fred Thompson and Vincent Lawrence
music: George Gershwin
lyrics: Ira Gershwin
staging: Bertram Harrison
choreography: Bobby Connelly
opened: November 8, 1928

Life (New York) 92:11, Nov 12, 1928
New York Times page 22, Nov 9, 1928
Outlook 150:1195, Nov 21, 1928
Vogue 72:82, Dec 22, 1928

Ups-A-Daisy (64 performances)
book: Clifford Grey and Robert A. Simon
music: Lewis E. Gensler
lyrics: Clifford Grey
staging: Edgar MacGregor and Earl Lindsey
opened: October 8, 1928
   Life (New York) 92:21, Nov 2, 1928
   New York Times page 34, Oct 9, 1928

Vanities (203 performances)
assembled by: Earl Carroll
music: Louis Alter, Jesse Greer, Richard
               Whiting
lyrics: Ray Klages and Joe Burke
staging: Earl Carroll
opened: August 6, 1928
   Life (New York) 92:12, Aug 23, 1928
   New Republic 56:21-2, Aug 22, 1928
   New York Times page 25, Aug 7, 1928
   Outlook 149:670, Aug 22, 1928
   Vogue 72:66, Sep 29, 1928

White Lilacs (136 performances)
book: Harry B. Smith, based on the life of
               Frederic Chopin from the German
               original by Sigurd Johannsen
music: Karl Hajos, based on melodies by
               Chopin
lyrics: Harry B. Smith
staging: J. J. Shubert and George Marion
opened: September 10, 1928
   New York Times page 31, Sep 11, 1928
               X, page 5, Oct 14, 1928
               page 25, Oct 22, 1928
   Theatre Magazine 48:80, Nov 1928

Whoopee (379 performances)
book: William Anthony McGuire, based on

43

Owen Davis's The Nervous Wreck
music: Walter Donaldson
lyrics: Gus Kahn
staging: William Anthony McGuire and Seymour
                Felix
opened: December 4, 1928
    New York Times X, page 2, Nov 11, 1928
                  X, page 4, Dec 9, 1928
                  page 18, Sep 23, 1929
    Outlook 152:434, Jul 10, 1929
    Theatre Magazine 49:50, Feb 1929

Season of 1929-1930

Almanac (1929) (See Murray Anderson's Almanac)

Artists and Models (55 performances)
book: adapted from the English musical
                comedy Dear Love
music: Harold Stern
lyrics: Ernie Golden   •
staging: Frank Smithson and Pal'mere Brandeaux
opened: June 10, 1930
    Life (New York) 95:16, Jul 11, 1930
    New York Times page 33, Jun 11, 1930
    Theatre Magazine 52:25, Aug 1930

Bamboola (34 performances)
book: D. Frank Marcus
music: D. Frank Marcus and Bernard Maltin
lyrics: D. Frank Marcus
staging: Sam Rose
opened: June 26, 1929
    New York Times page 17, Jun 27, 1929

Broadway Nights (40 performances)
music: Sam Timberg, Lee David, Maurice
                Rubens
lyrics: Moe Jaffe
staging: Busby Berkeley and Stanley Logan
opened: July 15, 1929
    New York Times page 23, Jul 16, 1929
    Outlook 152:595, Aug 7, 1929

44

Cape Cod Follies (30 performances)
book: Stewart Baird
music: Alexander Fogarty
lyrics: Stewart Baird
staging: Stewart Baird
choreography: John Lonergan
opened: September 18, 1929
    New York Times page 37, Sep 19, 1929
    Outlook 153:192, Oct 2, 1929

Change Your Luck (17 performances)
book: Garland Howard
music: J. C. Johnson
lyrics: Garland Howard
staging: Cleon Throckmorton
choreography: Lawrence Deas and Speedy Smith
opened: June 6, 1930
    New Republic 63:150-1, Jun 25, 1930
    New York Times page 10, Jun 7, 1930

Earl Carroll's Sketch Book (400 performances)
book: Eddie Cantor and E. Y. Harburg
music: Jay Gorney and Vincent Rose
lyrics: E. Y. Harburg, Charles and Harry
                 Tobias
staging: Earl Carroll, Edgar MacGregor,
                 Leroy Prinz
opened: July 1, 1929
    New Republic 59:262, Jul 24, 1929
    New York Times page 33, Jul 2, 1929
    Outlook 152:471, Jul 17, 1929
    Theatre Magazine 50:39, Sep 1929

Fifty Million Frenchmen (254 performances)
book: Herbert Fields
music: Cole Porter
lyrics: Cole Porter
staging: Edgar M. Wooley (Monty Woolley)
choreography: Larry Ceballos
opened: November 27, 1929
    Nation 129:756-8, Dec 18, 1929

New York Times page 34, Nov 28, 1929
                X, page 1, Dec 8, 1929
                VIII, page 1, Jan 5, 1930
Theatre Magazine 51:49, Jan 1930
Vogue 75:100, Jan 18, 1930

Flying High (357 performances)
book: B. G. DeSylva, John McGowan
music: Ray Henderson
lyrics: B. G. DeSylva and Lew Brown
staging: Edward Clark Lilley
choreography: Bobby Connelly
opened: March 3, 1930
Life (New York) 95:18, Mar 28, 1930
New York Times VIII, page 4, Feb 9, 1930
                page 24, Mar 4, 1930
                VIII, page 4, Mar 30, 1930
Outlook 155:29, May 7, 1930
Theatre Magazine 51:43, May 1930
Vogue 75:126, May 10, 1930

Garrick Gaieties (158 performances)
sketches: H. Alexander, Carroll Carroll, Ruth
                 Chorpenning, Leopoldine Damrosch,
                 Gretchen Damrosch Finletter, Landon
                 Herrick, Sterling Holloway, Benja-
                 min M. Kaye, Newman Levy, Dorian
                 Otvos, Louis M. Simon
music: Marc Blitzstein, Aaron Copland,
                 Vernon Duke, Basil Fomeen, Harold
                 Goldman, William Irwin, Ned Lehak,
                 Everett Miller, Peter Nolan, Willard
                 Robison, Charles M. Schwab, Kay
                 Swift
lyrics: Allen Boretz, Ruth Chorpenning, Ira
                 Gershwin, E. Y. Harburg, Sterling
                 Holloway, Paul James, Ronald Jeans,
                 Malcolm McComb, John Mercer,
                 Henry Myers, Louis M. Simon,
                 Josiah Titzell
staging: Philip Loeb and Olin Howard
opened: June 4, 1930
Life (New York) 95:16, Jun 27, 1930

New Republic 63:127-8, Jun 18, 1930
New York Times page 29, Jun 5, 1930
            VIII, page 1, Jun 22, 1930
Theatre Magazine 52:24, Aug 1930

George White's Scandals (161 performances)
book: W. K. Wells and George White
music: Cliff Friend, George White, Irving
                   Caesar
lyrics: Cliff Friend, George White, Irving
                   Caesar
staging: George White
choreography: Florence Wilson
opened: September 23, 1929
   Life (New York) 94:26, Oct 18, 1929
   New York Times page 29, Sep 24, 1929
                   page 21, Dec 25, 1929
   Theatre Magazine 50:70, Nov 1929

Great Day (36 performances)
book: William Cary Duncan and John Wells
music: Vincent Youmans
lyrics: William Rose
staging: R. H. Burnside and Frank M. Gillespie
choreography: LeRoy Prinz
opened: October 17, 1929
   New York Times VIII, page 1, Jun 9, 1929
                   page 24, Oct 18, 1929
                   IX, page 1, Nov 3, 1929
   Theatre Magazine 50:16, Oct 1929

Heads Up (144 performances)
book: John McGowan and Paul Gerard Smith
music: Richard Rodgers
lyrics: Lorenz Hart
staging: George Hale
opened: November 11, 1929
   New York Times page 34, Nov 12, 1929
                   IX, page 14, Nov 17, 1929
   Theatre Magazine 51:49, Jan 1930
   Vogue 75:60+, Jan 18, 1930

Hot Chocolates (219 performances)

book: Andy Razaf
music: Thomas Waller and Harry Brooks
staging: Leonard Harper
opened: June 20, 1929
    New York Times page 17, Jun 21, 1929
    Outlook 152:553, Jul 31, 1929
    Theatre Magazine 50:43, Aug 1929

The International Revue (95 performances)
book: Nat N. Dorfman and Lew Leslie
music: Jimmy McHugh
lyrics: Dorothy Fields
staging: Lew Leslie and E. C. Lilley
choreography: Busby Berkeley and Harry Crosley
opened: February 25, 1930
    Life (New York) 95:18, Mar 28, 1930
    New York Times VIII, page 4, Feb 9, 1930
                     page 22, Feb 26, 1930
    Outlook 155:109, May 21, 1930

Jonica (40 performances)
book: Dorothy Heyward and Moss Hart
music: Joseph Meyer
lyrics: William Moll
staging: William B. Friedlander
choreography: Pal'mere Brandeaux
opened: April 7, 1930
    New York Times VIII, page 2, Mar 30, 1930
                     page 27, Apr 8, 1930
    Outlook 154:671, Apr 23, 1930

Keep It Clean (16 performances)
book: Jimmy Duffy and Will Morrissey
music: Lester Lee, Jimmy Duffy, Harry
                     Archer, Benny Ryan, James Hanley,
                     Clarence Gaskill, Violinsky, Charles
                     Tobias, Harry Converse
staging: Will Morrissey and Russell Markert
opened: June 24, 1929
    New York Times page 35, Jun 25, 1929

Murray Anderson's Almanac (69 performances)
book: Noel Coward, Rube Goldberg, Ronald

```
                    Jeans, Paul Gerard Smith, Harry
                    Ruskin, John McGowan, Peter Arno,
                    Ed Wynn
music:              Milton Agar and Henry Sullivan
lyrics:             Jack Yellen
staging:            John Murray Anderson, William
                    Holbrook, Harry Ruskin
opened:             August 14, 1929
   Life (New York) 94:24, Sep 6, 1929
   New York Times VIII, page 1, Aug 4, 1929
                    page 20, Aug 15, 1929
   Outlook 152:712, Aug 28, 1929
   Theatre Magazine 50:42, Oct 1929
```

Ripples (55 performances)
```
book:               William Anthony McGuire
music:              Oscar Levant and Albert Sirmay
lyrics:             Irving Caesar and Graham John
staging:            William Anthony McGuire
choreography:       William Holbrook
opened:             February 11, 1930
   Life (New York) 95:18, Mar 14, 1930
   New York Times VIII, page 2, Feb 2, 1930
                    page 26, Feb 12, 1930
                    page 31, Mar 18, 1930
   Outlook 154:512, Mar 26, 1930
   Theatre Magazine 51:46, Apr 1930
   Vogue 75:55+, Mar 29, 1930
```

Scandals (1929) (see George White's Scandals)

Show Girl (111 performances)
```
book:               William Anthony McGuire, based
                    on the novel by J. P. McEvoy
music:              George Gershwin
lyrics:             Ira Gershwin and Gus Kahn
staging:            Florenz Ziegfeld, Bobby Connelly,
                    Albertina Rasch
opened:             July 2, 1929
   Life (New York) 94:22, Aug 30, 1929
   New Republic 59:262-3, Jul 24, 1929
   New York Times page 19, Jul 3, 1929
                    page 29, Aug 8, 1929
```

Outlook 152:515, Jul 24, 1929
Theatre Magazine 50:39, Sep 1929

The Silver Swan (21 performances)
book: William S. Brady and Alonzo Price
music: H. Maurice Jacquet
lyrics: William S. Brady and Alonzo Price
staging: Alonzo Price and Leroy J. Prinz
opened: November 27, 1929
    New York Times IX, page 1, Nov 3, 1929
                    page 34, Nov 28, 1929

Simple Simon (135 performances)
book: Ed Wynn and Guy Bolton
music: Richard Rodgers
lyrics: Lorenz Hart
staging: Zeke Colvan
choreography: Seymour Felix
opened: February 18, 1930
    Life (New York) 95:18, Mar 28, 1930
    New York Times VIII, page 2, Feb 2, 1930
                    page 22, Feb 19, 1930
                    page 23, Mar 10, 1931
    Theatre Magazine 51:46, Apr 1930

Sketch Book (1929) (see Earl Carroll's Sketch Book)

Sons O'Guns (295 performances)
book: Fred Thompson and Jack Donahue
music: J. Fred Coots
lyrics: Arthur Swanstrom and Benny Davis
staging: Bobby Connelly
choreography: Albertina Rasch
opened: November 26, 1929
    New York Times page 30, Nov 27, 1929
                    X, page 2, Dec 15, 1929
                    VIII, page 1, Jan 12, 1930
    Theatre Magazine 51:49, Jan 1930

Street Singer (191 performances)
book: Cyrus Wood and Edgar Smith
music: John Gilbert, Nicholas Kempner, Sam
                Timberg

lyrics: Graham John
staging: Busby Berkeley
opened: September 17, 1929
   New York Times page 35, Sep 18, 1929
   Outlook 153:192, Oct 2, 1929
   Theatre Magazine 50:72, Nov 1929

Strike Up the Band (191 performances)
book: Morrie Ryskind, based on George S.
                 Kaufman's libretto
music: George Gershwin
lyrics: Ira Gershwin
staging: Alexander Leftwich
choreography: George Hale
opened: January 14, 1930
   Christian Century 48:899-901, Jul 8, 1931
   Life (New York) 95:18, Feb 7, 1930
   Nation 130:226, Feb 19, 1930
   New York Times VIII, page 4, Dec 29, 1929
                    page 29, Jan 15, 1930
   Outlook 154:191, Jan 29, 1930
   Theatre Magazine 51:48, Mar 1930
   Vogue 75:106+, Mar 1, 1930

Sweet Adeline (234 performances)
book: Oscar Hammerstein II
music: Jerome Kern
lyrics: Oscar Hammerstein II
staging: Reginald Hammerstein and Danny Dare
choreography: Danny Dare
opened: September 3, 1929
   Arts and Decoration 32:67, Nov 1929
   Catholic World 131:81, Apr 1930
   Commonweal 10:564, Oct 2, 1929
   Life (New York) 94:23, Sep 27, 1929
   Nation 129:310-11, Sep 18, 1929
   New York Times VIII, page 3, Aug 25, 1929
                    page 33, Sep 23, 1929
   Theatre Magazine 50:45, Nov 1929
   Vogue 74:63+, Oct 26, 1929

Three Little Girls (104 performances)
book: Herman Feiner and Bruno Hardt-Warden,

51

                    adapted by Marie Hecht and
                    Gertrude Purcell
music: Walter Kollo
lyrics: Harry B. Smith
staging: J. J. Shubert
opened: April 14, 1930
   Life (New York) 95:18, May 2, 1930
   New York Times page 29, Apr 15, 1930
   Theatre Magazine 51:48, Jun 1930

Top Speed (102 performances)
book: Guy Bolton
music: Harry Ruby
lyrics: Bert Kalmar
staging: John Harwood
choreography: John Boyle
opened: December 25, 1929
   Life (New York) 95:20, Jan 17, 1930
   New York Times IX, page 4, Nov 17, 1929
                    page 20, Dec 26, 1929
   Theatre Magazine 51:63, Feb 1930
   Vogue 75:122, Feb 15, 1930

Wake Up and Dream (136 performances)
book: J. H. Turner
music: Cole Porter
lyrics: Cole Porter
staging: Frank Collins
choreography: Tilly Losch, Jack Buchanan, Max
                    Rivers
opened: December 30, 1929
   Life (New York) 95:20, Jan 24, 1930
   Nation 130:106, Jan 22, 1930
   New York Times X, page 1, Apr 14, 1929
                    page 14, Dec 31, 1929
                    VIII, page 1, Jan 5, 1930
   Theatre Magazine 51:63, Feb 1930
   Vogue 75:122, Feb 15, 1930

Woof, Woof (45 performances)
book: Estelle Hunt, Sam Summers, Cyrus
                    Wood
music: Edward Pola and Eddie Brandt

52

lyrics: Edward Pola and Eddie Brandt
staging: Leonide Massine
opened: December 25, 1929
  New York Times page 20, Dec 26, 1929
  Theatre Magazine 51:63, Feb 1930
                  Season of 1930-1931

America's Sweetheart (135 performances)
book: Herbert Fields
music: Richard Rodgers
lyrics: Lorenz Hart
staging: Bobby Connelly and Monty Woolley
opened: February 10, 1931
  New York Times VIII, page 2, Jan 25, 1931
                 page 23, Feb 11, 1931
  Theatre Magazine 53:25, Apr 1931
  Vogue 77:116, Apr 1, 1931

Ballyhoo (68 performances)
book: Harry Ruskin and Leighton K. Brill
music: Louis Alter
lyrics: Harry Ruskin and Leighton K. Brill
staging: Reginald Hammerstein
choreography: Earl Lindsey
opened: December 22, 1930
  Nation 132:24-5, Jan 7, 1931
  New York Times IX, page 3, Dec 14, 1930
                 page 24, Dec 23, 1930
                 page 26, Jan 9, 1931
  Theatre Magazine 53:26, Feb 1931
  Vogue 77:102, Feb 15, 1931

The Band Wagon (260 performances)
book: George S. Kaufman and Howard Dietz
music: Arthur Schwartz
lyrics: George S. Kaufman and Howard Dietz
staging: Hassard Short
choreography: Albertina Rasch
opened: June 3, 1931
  Bookman 73:633-4, Aug 1931
  Catholic World 133:463-4, Jul 1931
  Life (New York) 97:18, Jun 19, 1931
  New York Times VIII, page 3, May 17, 1931
                 page 31, Jun 4, 1931

VIII, page 8, Jun 7, 1931
VIII, page 1, Jun 14, 1931
VIII, page 2, Jun 14, 1931
page 28, Dec 21, 1931
Outlook 158:219, Jun 17, 1931
Theatre Arts 15:625+, Aug 1931
Theatre Guild Magazine 8:18-19, Aug 1931

Billy Rose's Crazy Quilt (79 performances)
assembled by: Billy Rose
music: Harry Warren, Ned Lehak, Louis Alter
lyrics: Bud Green, Edward Eliscu, Billy Rose,
               Mort Dixon, E. Y. Harburg
staging: Billy Rose
opened: May 19, 1931
  New York Times VIII, page 2, May 3, 1931
                VIII, page 2, May 31, 1931
  Stage 9:13, May 1932

Blackbirds (1930) (see Lew Leslie's Blackbirds)

Brown Buddies (111 performances)
book: Carl Rickman
music: Joe Jordan and Millard Thomas
lyrics: Carol Rickman
opened: October 7, 1930
  New York Times page 29, Oct 8, 1930

Crazy Quilt (see Billy Rose's Crazy Quilt)

Earl Carroll's Vanities (215 performances)
assembled by: Earl Carroll
music: Harold Arlen and Ted Koehler
lyrics: E. Y. Harburg
staging: Earl Carroll, Priestly Morrison,
               LeRoy Prinz
opened: July 1, 1930
  New York Times page 28, Jul 2, 1930
  Theatre Magazine 52:24, Aug 1930

Fine and Dandy (255 performances)
book: Donald Ogden Stewart
music: Kay Swift

54

lyrics: Paul James
staging: Morris Green, Frank McCoy, Dave
                 Gould, Tom Nip
opened: September 23, 1930
  Bookman 72:411, Dec 1930
  Commonweal 12:583, Oct 8, 1930
  Life (New York) 96:18, Oct 10, 1930
  Nation 131:422, Oct 15, 1930
  New York Times IX, page 2, Sep 7, 1930
                 page 26, Sep 24, 1930
                 IX, page 1, Oct 5, 1930
  Outlook 156:233, Oct 8, 1930
  Theatre Magazine 52:64, Dec 1930
  Vogue 76:116, Nov 10, 1930

The Gang's All Here (23 performances)
book: Russel Crouse, Oscar Hammerstein II,
                 Morrie Ryskind
music: Lewis E. Gensler
lyrics: Owen Murphy and Robert A. Simon
staging: Oscar Hammerstein II
choreography: Dave Gould and Tilly Losch
opened: February 18, 1931
  New York Times page 31, Feb 19, 1931
  Theatre Magazine 53:27, Mar 1931
                 53:36, Apr 1931

Girl Crazy (272 performances)
book: Guy Bolton and John McGowan
music: George Gershwin
lyrics: Ira Gershwin
staging: Alexander Leftwich
choreography: George Hale
opened: October 14, 1930
  Life (New York) 96:16, Nov 7, 1930
  Nation 131:479, Oct 29, 1930
  New York Times IX, page 4, Oct 5, 1930
                 page 27, Oct 15, 1930
  Theatre Magazine 52:64, Dec 1930
  Vogue 76:136, Dec 8, 1930

Hello Paris (33 performances)
book: Edgar Smith, adapted from Homer

Croy's novel

music: Russell Tarbox and Michael Cleary
lyrics: Edgar Smith
staging: Ben Holmes
opened: November 15, 1930
   Life (New York) 96:35, Dec 5, 1930
   New York Times page 29, Nov 19, 1930

Hot Rhythm (68 performances)
sketches: Ballard Mcdonald, Will Morrissey,
              Edward Hurley
music: Porter Grainger and Donald Heywood
lyrics: Porter Grainger and Donald Heywood
staging: Will Morrissey and Nat Cash
opened: August 21, 1930
   Life (New York) 96:16, Sep 12, 1930
   New York Times page 18, Aug 22, 1930

Lew Leslie's Blackbirds (57 performances)
book: Flourney Miller
music: Eubie Blake
lyrics: Andy Razaf
staging: Lew Leslie
opened: October 22, 1930
   Bookman 72:409-10, Dec 1930
   Life (New York) 96:17, Nov 14, 1930
   New York Times page 34, Oct 23, 1930

Luana (21 performances)
book: Howard Emmett Rogers, based on
              Richard Walton Tully's The Bird of
              Paradise
music: Rudolf Friml
lyrics: J. Kiern Brennan
staging: Arthur Hammerstein, Howard Rogers,
              Earl Lindsey
opened: September 17, 1930
   Life (New York) 96:18, Oct 10, 1930
   New York Times page 28, Sep 18, 1930
   Theatre Magazine 52:26, Nov 1930

Meet My Sister (167 performances)
book: Harry Wagstaffe Gribble, from the

```
                    French of Berr, Verneuil, and Blum
music:          Ralph Benatsky
lyrics:         Ralph Benatsky
staging:        William Mollison
choreography:   John Pierce
opened:         December 30, 1930
   Catholic World 132:596, Feb 1931
   New York Times, page 11, Dec 31, 1930
   Theatre Magazine 53:60, Mar 1931
```

Mystery Moon (1 performance)
```
book:           Fred Herendeen
music:          Carlo and Sanders
lyrics:         Carlo and Sanders
opened:         June 23, 1930
   New York Times page 23, Jun 24, 1930
```

The New Yorkers (168 performances)
```
book:           Herbert Fields, suggested by Peter
                Arno and Ray Goetz
music:          Cole Porter
lyrics:         Cole Porter
staging:        Monty Woolley
choreography:   George Hale
opened:         December 8, 1930
   Catholic World 132:596, Feb 1931
   Life (New York) 96:18, Dec 26, 1930
   New York Times VIII, page 3, Nov 16, 1930
                page 31, Dec 9, 1930
   Outlook 156:671, Dec 24, 1930
```

Nina Rosa (137 performances)
```
book:           Otto Harbach
music:          Sigmund Romberg
lyrics:         Irving Caesar
staging:        J. J. Shubert and J. C. Huffman
opened:         September 20, 1930
   Life (New York) 96:18, Oct 10, 1930
   National Magazine 59:107, Nov 1930
   New York Times page 13, May 30, 1930
                page 19, May 31, 1930
                page 22, Sep 22, 1930
   Theatre Magazine 52:26, Nov 1930
```

Vogue 76:118, Nov 10, 1930

Rhapsody in Black (80 performances)
assembled by: Lew Leslie
music: Alberta Nichols
lyrics: Mann Holiner
staging: Lew Leslie
opened: May 4, 1931
    New York Times page 33, May 5, 1931

Second Little Show (63 performances)
assembled by: Dwight Deere Wiman
music: Arthur Schwartz
lyrics: Howard Dietz
staging: Dwight Deere Wiman, Dave Gould,
                 Monty Woolley
opened: September 2, 1930
    Life (New York) 96:16, Sep 19, 1930
    New York Times VIII, page 2, Aug 17, 1930
                   page 36, Sep 3, 1930
    Vogue 76:60+, Oct 27, 1930

Smiles (63 performances)
book: William Anthony McGuire
music: Vincent Youmans
lyrics: Clifford Grey, Harold Adamson, Ring
                 Lardner
staging: Ned Wayburn and William Anthony
                 McGuire
opened: November 18, 1930
    Life (New York) 96:18, Dec 12, 1930
    New York Times page 19, Nov 19, 1930

Sweet and Low (184 performances)
book: David Freedman
music: Billy Rose
lyrics: David Freedman
staging: Alexander Leftwich
opened: November 17, 1930
    Nation 131:632, Dec 3, 1930
    New York Times page 28, Nov 18, 1930

The Third Little Show (136 performances)

assembled by: Dwight Deere Wiman
music: Noel Coward, Henry Sullivan, Michael
Cleary, Morris Hamilton, Burton
Lane, Herman Hupfeld, Ned Lehak,
William Lewis, Jr.
lyrics: Noel Coward, Earle Crooker, Max
and Nathaniel Lief, Grace Henry,
Harold Adamson, Herman Hupfeld,
Edward Eliscu, Ted Fetter
staging: Alexander Leftwich
opened: June 1, 1931
Bookman 73:632-3, Aug 1931
Catholic World 133:463, Jul 1931
Commonweal 14:188, Jun 17, 1931
Life (New York) 97:19, Jun 26, 1931
New York Times VIII, page 2, May 10, 1931
page 34, Jun 2, 1931
Outlook 158:219, Jun 17, 1931

Three's A Crowd (272 performances)
book: Howard Dietz
music: Arthur Schwartz and others
lyrics: Howard Dietz
staging: Hassard Short
choreography: Albertina Rasch
opened: October 15, 1930
Bookman 72:411-12, Dec 1930
Catholic World 132:721-2, Mar 1931
Life (New York) 96:21, Oct 31, 1930
Nation 131:480, Oct 29, 1930
New York Times page 28, Oct 16, 1930
IX, page 4, Oct 5, 1930
VIII, page 1, Oct 26, 1930
Theatre Magazine 53:42, Jan 1931
53:20, Feb 1931
Vogue 76:76+, Dec 8, 1930

The Vanderbilt Revue (13 performances)
assembled by: Lew Fields
sketches: Kenyon Nicholson, Ellis O. Jones,
Sig Herzig, E. North
music and
lyrics: Dorothy Fields, Jimmy McHugh,

                    Jacques Fray, Mario Braggiotti,
                    E. Y. Harburg
staging: John E. Lonergan, Jack Haskell,
                    Theodore J. Hammerstein
opened: November 5, 1930
    Bookman 72:409, Dec 1930
    New York Times VIII, page 3, Oct 26, 1930
                    page 22, Nov 6, 1930

Vanities (1930) (see Earl Carroll's Vanities)

Who Cares (32 performances)
sketches: Edward Clarke Lilley, Bertrand
                    Robinson, Kenneth Webb, John
                    Cantwell
music: Percy Wenrich
lyrics: Harry Clarke
staging: George Vivian, Edward Clarke Lilley,
                    William Holbrook
opened: July 8, 1930
    Life (New York) 96:16, Aug 1, 1930
    New York Times page 27, Jul 9, 1930
    Theatre Magazine 52:26, Aug 1930

You Said It (192 performances)
book: Jack Yellen and Sid Silvers
music: Harold Arlen
lyrics: Jack Yellen
staging: John Harwood and Danny Dare
opened: January 19, 1931
    Life (New York) 97:18, Feb 6, 1931
    New York Times page 21, Jan 20, 1931

                    Season of 1931-1932

Blackberries of 1932 (24 performances)
assembled by: Lee Posner
book: Eddie Green
music: Donald Heywood and Tom Peluso
lyrics: Donald Heywood and Tom Peluso
staging: Ben Bernard
opened: April 4, 1932
    New York Times page 27, Apr 5, 1932

The Cat and the Fiddle (395 performances)
book: Otto Harbach
music: Jerome Kern
lyrics: Otto Harbach
staging: Jose Ruben
opened: October 15, 1931
   Catholic World 134:335-6, Dec 1931
   Life 98:18, Nov 6, 1931
   New Statesman 3:330-1, Mar 12, 1932
   New York Times VIII, page 3, Sep 27, 1931
                     page 26, Oct 16, 1931
                 VIII, page 2, Oct 18, 1931
                     page 17, Aug 4, 1932
   Vogue 78:102, Dec 15, 1931

Earl Carroll's Vanities (278 performances)
sketches: Ralph Spence and Eddie Welch
music: Burton Lane
lyrics: Harold Adamson
staging: Earl Carroll
opened: August 27, 1931
   New Republic 68:127-8, Sep 16, 1931
   New York Times page 28, Aug 11, 1931
                     VIII, page 1, Aug 16, 1931
                     page 18, Aug 28, 1931
                     VIII, page 1, Sep 6, 1931
   Outlook 159:55, Sep 9, 1931
           159:570, Dec 30, 1931
   Vogue 78:79+, Oct 15, 1931

East Wind (23 performances)
book: Oscar Hammerstein II and Frank
                  Mandel
music: Sigmund Romberg
lyrics: Oscar Hammerstein II
staging: Oscar Hammerstein II
choreography: Bobby Connelly
opened: October 27, 1931
   New York Times page 18, Oct 28, 1931

Everybody's Welcome (139 performances)
book: Harold Atteridge, based on Frances
                  Goodrich and Albert Hackett's Up

61

Pops the Devil

music: Sammy Fain
lyrics: Irving Kahal
staging: William Mollison
opened: October 13, 1931
   New York Times VIII, page 3, Sep 20, 1931
               page 26, Oct 14, 1931

Face the Music (165 performances)
book: Moss Hart
music: Irving Berlin
lyrics: Irving Berlin
staging: Hassard Short and George S. Kaufman
choreography: Albertina Rasch
opened: February 17, 1932
   Arts and Decoration 36:45+, Apr 1932
   Bookman 74:666, Mar 1932
   Catholic World 135:75-6, Apr 1932
   Commonweal 15:495, Mar 2, 1932
   Nation 134:294, Mar 9, 1932
   New Outlook 161:48, Mar 1933
   New Republic 70:97, Mar 9, 1932
   New York Times page 25, Feb 4, 1932
               page 24, Feb 18, 1932
               VIII, page 1, Mar 20, 1932
               page 13, Feb 1, 1933
   Outlook 160:189, Mar 1932
   Theatre Guild Magazine 9:28-30, Mar 1932
                   9:23, Apr 1932
   Vogue 79:56+, Apr 15, 1932

Fast and Furious (7 performances)
assembled by: Forbes Randolph
music: Joe Jordan and Harry Revel
lyrics: Rosamond Johnson, Mack Gordon,
               Harold Adamson
staging: Forbes Randolph
opened: September 15, 1931
   New York Times page 15, Sep 16, 1931

Follies (1931) (see Ziegfeld Follies)

Free for All (15 performances)

62

book: Oscar Hammerstein II and Laurence
                 Schwab
music: Richard A. Whiting
lyrics: Oscar Hammerstein II
staging: Oscar Hammerstein II
choreography: Bobby Connelly
opened: September 8, 1931
    Arts and Decoration 36:73, Nov 1931
    New York Times VIII, page 1, Aug 16, 1931
    Outlook 159:119, Sep 23, 1931

George White's Scandals (202 performances)
sketches: George White, Lew Brown, Irving
                 Caesar
music: Ray Henderson
lyrics: Lew Brown
staging: George White
opened: September 14, 1931
    New York Times page 28, Aug 11, 1931
                 VIII, page 1, Aug 16, 1931
                 page 30, Sep 15, 1931
                 page 26, Feb 10, 1932
    Vogue 78:55+, Nov 15, 1931

Here Goes the Bride (7 performances)
book: Peter Arno
music: John W. Green and Richard Myers
lyrics: Peter Arno
staging: Edward Clarke Lilley
choreography: Russell Markert
opened: November 3, 1931
    New York Times page 31, Nov 4, 1931
                 page 22, Nov 9, 1931

Hey Nonny Nonny! (32 performances)
book: Max and Nathaniel Lief
music: Michale H. Cleary
lyrics: Max and Nathaniel Lief
staging: Alexander Leftwich
opened: June 6, 1932
    Nation 134:708, Jun 22, 1932
    New York Times page 22, Jun 7, 1932

63

Hot-Cha! (119 performances)
book: Lew Brown, Ray Henderson, Mark
               Hellinger, H. S. Kraft
music: Ray Henderson
lyrics: Lew Brown
staging: Edgar McGregor
choreography: Bobby Connelly
opened: March 8, 1932
    Bookman 75:77, Apr 1932
    New York Times VIII, page 2, Feb 21, 1932
                    page 17, Mar 9, 1932
                    VIII, page 1, Mar 20, 1932
    Outlook 160:229, Apr 1932
    Vogue 79:60+, May 1, 1932

The Laugh Parade (231 performances)
book: Ed Wynn and Ed Preble
music: Harry Warren
lyrics: Mort Dixon and Joe Young
staging: Ed Wynn
choreography: Albertina Rasch
opened: November 2, 1931
    Catholic World 134:471, Jan 1932
    Nation 133:582, Nov 25, 1931
    New York Times VIII, page 3, Sep 20, 1931
                    page 31, Nov 3, 1931
                    VIII, page 1, Dec 6, 1931

A Little Racketeer (48 performances)
book: Harry Clarke, adapted from the
               German of F. Kalbfuss and R. Wilde
music: Haskell Brown
lyrics: Edward Eliscu
staging: William Caryl
choreography: Albertina Rasch
opened: January 18, 1932
    New York Times VIII, page 4, Oct 18, 1931
                    page 24, Jan 19, 1932
                    page 13, Feb 15, 1932

Marching By (12 performances)
book: Ernst Neubach, adapted by Harry
               Clarke and Harry B. Smith

music: Jean Gilbert, Mark Gordon and
                    Harry Revel
lyrics: Ernst Neubach
staging: J. C. Huffman
opened: March 3, 1932
    New York Times page 17, Mar 4, 1932

Nikki (39 performances)
book: John Monk Saunders
music: Philip Charig
lyrics: John Monk Saunders
staging: William B. Friedlander
opened: September 29, 1931
    New York Times page 23, Sep 30, 1931

Of Thee I Sing (441 performances)
book: George S. Kaufman and Morrie
                    Ryskind
music: George Gershwin
lyrics: Ira Gershwin
staging: George S. Kaufman
choreography: Chester Hale
opened: December 26, 1931
    Arts and Decoration 36:39+, Feb 1932
                        37:43+, Sep 1932
    Bookman 74:561-2, Jan 1932
    Catholic World 134:587-8, Feb 1932
                    175:310, Jul 1952
    Commonweal 15:302, Jan 13, 1932
                    56:196-7, May 30, 1952
    Harper 205:92, Jul 1952
    Literary Digest 112:18, Jan 16, 1932
    Nation 134: 56, Jan 13, 1932
            134:294, Mar 9, 1932
            174:486, May 17, 1952
    New Republic 69:243, Jan 13, 1932
                    70:97, Mar 9, 1932
    New York Theatre Critics' Reviews 1952:289
    New York Times VIII, page 2, Dec 13, 1931
                    VIII, page 1, Mar 20, 1932
                    page 1, May 3, 1932
                    VIII, page 1, May 8, 1932
                    page 28, Jan 2, 1933

                    page 23, Jan 6, 1933
                    page 22, Aug 10, 1937
                    page 14, Aug 18, 1937
                    II, page 1, May 4, 1952
                    page 34, May 6, 1952
                    II, page 1, May 11, 1952
New Yorker 28:87, May 17, 1952
Newsweek 39:101, May 19, 1952
Outlook 160:54+, Jan 13, 1932
Saturday Review 9:385-6, Jan 21, 1933
                    35:30-2, May 24, 1952
Theatre Arts 36:17+, Jul 1952
Theatre Guild Magazine 9:16-20, Feb 1932
                            9:23, Apr 1932
Time 59:83, May 19, 1952
Vogue 79:73+, Feb 15, 1932

Scandals (1931) (see George White's Scandals)

Shoot the Works (87 performances)
assembled by: Heywood Brown and Milton Raison
contributors: Heywood Brown, H. I. Phillips,
                Peter Arno, Sig Herzig, Edward J.
                McNamara, Michael H. Cleary,
                Philip Charig, Jay Gorney, Dorothy
                Fields, Ira Gershwin, Alexander
                Williams, Robert Stolz, A. Robin-
                son, Dorothy Parker, Nunnally
                Johnson, E. B. White, Jack
                Hazzard, Irving Berlin, Max Lief,
                Nathaniel Lief, E. Y. Harburg,
                Jimmie McHugh, Vernon Duke,
                Herbert Goode, Walter Reisch
opened: July 21, 1931
    Arts and Decoration 35:45+, Oct 1931
    Commonweal 14:346, Aug 5, 1931
    Nation 133:148, Aug 12, 1931
    New Republic 67: 317-18, Aug 5, 1931
    New York Times page 19, Jul 22, 1931
                    VIII, page 2, Jul 26, 1931
                    VIII, page 2, Aug 16, 1931
                    page 35, Oct 6, 1931
    Outlook 158:437, Aug 5, 1931

The Singing Rabbi (4 performances)
book: Bores and Harry Thomashefsky
music: J. Rumshinsky and Harry Lubin
staging: William E. Morris
opened: September 10, 1931
    New York Times page 24, Sep 11, 1931

Sugar Hill (11 performances)
book: Charles Tazewell
music: Jimmy Johnson
lyrics: Jo Trent
opened: December 25, 1931
    New York Times page 15, Dec 26, 1931

There You Are (8 performances)
book: Carl Bartfield
music: William Heagney
lyrics: William Heagney and Tom Connell
staging: Horace Sinclair
opened: May 16, 1932
    New York Times page 25, May 17, 1932

Through the Years (20 performances)
book: Brian Hooker, based on Jane Cowl's
                     Smilin' Through
music: Vincent Youmans
lyrics: Edward Heyman
staging: Edgar McGregor
choreography: Jack Haskell and Max Scheck
opened: January 28, 1932
    New York Times VIII, page 3, Jan 3, 1932
                 page 23, Feb 13, 1932

Vanities (1931) (see Earl Carroll's Vanities)

Yeah Man (4 performances)
book: Leigh Whipper and Billy Mills
music: Al Wilson, Charles Weinberg, Ken
                     Macomber
lyrics: Al Wilson, Charles Weinberg, Ken
                     Macomber

staging: Walter Campbell
opened: May 26, 1932
    New York Times page 27, May 27, 1932

Ziegfeld Follies, 1931 (165 performances)
assembled by: Florenz Ziegfeld
contributors: Gene Buck, Mark Hellinger, J. P.
                 Murray, Barry Trivers, Ben Oak-
                 land, Walter Donaldson, Dave
                 Stamper, Hugo Reisenfeld, Mack
                 Gordon, Harry Revel, Dmitri
                 Tiomkin
staging: Florenz Ziegfeld and Gene Buck
choreography: Bobby Connelly and Albertina Rasch
opened: July 1, 1931
    New Republic 67:262-3, Jul 22, 1931
    New York Times page 30, Jul 2, 1931
                     VIII, page 2, Aug 16, 1931
    Outlook 158:343, Jul 15, 1931

Season of 1932-1933

Americana (77 performances)
book: J. P. McEvoy
music: Jay Gorney, Harold Arlen, Herman
                  Hupfeld, Richard Meyers
lyrics: E. Y. Harburg
staging: Harold Johnsrud
sets: Albert R. Johnson
opened: October 5, 1932
    Catholic World 136:210, Nov 1932
    New York Times IX, page 1, Sep 23, 1932
                     page 19, Oct 6, 1932
    Stage 10:49, Dec 15, 1932
    Theatre Arts 16:863+, Nov-Dec 1932

Ballyhoo of 1932 (95 performances)
book: Norman B. Anthony
music: Lewis E. Gensler
lyrics: E. Y. Harburg
staging: Norman B. Anthony, Lewis E.
                  Gensler, Bobby Connelly, Russell
                  Patterson

68

```
sets:            Russell Patterson
opened:          September 6, 1932
   Nation 135:266, Sep 21, 1932
   New York Times page 14, Sep 7, 1932
                 page 23, Nov 29, 1932
   Stage 10:10-11, Oct 1932
   Vogue 80:100, Oct 15, 1932
```

Belmont Varieties (8 performances)
```
book:            Helen and Nolan Leary and Sam
                 Bernard II
music and
 lyrics:         Serge Walter, Alvin Kaufman, Charles
                 Kenny, Henry Lloyd, Mildred
                 Kaufman, Robert Burk
staging:         Max Scheck and Sam Bernard II
opened:          September 26, 1932
```

Cosmo Vanities (see Belmont Varieties)

Earl Carroll Vanities (87 performances)
```
book:            Jack McGowan
music:           Harold Arlen
lyrics:          Ted Koehler
staging:         Earl Carroll
sets:            Vincente Minnelli
opened:          September 27, 1932
   Nation 135:375, Oct 19, 1932
   New Outlook 161:46, Dec 1932
   New York Times IX, page 2, Sep 18, 1932
                 page 22, Sep 28, 1932
```

Flying Colors (188 performances)
```
book:            Howard Dietz
music:           Arthur Schwartz
lyrics:          Howard Dietz
staging:         Howard Dietz
sets:            Norman Bel-Geddes
opened:          September 15, 1932
   Arts and Decoration 38:45+, Nov 1932
   Catholic World 136:210-11, Nov 1932
```

69

New Outlook 161:47, Jan 1933
Nation 135:318, Oct 5, 1932
New York Times page 24, Sep 16, 1932
Stage 10:11, Oct 1932
       10:18-21, Nov 1932
Theatre Arts 16:873, Nov 1932
Vogue 80:89, Nov 1, 1932

Gay Divorce (248 performances)
book: Dwight Taylor, based on J. Hartley
                 Manners' unproduced play. Musical
                 adaption by Kenneth Webb and
                 Samuel Hoffenstein
music: Cole Porter
lyrics: Cole Porter
staging: Howard Lindsay
sets: Jo Mielziner
opened: November 29, 1932
  New Outlook 161:47, Jan 1933
  New Republic 73:89, Dec 28, 1932
  New York Times page 23, Nov 30, 1932
                  page 15, Apr 19, 1933
                  IX, page 3, Nov 19, 1933
                  page 39, Apr 4, 1960
  New Yorker 36:136, Apr 16, 1960

George White's Music Hall Varieties (72 performances)
book: William K. Wells and George White
music and
 lyrics: Irving Caesar and others
staging: George White and Russell Markert
opened: November 22, 1932
  New Outlook 161:47, Jan 1933
  New York Times page 15, Nov 15, 1932
                  page 19, Jan 3, 1933
  Vogue 81:73, Jan 15, 1933
        81:88, Mar 1, 1933

Manhattan Vanities (see Belmont Varieties)

Melody (79 performances)
book: Edward Childs Carpenter
music: Sigmund Romberg

lyrics: Irving Caesar
staging: Bobby Connelly
sets: Joseph Urban
choreography: Bobby Connelly
opened: February 14, 1933
  Arts and Decoration 38:59+, Apr 1933
  Catholic World 137:81-2, Apr 1933
  Nation 136:244, Mar 1, 1933
  New Outlook 161:48, Mar 1933
  New York Times page 17, Feb 15, 1933
  Newsweek 1:26, Feb 17, 1933
  Stage 10:16-17, Mar 1933

Music Hall Varieties (see George White's Music Hall
  Varieties)

Music in the Air (342 performances)
book: Oscar Hammerstein II
music: Jerome Kern
lyrics: Oscar Hammerstein II
staging: Oscar Hammerstein II and Jerome Kern
sets: Joseph Urban
opened: November 8, 1932
  Arts and Decoration 38:50, Jan 1933
  Catholic World 136:462-3, Jan 1933
                 174:228, Dec 1951
  Commonweal 17:131, Nov 30, 1932
                 55:62, Oct 26, 1951
  New Republic 125:22, Nov 12, 1951
  New York Theatre Critics' Reviews 1951:215
  New York Times IX, page 3, Oct 23, 1932
                 page 28, Nov 9, 1932
                 IX, page 1, Nov 20, 1932
                 page 11, May 20, 1933
                 II, page 1, Oct 7, 1951
                 page 32, Oct 9, 1951
                 II, page 1, Oct 21, 1951
  New Yorker 27:60+, Oct 20, 1951
  Newsweek 38:93, Oct 22, 1951
  Stage 10:32-3, Dec 1932
  Theatre Arts 17:4-5, Jan 1933
                 35:3+, Dec 1951
  Time 58:56, Oct 22, 1951

Pardon My English (46 performances)
book: Herbert Fields
music: George Gershwin
lyrics: Ira Gershwin
staging: George Hale
sets: John Wenger
opened: January 20, 1933
   New Outlook 161:48, Mar 1933
   New York Times IX, page 5, Dec 11, 1932
                 page 11, Jan 21, 1933

Shuffle Along of 1933 (17 performances)
book: Flournoy E. Miller
music: Eubie Blake
lyrics: Noble Sissle
staging: Walter Brooks
sets: Karl Amend
choreography: Davis and Carey
opened: December 26, 1932
   New York Times page 11, Dec 27, 1932

Smiling Faces (33 performances)
book: Harry Clarke
music: Harry Revel
lyrics: Mack Gordon
staging: R. H. Burnside
opened: August 30, 1932
   Catholic World 136:84-5, Oct 1932

Strike Me Pink (105 performances)
book: Ray Henderson and Lew Brown,
                   additional dialogue by Mack Gordon
music: Ray Henderson
lyrics: Lew Brown
staging: Ray Henderson and Lew Brown
sets: Henry Dreyfuss
choreography: Seymour Felix
opened: March 4, 1933
   Nation 136:356, Mar 29, 1933
   New Outlook 161:46, Apr 1933
   New York Times page 16, Mar 6, 1933
                 IX, page 2, Apr 9, 1933
   Stage 10:19-22, Apr 1933

Time 21:40, Mar 13, 1933

Take A Chance (243 performances)
book: B. G. DeSylva and Laurence Schwab,
                   additional dialogue by Sid Silvers
music: Herb Brown Nacio and Richard Whit-
                   ing, additional songs by Vincent
                   Youmans
lyrics: B. G. DeSylva
staging: Edgar MacGregor
sets: Cleon Throckmorton
choreography: Bobby Connelly
opened: November 26, 1932
   New Outlook 161:47, Jan 1933
   New York Times page 11, Nov 18, 1932
                   III, page 2, Dec 4, 1932

Tattle Tales (28 performances)
book: Frank Fay and Nick Copeland
music and
   lyrics: Howard Jackson, Edward Ward, Leo
                   Robin, Ralph Rainger, George
                   Waggoner, Willard Robison, Edward
                   Eliscu, Eddie Beinbryer, William
                   Walsh
staging: Frank Fay
opened: June 1, 1933
   New Outlook 162:43, Jul 1933
   New York Times page 22, Jun 2, 1933

Tell Her the Truth (11 performances)
book: R. P. Weston and Bert Lee, adapted
                   from Frederick Isham and James
                   Montgomery's Nothing But the Truth
music: Jack Waller and Joseph Tunbridge
lyrics: R. P. Weston and Bert Lee
staging: Morris Green and Henry Thomas
opened: October 28, 1932
   New York Times page 18, Oct 29, 1932
                   page 20, Nov 7, 1932

Walk A Little Faster (119 performances)
sketches: S. J. Perelman and Robert Mac

Gunigle
music: Vernon Duke
lyrics: E. Y. Harburg
staging: E. M. Woolley (Monty Wooley)
sets: Boris Aronson
choreography: Albertina Rasch
opened: December 7, 1932
   New Outlook 161:47, Jan 1933
   New Republic 73:189, Dec 28, 1932
   New York Times page 24, Dec 8, 1932
   Vogue 81:56+, Feb 1, 1933

Season of 1933-1934

All the King's Horses (120 performances)
book: Frederick Herendeen
music: Edward A. Horan
lyrics: Frederick Herendeen
staging: Jose Ruben
sets: Herbert Ward
opened: January 30, 1934
   Catholic World 138:734, Mar 1934
   New Outlook 163:32, Mar 1934
   New York Times page 21, Jan 31, 1934
   Review of Reviews 89:58, Apr 1934

As Thousands Cheer (400 performances)
book: Irving Berlin and Moss Hart
music: Edward Heyman and Richard Meyers
lyrics: Edward Heyman and Richard Meyers
staging: Hassard Short
sets: Albert Johnson
choreography: Charles Weidman
opened: September 30, 1933
   Canadian Forum 15:274, Apr 1935
   Catholic World 138:337, Dec 1933
   Collier's 94:17+, Aug 18, 1934
   Commonweal 18:591-2, Oct 20, 1933
   Literary Digest 116:18, Oct 21, 1933
   New Outlook 162:42, Nov 1933
   New Republic 76:279, Oct 18, 1933
   New York Times II, page 5, Sep 10, 1933
                        page 22, Oct 2, 1933

74

                    IX, page 1, Oct 15, 1933
                    page 26, Mar 20, 1934
                    page 24, Jul 10, 1934
                    IX, page 1, Nov 11, 1934
    Review of Reviews 89:40, Feb 1934
    Stage 11:12-17, Oct 1933
        11:13, Nov 1933
    Theatre Arts 17:919, Dec 1933
    Time 22:27, Oct 9, 1933
    Vanity Fair 41:42, Dec 1933

Blackbirds of 1933 (25 performances)
book: Nat N. Dorfman, Mann Holiner, Lew
                     Leslie
music and
  lyrics: Mann Holiner, Alberta Nichols,
                     Joseph Young, Ned Washington,
                     Victor Young
staging: Lew Leslie
sets: Mabel A. Buell
opened: December 2, 1933
    New York Times page 32, Dec 4, 1933
                    II, page 6, Aug 26, 1934

Caviar (30 performances)
book: Leo Randole
music: Harden Church
lyrics: Edward Heyman
staging: Clifford Brooke
sets: Steele Savage
choreography: John Lonergan
opened: June 7, 1934
    New York Times page 19, Jun 8, 1934

Follies (1934) (see Ziegfeld Follies)

Hold Your Horses (88 performances)
book: Russel Crouse and Corey Ford, based
                     on a play by Crouse, Ford, and
                     Charles Beahan
music and
  lyrics: Russell Bennett, Robert A. Simon,
                     Louis Alter, Arthur Swanstrom, Ben

                          75

                    Oakland, Owen Murphy
staging: Russell Patterson
choreography: Robert Alton and Harriet Hoctor
opened: September 25, 1933
     Catholic World 138:218, Nov 1933
     Commonweal 18:592, Oct 20, 1933
     New Outlook 162:43, Nov 1933
     New York Times page 20, Aug 31, 1933
                         X, page 1, Sep 10, 1933
                         page 26, Sep 26, 1933
                         IX, page 2, Oct 29, 1933
     Stage 11:9-11, Oct 1933

Let'Em Eat Cake (90 performances)
book: George S. Kaufman and Morrie
                    Ryskind
music: George Gershwin
lyrics: Ira Gershwin
staging: George S. Kaufman
sets: Albert R. Johnson
choreography: Van Grona and Ned McGurn
opened: October 21, 1933
     Catholic World 138:338, Dec 1933
     Commonweal 19:47, Nov 10, 1933
     Nation 137:550, Nov 8, 1933
     New Outlook 162:47, Dec 1933
     New York Times page 16, Apr 17, 1933
                         page 26, Oct 3, 1933
                         X, page 2, Oct 8, 1933
                         page 18, Oct 23, 1933
                         IX, page 1, Nov 12, 1933
     Stage 11:9-10, Dec 1933
     Time 22:29-30, Oct 30, 1933

Murder at the Vanities (207 performances)
book: Earl Carroll and Rufus King
music and
 lyrics: John Green, Edward Heyman, Richard
                    Meyers, Ned Washington, Victor
                    Young, Herman Hupfeld, John J.
                    Loeb, Paul Francis Webster
staging: Earl Carroll
opened: September 8, 1933

Nation 137:362-3, Sep 27, 1933
New Outlook 162:49, Oct 1933
New York Times page 20, Aug 31, 1933
                page 22, Sep 13, 1933
Theatre Arts 17:839, Nov 1933

New Faces (149 performances)
sketches: Viola Brothers Shore, Nancy Hamilton,
               June Sillman
music: Warburton Guilbert, Donald Honrath,
               Martha Caples, James Shelton,
               Morgan Lewis
lyrics: Viola Brothers Shore, Nancy Hamilton,
               June Sillman
staging: Elsie Janis
sets: Sergei Soudeikine
opened: March 15, 1934
   Catholic World 139:215, May 1934
   Commonweal 19:609, Mar 30, 1934
   Nation 138:370, Mar 28, 1934
   New Outlook 163:45, Apr 1934
   New York Times page 24, Mar 16, 1934
                   X, page 2, Apr 1, 1934
   Newsweek 3:39, Mar 24, 1934
   Stage 11:10-11, May 1934

Roberta (295 performances)
book: Otto Harbach, adapted from Alice
               Duer Miller's novel Gowns
music: Jerome Kern
lyrics: Otto Harbach
staging: Hassard Short
sets: Clark Robinson
choreography: John Lonergan
opened: November 18, 1933
   Catholic World 138:733-4, Mar 1934
   Fortune 9:69-76+, May 1934
   New Outlook 163:43, Jan 1934
   New York Times page 18, Nov 20, 1933
                   IX, page 3, Jan 13, 1935
                   II, page 3, Aug 18, 1935
   Newsweek 2:32, Nov 25, 1933
   Review of Reviews 89:48, Mar 1934

Stage 11:8-9+, Dec 1933
Time 22:45, Nov 27, 1933

Shady Lady (30 performances)
book: Estelle Morando, revised by Irving
                 Caesar
music and
 lyrics: Sam H. Sept, Bud Green, Jesse Greer,
                 Stanley Adams
staging: Theodore Hammerstein
sets: Tom Adrian Cracraft
choreography: Jack Donohue
opened: July 5, 1933
    New York Times page 26, Jul 26, 1933

Ziegfeld Follies (182 performances)
sketches and
 songs: Vernon Duke, Samuel Pokrass, Billy
                 Hill, H. I. Phillips, Fred Allen,
                 Harry Tugend, Ballard McDonald,
                 David Freedman
lyrics: E. Y. Harburg
staging: Edward C. Lilley
sets: Watson Barratt and Albert R. Johnson
choreography: Robert Alton
opened: January 4, 1934
    Commonweal 19:441, Feb 16, 1934
    Nation 138:310, Mar 14, 1934
    New Outlook 163:48, Feb 1934
    New York Times X, page 1, Jan 21, 1934
                  IX, page 1, Nov 11, 1934
    Review of Reviews 89:40, Feb 1934
    Time 23:40, Jan 15, 1934
    Vanity Fair 42:38-9, Mar 1934

Season of 1934-1935

Anything Goes (420 performances)
book: Guy Bolton, P. G. Wodehouse,
                 Howard Lindsay and Russel Crouse
music: Cole Porter
lyrics: Cole Porter
staging: Howard Lindsay

78

sets: Donald Oenslager
choreography: Robert Alton
opened: November 21, 1934
    Catholic World 140:469-70, Jan 1935
    Dance Magazine 36:26, Jul 1962
    Literary Digest 118:18, Dec 8, 1934
    New Republic 81:131, Dec 12, 1934
    New York Times IX, page 1, Nov 18, 1934
                   page 26, Nov 22, 1934
                   IX, page 3, Nov 25, 1934
                   page 20, Jun 15, 1935
                   X, page 1, Jul 28, 1935
                   IX, page 1, Aug 18, 1935
                   IX, page 1, Sep 15, 1935
                   page 23, Aug 17, 1937
                   page 24, Aug 26, 1937
    New Yorker 38:92-3, May 26, 1962
    Newsweek 4:23, Dec 1, 1934
    Theatre Arts 19:19, Jan 1935
                46:59, Aug 1962
    Time 24:24, Dec 3, 1934

Calling All Stars (36 performances)
sketches: Lew Brown
music: Harry Akst
lyrics: Lew Brown
staging: Lew Brown and Thomas Mitchell
sets: Nat Karson
choreography: Sara Mildred Strauss
opened: December 13, 1934
    New York Times page 28, Dec 14, 1934
    Time 24:13, Dec 24, 1934

Earl Carroll Sketch Book (207 performances)
sketches: Eugene Conrad and Charles Sherman
music and
  lyrics: Charles Tobias, Murray Mencher,
                   Charles Newman, Norman Zeno,
                   Will Irwin
staging: Earl Carroll
sets: Clark Robinson
choreography: Boots McKenna
opened: June 4, 1935

Nation 140:724, Jun 19, 1935
New York Times page 22, Jun 5, 1935

The Great Waltz (298 performances)
book: Moss Hart, based on libretti by Dr.
                 A. M. Willner, Heinz Reichert,
                 Ernst Marischka, Caswell Garth
music: Johann Strauss, father and son
lyrics: Desmond Carter
staging: Hassard Short
sets: Albert Johnson
choreography: Albertina Rasch
opened: September 22, 1934
    Catholic World 140:213, Nov 1934
    Golden Book Magazine 20:508+, Nov 1934
    Literary Digest 118:19, Oct 6, 1934
    New York Times page 14, Sep 23, 1934
                 IX, page 1, Sep 30, 1934
    Newsweek 4:27, Sep 29, 1934
    Stage 12:3+, Nov 1934
    Time 24:34, Oct 1, 1934

Gypsy Blonde (24 performances)
book: Kenneth Johns, based on Michael
                 Balfe's opera Bohemian Girl
music: Michael Balfe
lyrics: Frank Gabrielson
staging: Dmitri Ostrov
sets: Karl Amend
choreography: Vaughn Godfrey
opened: June 25, 1934
    New York Times page 22, Jun 26, 1934

Keep Moving (20 performances)
sketches: Newman Levy and Jack School
music: Max Rich
lyrics: Newman Levy and Jack School
staging: George Rosener and Harry Losee
sets: Clark Robinson
opened: August 23, 1934
    New York Times page 10, Aug 24, 1934

Life Begins at 8:40 (237 performances)

book: David Freedman
music: Harold Arlen
lyrics: Ira Gershwin and E. Y. Harburg
staging: John Murray Anderson and Philip Loeb
sets: Albert Johnson
choreography: Robert Alton and Charles Weidman
opened: August 27, 1934
   Catholic World 140:88, Oct 1934
   Literary Digest 118:20, Sep 8, 1934
   New York Times page 20, Aug 7, 1934
                         IX, page 1, Aug 12, 1934
                         page 24, Aug 28, 1934
                         IX, page 1, Sep 2, 1934
   Stage 12:8-9, Oct 1934
   Time 24:30, Sep 10, 1934

Music Hath Charms (29 performances)
book: Rowland Leigh, George Rosener, John
                   Shubert
music: Rudolf Friml
lyrics: Rowland Leigh and John Shubert
staging: George Rosener
sets: Watson Barratt
choreography: Alex Yakovleff
opened: December 29, 1934
   Catholic World 140:601, Feb 1935
   New York Times page 8, Dec 31, 1934

Parade (40 performances)
sketches: Paul Peters, George Sklar, Frank
                   Gabrielson, David Lesan, Kyle
                   Crichton
music: Jerome Moross
staging: Philip Loeb
sets: Lee Simonson
choreography: Robert Alton
opened: May 20, 1935
   Commonweal 22:160, Jun 7, 1935
   Nation 140:666+, Jun 5, 1935
   New Republic 83:106, Jun 5, 1935
   New York Times page 26, May 7, 1935
                      X, page 2, May 12, 1935
                      page 22, May 21, 1935

XI, page 22, May 26, 1935
Newsweek 5:24-5, Jun 1, 1935
Time 25:26+, Jun 3, 1935

Revenge With Music (158 performances)
book: Howard Dietz and Arthur Schwartz,
               from the Spanish fable "The Three
               Cornered Hat"
music: Arthur Schwartz
lyrics: Howard Dietz
staging: Komisarjevsky
sets: Albert Johnson
choreography: Michael Mordkin
opened: November 28, 1934
   Catholic World 140:469, Jan 1935
   Golden Book Magazine 21:32a, Feb 1935
   New York Times page 33, Nov 29, 1934
               IX, page 2, Dec 23, 1934
   Time 24:50, Dec 10, 1934

Saluta (39 performances)
book: Will Morrissey, revised by Eugene
               Conrad and Maurice Marks
music: Frank D'Armond
lyrics: Will Morrissey
staging: William Morrissey and Edwin Saul-
               paugh
sets: Hugh Willoughby
choreography: Boots McKenna
opened: August 28, 1934
   New York Times page 13, Aug 29, 1934

Say When (76 performances)
book: Jack McGowan
music: Ray Henderson
lyrics: Ted Koehler
staging: Bertram Harrison and Russell Markert
sets: Clark Robinson
opened: November 8, 1934
   New York Times page 24, Nov 9, 1934
   Stage 12:9, Dec 1934

Sketch Book (1935) (see Earl Carroll's Sketch Book)

82

Thumbs Up (156 performances)
sketches: H. I. Phillips, Harold Atteridge,
                Alan Baxter, Ballard MacDonald,
                Earle Crooker
music: James Hanley and Henry Sullivan
lyrics: H. I. Phillips, Harold Atteridge, Alan
                Baxter, Ballard McDonald, Earle
                Crooker
staging: John Murray Anderson
sets: Ted Weidhaas, James Reynolds,
                Raoul Pene duBois
choreography: Robert Alton
opened: December 27, 1934
   Catholic World 140:723, Mar 1935
   Commonweal 21:346, Jan 18, 1935
   New York Times page 24, Dec 28, 1934
               VIII, page 2, Feb 3, 1934
               IX, page 1, Aug 18, 1934
   Newsweek 5:26, Jan 5, 1935

Season of 1935-1936

Follies (1936) (see Ziegfeld Follies)

George White's Scandals (110 performances)
sketches: George White, William K. Wells,
                Howard A. Shiebler
music: Ray Henderson
lyrics: Jack Yellen
staging: George White
sets: Russell Patterson and Walter Jage-
                mann
costumes: Charles LeMaire
choreography: Russell Markert
opened: December 25, 1935
   Nation 142:56, Jan 8, 1936
   New York Times page 20, Dec 26, 1935
               page 17, Mar 30, 1936
   Newsweek 7:25, Jan 4, 1936
   Time 27:24, Jan 6, 1936

The Illustrator's Show (5 performances)
assembled by: The Society of Illustrators, edited by

83

Tom Weatherly

music: Frank Loesser and Irving Actman
lyrics: Frank Loesser and Irving Actman
staging: Tom Weatherly
sets: Arne Lundborg
costumes: Carl Sidney
choreography: Carl Randall
opened: January 22, 1936
   New York Times page 25, Jan 23, 1936

Jubilee (169 performances)
book: Moss Hart
music: Cole Porter
lyrics: Cole Porter
staging: Hassard Short
sets: Jo Mielziner
costumes: Irene Sharaff and Connie de Pinna
choreography: Albertina Rasch
opened: October 12, 1935
   Catholic World 142:340, Dec 1935
   Commonweal 22:642, Oct 1935
   Nation 141:548, Nov 6, 1935
   New York Times IX, page 2, Sep 15, 1935
                  page 20, Sep 23, 1935
                  X, page 1, Sep 29, 1935
                  page 20, Oct 14, 1935
                  X, page 3, Oct 20, 1935
                  IX, page 1, Oct 27, 1935
                  IX, page 8, Nov 24, 1935
   Newsweek 6:26-7, Oct 19, 1935
   Stage 13:30-1, Oct 1935
        13:33-4, Dec 1935
   Theatre Arts 19:901-2, Dec 1935
   Time 26:51, Oct 21, 1935
   Vanity Fair 45:68, Dec 1935

Jumbo (233 performances)
book: Ben Hecht and Charles MacArthur
music: Richard Rodgers
lyrics: Lorenz Hart
staging: John Murray Anderson
sets: Albert Johnson
costumes: Raoul Pene duBois and James

84

                        Reynolds
choreography: Allan K. Foster and Marjery Fielding
opened: November 16, 1935
    Literary Digest 120:18-19, Nov 30, 1935
    Nation 141:660, Dec 4, 1935
    New Republic 85:134, Dec 11, 1935
    New York Times page 12, Aug 8, 1935
                        IX, page 1, Aug 11, 1935
                        page 20, Nov 18, 1935
                        IX, page 1, Nov 24, 1935
                        IX, page 4, Dec 22, 1935
    Newsweek 6:30-2, Nov 23, 1935
    Stage 13:49-51, Jan 1936
    Theatre Arts 20:12+, Jan 1936
    Time 26:47, Nov 25, 1935
    Vanity Fair 45:57, Jan 1936

May Wine (213 performances)
book: Frank Mandel, adapted from The
                        Happy Alienist by Eric von Stroheim
                        and Wallace Smith
music: Sigmund Romberg
lyrics: Oscar Hammerstein II
staging: Jose Ruben
sets: Raymond Sovey
costumes: Kay Morrison
opened: December 5, 1935
    Catholic World 142:601, Feb 1936
    Commonweal 23:218, Dec 20, 1935
    Literary Digest 120:20, Dec 21, 1935
    New York Times page 23, Nov 23, 1935
                        page 30, Dec 6, 1935
    Newsweek 6:38, Dec 14, 1935
    Theatre Arts 20:103, Feb 1936
    Time 26:61, Dec 16, 1935

New Faces of 1936 (193 performances)
sketches: Mindret Lord and Everett Marcy
music: Alexander Fogarty and Irvin Graham
lyrics: June Sillman, Edwin Gilbert, Bickley
                        Reichner
staging: Leonard Sillman
sets: Stewart Chaney

                        85

costumes: Stewart Chaney
choreography: Ned McGurn
opened: May 19, 1936
    Catholic World 143:474, 602, Jul-Aug, 1936
    Commonweal 24:160, Jun 5, 1936
    Literary Digest 121:26, May 30, 1936
    New York Times page 24, May 20, 1936
                    IX, page 2, Jun 21, 1936

On Your Toes (315 performances)
book: George Abbott
music: Richard Rodgers
lyrics: Lorenz Hart
staging: Worthington Miner
sets: Jo Mielziner
costumes: Irene Sharaff
choreography: George Balanchine
opened: April 11, 1936
    America 92:163, Nov 6, 1954
    Catholic World 143:340, Jun 1936
                   180:228, Dec 1954
    Commonweal 23:724, Apr 24, 1936
                   61:166, Nov 12, 1954
    Mademoiselle 40:142, Nov 1954
    Nation 142:559, Apr 29, 1936
           179:390, Oct 30, 1954
    New Republic 131:22-3, Nov 1, 1954
    New York Times page 22, Mar 23, 1936
                    page 14, Apr 13, 1936
                    page 15, Feb 6, 1937
                    page 21, Aug 3, 1937
                    II, page 1, Oct 10, 1954
                    page 24, Oct 12, 1954
    New Yorker 30:84-6, Oct 23, 1954
    Newsweek 7:28-9, Apr 25, 1936
             44:93, Oct 25, 1954
    Theatre Arts 20:415, Jun 1936
                 38:22-3+, Dec 1954
    Time 37:56, Apr 20, 1936
         64:41, Oct 25, 1954
    Vogue 124:100-1, Oct 15, 1954

Porgy and Bess (124 performances)

86

```
book:            Dubose Heyward, adapted from Dubose
                 and Dorothy Heyward's play Porgy
music:           George Gershwin
lyrics:          DuBose Heyward and Ira Gershwin
staging:         Rouben Mamoulian
sets:            Sergei Soudekine
opened:          October 10, 1935
   America 88:687, Mar 21, 1953
            105:473, Jun 24, 1961
   Catholic World 142:340-1, Dec 1935
            177:148-9, May 1953
   Commonweal 22:642, Oct 25, 1935
            57:624-5, Mar 27, 1953
   Etude 74:14-15, Mar 1956
   Good Housekeeping 141:17+, Oct 1955
   Life 12:65, Feb 23, 1942
   Literary Digest 120:18, Oct 26, 1935
   Look 17:17, May 19, 1953
   Modern Music 19:195, Mar-Apr 1942
   Musical America 73:33, Apr 15, 1953
   Musical Courier 111:7, Oct 12, 1935
   Nation 141:518-19, Oct 30, 1935
          176:272, Mar 28, 1953
   New Republic 84:338, Oct 30, 1935
                128:30-1, Apr 6, 1953
   New York Theatre Critics' Reviews 1942:373+
                                     1953:337+
   New York Times IX, page 2, Sep 15, 1935
                      page 27, Oct 1, 1935
                      XI, page 3, Oct 6, 1935
                      page 30, Oct 11, 1935
                      X, page 1, Oct 20, 1935
                      X, page 7, Oct 20, 1935
                      page 25, Mar 17, 1936
                      page 16, Jan 23, 1942
                      IX, page 1, Feb 1, 1942
                      VIII, page 7, Nov 15, 1942
                      page 26, Sep 14, 1943
                      page 13, Feb 8, 1944
                      II, page 4, Jun 17, 1945
                      II, page 7, Nov 26, 1950
                      II, page 1, Sep 7, 1952
                      page 18, Sep 8, 1952
```

          19:893-4, Dec 1935
          37:89, Jun 1952
          37:64-5, May 1953
          39:66-7+, May 1955
          45:10-11, Jul 1961
   Time 26:49-50, Sep 30, 1935
          26:48-9, Oct 21, 1935
          39:45, Feb 2, 1942
          61:80, Mar 23, 1953
          65:83, Mar 7, 1955
   Vanity Fair 45:68, Dec 1935

Provincetown Follies (63 performances)
sketches: Frederick Herendeen, Gwynn Langdon,
                Barrie Oliver, George K. Arthur
music: Sylvan Green, Mary Schaeffer,
                Arthur Jones, Trevor Jones, Dave
                Stamper
lyrics: Frederick Herendeen, Gwynn Langdon,
                Barrie Oliver, George K. Arthur
staging: Lee Morrison
choreography: Mary Read
opened: November 3, 1935
   New York Times page 24, Nov 4, 1935

Scandals (1935) (see George White's Scandals)

Smile at Me (27 performances)
sketches: Edward J. Lambert
music: Gerald Dolin
lyrics: Edward J. Lambert
staging: Frank Merlin
sets: Karl Amend
costumes: Dorothy Van Winkle
choreography: Paul Florenz
opened: August 23, 1935
   New York Times page 18, Aug 24, 1935

Strip Girl (33 performances)
book: Henry Rosendahl
music: Harry Archer
lyrics: Jill Rainsford
staging: Jose Ruben

sets: Cirker and Robbins
opened: October 19, 1935
     New York Times page 22, Oct 21, 1935

Ziegfeld Follies (115 performances)
book: Ira Gershwin and David Freedman
music: Vernon Duke
lyrics: Ira Gershwin and David Freedman
staging: John Murray Anderson
sets: Vincente Minnelli
costumes: Vincente Minnelli
choreography: Robert Alton
opened: January 30, 1936
     Nation 142:231, Feb 19, 1936
     New York Times page 10, Dec 31, 1935
                 IX, page 3, Jan 5, 1936
                 page 17, Jan 31, 1936
     Time 27:47, Feb 10, 1936

                Season of 1936-1937

Babes in Arms (289 performances)
book: Lorenz Hart
music: Richard Rodgers
lyrics: Lorenz Hart
staging: Robert Sinclair
sets: Raymond Sovey
costumes: Helene Pons
choreography: George Balanchine
opened: April 14, 1937
     Catholic World 145:343, Jun 1937
     Commonweal 26:48, May 7, 1937
     New York Times page 18, Apr 15, 1937
     Newsweek 9:20+, Apr 24, 1937
     Theatre Arts 21:424-5, Jun 1937
     Time 29:26+, Apr 26, 1937

Black Rhythm (6 performances)
book: Donald Heywood
music: Donald Heywood
lyrics: Donald Heywood
staging: Earl Dancer and Donald Heywood
opened: December 19, 1936

                      90

New York Times page 19, Dec 21, 1936

Follies (1936-1937) (see Ziegfeld Follies of 1936-1937)

Forbidden Melody (32 performances)
book: Otto Harbach
music: Sigmund Romberg
lyrics: Otto Harbach
staging: Macklin Megley
sets: Sergei Soudeikine
costumes: Ten Eyck
opened: November 2, 1936
    New York Times page 30, Oct 13, 1936

Naughty Naught '00 (173 performances)
book: John Van Antwerp
music: Richard Lewine
lyrics: Ted Fetter
staging: Morgan Lewis
sets: Eugene Dunkel
opened: January 23, 1937
    New York Times page 23, Jan 25, 1937
                page 27, Oct 21, 1946
    Newsweek 9:35, Feb 6, 1937
    Time 48:63, Oct 28, 1946

Orchids Preferred (7 performances)
book: Fred Herendeen
music: Dave Stamper
lyrics: Fred Herendeen
staging: Alexander Leftwich
sets: Frederick Fox
choreography: Robert Sanford
opened: May 11, 1937
    New York Times page 16, Aug 29, 1937
                page 26, May 12, 1937

The Pepper Mill (6 performances)
sketches: W. H. Auden, Klaus Mann, Erich
                Muhsam, Ernst Toller, Erica Mann;
                English adaptation by John Latouche
                and Edwin Denby
music: Magnus Henning, Aaron Copland,

                    Peter Krender, Herbert Murril,
                    Werner Kruse
staging: Therese Giehse
sets: Anton Refregier
opened: January 5, 1937
    New York Times page 19, Jan 6, 1937
    Theatre Arts 21:6, Jan 1937

Red, Hot and Blue (183 performances)
book: Howard Lindsay and Russel Crouse
music: Cole Porter
lyrics: Cole Porter
staging: Howard Lindsay
sets: Donald Oenslager
costumes: Constance Ripley
choreography: George Hale
opened: October 29, 1936
    Catholic World 144:338-9, Dec 1936
    Nation 143:585, Nov 14, 1936
    New York Times page 28, Oct 8, 1936
                    X, page 3, Oct 11, 1936
                    page 26, Oct 30, 1936
                    X, page 1, Nov 8, 1936
    Newsweek 8:41, Nov 7, 1936
                34:88, Nov 14, 1949
    Photoplay 36:19, Dec 1949
    Stage 14:49, Oct 1936
    Time 28:21, Nov 9, 1936
            54:96, Nov 7, 1949

Sea Legs (15 performances)
book: Arthur Swanstrom
music: Michael H. Cleary
lyrics: Arthur Swanstrom
staging: Bertram Harrison
sets: Mabel Buell
choreography: Johnny Mattison
opened: May 18, 1937
    New York Times page 26, May 19, 1937

The Show Is On (237 performances)
assembled by: Vincente Minnelli
contributors: David Freedman, Moss Hart, Vernon

92

                    Duke, Ted Fetter, Howard Dietz,
                    Arthur Schwartz, Richard Rodgers,
                    Lorenz Hart
staging: Vincente Minnelli
sets: Vincente Minnelli
choreography: Harry Losee
opened: December 25, 1936
    Arts and Decoration 46:22-3, Jul 1937
    Catholic World 144:729-30, Mar 1937
    Nation 144:80, Jan 16, 1937
    New York Times page 22, Nov 9, 1936
                    XI, page 2, Nov 15, 1936
                    page 14, Dec 26, 1936
                    X, page 1, Jan 10, 1937
                    X, page 2, Feb 14, 1937
                    XI, page 8, Feb 28, 1937
                    page 18, Sep 20, 1937
                    X, page 3, Oct 31, 1937
    Newsweek 9:22, Jan 2, 1937
    Stage 13:33-5, Sep 1936
    Theatre Arts 21:97, Feb 1937
    Time 29:30-1, Jan 4, 1937
    Vogue 89:64, Feb 1, 1937

White Horse Inn (223 performances)
book: Hans Mueller, suggested by Oskar
                    Blumenthal and G. Kandelburg,
                    adapted by David Freedman
music: Ralph Benatsky
lyrics: Irving Caesar
staging: Erick Charell
sets: Ernst Stern
costumes: Irene Sharaff
choreography: Max Rivers
opened: October 1, 1936
    Catholic World 144:215, Nov 1936
    Collier's 98:64-6, Nov 7, 1936
    Commonweal 34:590, Oct 16, 1936
    Literary Digest 122:31-2, Oct 17, 1936
    New Republic 88:314, Oct 21, 1936
    New York Times X, page 1, Aug 16, 1936
                    page 28, Oct 2, 1936
                    X, page 2, Oct 11, 1936

Newsweek 8:28-9, Oct 10, 1936
Theatre Arts 20:848-9, Nov 1936
Time 28:53, Oct 12, 1936

Ziegfeld Follies of 1936-1937 (112 performances)
book: Ira Gershwin and David Freedman
music: Vernon Duke
lyrics: Ira Gershwin and David Freedman
staging: John Murray Anderson
sets: Vincente Minnelli
costumes: Vincente Minnelli
choreography: Robert Alton
opened: Sep 14, 1936
   New York Times page 37, Sep 15, 1936

Season of 1937-1938

Between the Devil (93 performances)
book: Howard Dietz
music: Arthur Schwartz
lyrics: Howard Dietz
staging: Hassard Short and John Hayden
sets: Albert Johnson
costumes: Kiviette
choreography: Robert Alton
opened: December 22, 1937
   Nation 146:754, Jan 1, 1938
   New York Times page 19, Oct 15, 1937
                    XI, page 2, Oct 24, 1937
                    page 24, Dec 23, 1937
   One Act Play Magazine 1:849, Jan 1938
   Stage 15:52-3, Feb 1938
   Time 31:22, Jan 3, 1938

The Cradle Will Rock (108 performances)
book: Marc Blitzstein
music: Marc Blitzstein
lyrics: Marc Blitzstein
staging: Marc Blitzstein
opened: January 3, 1938
   Catholic World 146:598-9, Feb 1938
   Commonweal 47:350, Jan 16, 1948
   Current History 48:53, Apr 1938

Forum 109:156, Mar 1948
Literary Digest 125:34, Jan 1, 1938
Magazine Art 32:356-7+, Jun 1939
Nation 146:107, Jan 22, 1938
        190:236, Mar 12, 1960
New Republic 93:310, Jan 19, 1938
            117:35-6, Dec 22, 1947
New York Theatre Critics' Reviews 1947:229+
New York Times page 19, Dec 6, 1937
                page 19, Jan 4, 1938
                II, page 7, Nov 23, 1947
                page 38, Nov 25, 1947
                II, page 9, Feb 7, 1960
                page 23, Feb 12, 1960
                II, page 9, Feb 21, 1960
                page 40, Nov 9, 1964
New Yorker 23:45, Jan 10, 1948
          36:142-3, Feb 20, 1960
Newsweek 10:20-1, Jul 3, 1937
         30:78, Dec 7, 1948
         64:102, Nov 23, 1964
Reporter 30:46+, May 21, 1964
Saturday Review 31:22-4, Jan 17, 1948
Scribner's Magazine 103:70-1, Mar 1938
Stage 15:54, Feb 1938
Theatre Arts 22:98-9, Feb 1938
Time 29:46+, Jun 28, 1937
     30:57, Dec 13, 1937
     51:64, Jan 5, 1948

The Fireman's Flame (204 performances)
book: John Van Antwerp
music: Richard Lewine
lyrics: Ted Fetter
staging: John and Jerrold Krimsky
sets: Eugene Dunkel
costumes: Kermit Love
choreography: Morgan Lewis
opened: October 9, 1937
  Life 3:62-5, Dec 27, 1937
  New York Times XI, page 3, Oct 3, 1937
                 page 26, Oct 10, 1937

A Hero Is Born (50 performances)
book: Theresa Helburn, based on a fairy tale
                by Andrew Lang
music: A. Lehman Engel
lyrics: Agnes Morgan
staging: Agnes Morgan
sets: Tom Adrian Cracraft
costumes: Alexander Saron
opened: October 1, 1937
    Catholic World 146:218, Nov 1937
    New York Times page 18, Oct 2, 1937
    Time 30:54, Oct 11, 1937

Hooray for What! (200 performances)
book: Howard Lindsay and Russel Crouse
                (conceived by E. Y. Harburg)
music: Harold Arlen
lyrics: E. Y. Harburg
staging: Howard Lindsay
sets: Vincente Minnelli
costumes: Raoul Pene du Bois
choreography: Robert Alton
opened: December 1, 1937
    Catholic World 146:470, Jan 1938
    Commonweal 27:220, Dec 17, 1937
    Life 3:44-6, Dec 20, 1937
    Literary Digest 124:34-5, Dec 25, 1937
    Nation 145:698, Dec 18, 1937
    New Republic 93:198, Dec 22, 1937
    New York Times XI, page 2, Nov 7, 1937
                    page 32, Dec 2, 1937
                X, page 3, Jan 9, 1938
    Stage 15:51-3, Dec 1937
    Time 30:57, Dec 13, 1937

I Married An Angel (338 performances)
book: Richard Rodgers and Lorenz Hart,
                adapted from John Veszary's
                Hungarian play
music: Richard Rodgers
lyrics: Lorenz Hart
staging: Joshua Logan
sets: Jo Mielziner

96

costumes: John Hambleton
choreography: George Balanchine
opened: May 11, 1938
   Catholic World 147:474-5, Jul 1938
   Commonweal 28:133, May 27, 1938
   Life 4:48-9, May 30, 1938
   New York Times page 26, May 12, 1938
                  XI, page 1, May 22, 1938
                  IX, page 8, Jul 17, 1938
   Newsweek 11:20, May 23, 1938
   Stage 15:13-15, Jun 1938
   Theatre Arts 22:464, Jul 1938
   Time 31:20, May 23, 1938

I'd Rather Be Right (290 performances)
book: George S. Kaufman and Moss Hart
music: Richard Rodgers
lyrics: Lorenz Hart
staging: George S. Kaufman
sets: Donald Oenslager
costumes: Irene Sharaff
choreography: Charles Weidman
opened: November 2, 1937
   Catholic World 146:339-40, Dec 1937
   Commonweal 27:106, Nov 19, 1937
   Independent Woman 16:351, Nov 1937
   Life 3:27-9, Oct 25, 1937
   Literary Digest 1:35, Nov 20, 1937
   New Republic 93:44, Nov 17, 1937
   New York Times page 27, Oct 12, 1937
                  IX, page 2, Oct 17, 1937
                  page 18, Oct 26, 1937
                  page 28, Nov 3, 1937
                  XI, page 2, Nov 7, 1937
   Newsweek 10:24-6, Oct 25, 1937
             10:29, Nov 15, 1937
   Scholastic 31:2, Oct 30, 1937
   Scribner's Magazine 103:70, Jan 1938
   Stage 15:52-4, Nov 1937
       15:94, Nov 1937
       15:56-9, Dec 1937
   Theatre Arts 21:924+, Dec 1937
   Time 30:45, Oct 25, 1937

30:25, Nov 15, 1937
Vogue 90:108+, Dec 1, 1937

Pins and Needles (1,108 performances)
book: Arthur Arent, Marc Blitzstein,
                Emanuel Eisenberg, Charles Fried-
                man, David Gregory
music: Harold J. Rome
lyrics: Harold J. Rome
staging: Charles Friedman
sets: S. Syrjala
choreography: Benjamin Zemach
opened: November 27, 1937
  Catholic World 147:215, May 1938
                 150:86-7, Oct 1939
  Collier's 102:34+, Nov 12, 1938
  Independent Woman 17:52, Feb 1938
                     17:359, Nov 1938
  Life 3:52-3, Dec 27, 1937
  Literary Digest 125:34, Jan 1, 1938
  Nation 145:698, Dec 18, 1937
  New York Theatre Critics' Reviews 1940:497+
  New York Times page 24, Jun 15, 1936
                  page 18, Nov 29, 1937
                  XI, page 1, Jan 23, 1938
                  IX, page 3, Aug 21, 1938
                  page 27, Dec 6, 1938
                  X, page 3, Dec 11, 1938
                  page 16, Jan 24, 1939
                  page 26, Apr 21, 1939
                  page 19, Nov 21, 1939
  Scholastic 32:19E, Mar 5, 1938
  Stage 15:54-5, Feb 1938
  Theatre Arts 22:4, Jan 1938
               23:403, Jun 1939
               24:20, Jan 1940
  Time 31:32+, Mar 14, 1938

Right This Way (15 performances)
book: Marianne Brown Waters; additional
                dialogue by Parke Levy and Allen
                Lipscott; additional songs by Sammy
                Fain and Irving Kahal

98

music:	Brad Greene and Fabian Storey
lyrics:	Marianne Brown Waters
staging:	Bertram Robinson and Alice Alexander
sets:	Nat Karson
costumes:	Miles White
choreography:	Marjery Fielding
opened:	January 4, 1938

New York Times VI, page 6, Oct 31, 1937
                 page 22, Jan 6, 1938

Swing It (60 performances)
book:	Cecil Mack and Milton Reddie
music:	Eubie Blake
lyrics:	Cecil Mack and Milton Reddie
staging:	Cecil Mack and Jack Mason
sets:	Walter Walden and Victor Zanoff
costumes:	Maxine and Alexander Jones
opened:	July 22, 1937

New York Times page 17, Jul 22, 1937

Three Waltzes (122 performances)
book:	Clare Kummer and Rowland Leigh, adapted from Paul Knepler and Armin Robinson's play
music:	Johann Strauss, Sr., Johann Strauss, Jr., Oscar Straus
lyrics:	Clare Kummer, Edwin Gilbert
staging:	Hassard Short
sets:	Watson Barratt
costumes:	Connie dePinna
choreography:	Chester Hale
opened:	December 25, 1937

Commonweal 27:300, Jan 7, 1938
New York Times page 15, Nov 15, 1937
                 page 10, Dec 27, 1937
One Act Play Magazine 1:849, Jan 1938
Stage 15:51, Feb 1938
Theatre Arts 22:100, Feb 1938
Time 31:24, Jan 3, 1938

Virginia (60 performances)
book:	Laurence Stallings and Owen Davis
music:	Arthur Schwartz

lyrics:	Albert Stillman
staging:	Leon Leonidoff
sets:	Lee Simonson
costumes:	Irene Sharaff
choreography:	Florence Rogge
opened:	Sep 2, 1937

   Catholic World 146:86, Oct 1937
   Commonweal 26:478, Sep 17, 1937
   Nation 145:303, Sep 18, 1937
   New York Times page 13, Sep 3, 1937
                 XI, page 1, Sep 12, 1937
                 page 29, Oct 5, 1937
   Newsweek 10:25, Sep 13, 1937
   Stage 14:34-5, Sep 1937
   Theatre Arts 21:836-7, Nov 1937

Who's Who (23 performances)

assembled by:	Leonard Sillman
sketches:	Leonard Sillman and Everett Marcy
music:	Baldwin Bergerson, James Shelton, Irvin Graham, Paul McGrane
lyrics:	June Sillman, Irvin Graham, James Shelton
staging:	Leonard Sillman
sets:	Mercedes
costumes:	Billi Livingston
opened:	March 1, 1938

   New York Times page 16, Mar 2, 1938
                 page 24, Mar 20, 1938

Season of 1938-1939

Blackbirds (1939) (see Lew Leslie's Blackbirds of 1939)

The Boys from Syracuse (235 performances)

book:	George Abbott, based on Shakespeare's The Comedy of Errors
music:	Richard Rodgers
lyrics:	Lorenz Hart
staging:	George Abbott
sets:	Jo Mielziner
costumes:	Irene Sharaff

choreography: George Balanchine
opened: November 23, 1938
   Catholic World 148:474-6, Jan 1939
   Commonweal 29:190, Dec 9, 1938
   Life 5:43-4, Dec 12, 1938
   Nation 147:638, Dec 10, 1938
   New Republic 97:173, Dec 14, 1938
   New York Times IX, page 2, Nov 13, 1938
                    page 36, Nov 24, 1938
                    X, page 5, Dec 4, 1938
                    II, page 1, Jun 2, 1963
                    page 14, Nov 9, 1963
                    page 37, Jun 19, 1964
   New Yorker 39:84, Apr 27, 1963
   North American Review 247 no1:159-60, Mar 1939
   Saturday Review 46:33, Aug 10, 1963
   Theatre Arts 23:10-11, Jan 1939
                47:13, Jun 1963
                47:14-15, Jun 1963
   Time 32:35, Sep 26, 1938
        32:44, Dec 5, 1938

The Devil and Daniel Webster (6 performances)
book: Douglas Moore, based on Stephen
               Vincent Benet's short story
music: Douglas Moore
lyrics: Douglas Moore
staging: John Houseman
sets: Robert Edmund Jones
choreography: Eugene Loring
opening: May 18, 1939
   Commonweal 30:160, Jun 2, 1939
   Life 6:37-8+, Jun 12, 1939
   Musical Courier 119:7, Jun 1, 1939
   New Republic 99:131, Jun 7, 1939
   New York Times page 26, May 19, 1939
                    X, page 1, May 21, 1939
   Newsweek 13:34, Jun 5, 1939
   Saturday Review 20:10, May 20, 1939
                    20:8, May 27, 1939
   Time 33:40, May 29, 1939

Great Lady (20 performances)

101

book:	Earle Crooker and Lowell Brentano
music:	Frederick Loewe
lyrics:	Earle Crooker and Lowell Brentano
staging:	Bretaigne Windust
sets:	Albert R. Johnson
costumes:	Lucinda Ballard and Scott Wilson
choreography:	William Dollar
opened:	December 1, 1938

Catholic World 148:477-8, Jan 1939
New York Times page 26, Dec 2, 1938
Time 32:32, Dec 12, 1938

Hellzapoppin (1,404 performances)
assembled by:	Ole Olson and Chic Johnson
music:	Sammy Fain
lyrics:	Charles Tobias
staging:	Edward Duryea Dowling
opened:	September 22, 1938

Catholic World 148:215, Nov 1938
Collier's 102:16-17+, Dec 10, 1938
Commonweal 31:227, Dec 29, 1939
Life 5:30-3, Oct 24, 1938
New York Theatre Critics' Reviews 1940:493+
                      1941:495+
New York Times page 34, Sep 23, 1938
                IX, page 1, Oct 2, 1938
                X, page 1, Sep 17, 1939
                page 36, Dec 12, 1939
                page 14, Sep 20, 1940
                page 39, Jan 19, 1941
                IX, page 2, Mar 2, 1941
                IX, page 1, Aug 3, 1941
                VIII, page 2, Feb 15, 1942
Newsweek 12:28, Oct 10, 1938
            14:28, Dec 25, 1939
Stage 16:20-2, Jan 1939
Theatre Arts 22:783, Nov 1938
            24:93-4, Feb 1940
Time 32:30, Oct 3, 1938
          34:24, Dec 25, 1939

Knickerbocker Holiday (168 performances)
book:	Maxwell Anderson

music: Kurt Weill
lyrics: Maxwell Anderson
staging: Joshua Logan
sets: Jo Mielziner
costumes: Frank Bevan
choreography: Carl Randall and Edwin Denby
opened: October 19, 1938
   Catholic World 148:343-4, Dec 1938
   Commonweal 29:48, Nov 4, 1938
   Life 5:27, Nov 21, 1938
   Modern Music 16:54-6, Nov 1938
   Nation 147:488-9, Nov 5, 1938
        147:673, Dec 17, 1938
   New Republic 97:18, Nov 9, 1938
   New York Times IX, page 1, Sep 25, 1938
             IX, page 3, Oct 2, 1938
             page 26, Oct 20, 1938
             IX, page 1, Nov 20, 1938
   Newsweek 12:29, Oct 31, 1938
   North American Review 246 no2:374-6, Dec 1938
   Theatre Arts 22:862, Dec 1938
   Time 32:55, Oct 31, 1938

Knights of Song (16 performances)
book: Glendon Allvine, based on a story by
                Glendon Allvine and Adele Gutman
                Nathan
music: excerpts from Gilbert and Sullivan
                operettas
lyrics: excerpts from Gilbert and Sullivan
                operettas
staging: Oscar Hammerstein and Avalon
                Collard
sets: Raymond Sovey
costumes: Kate Lawson
opened: October 17, 1938
   Commonweal 29:48, Nov 4, 1938
   Musical Courier 118:11, Aug 15, 1938
   New York Times page 29, Oct 18, 1938
   Time 32:54, Oct 31, 1938

Leave It to Me (307 performances)
book: Bella and Samuel Spewack

music: Cole Porter
lyrics: Cole Porter
staging: Samuel Spewack
sets: Albert Johnson
costumes: Raoul Pene duBois
choreography: Robert Alton
opened: November 9, 1938
   Catholic World 148:477, Jan 1939
   Commonweal 29:132, Nov 25, 1938
   Life 5:53-5, Nov 7, 1938
   Nation 147:572-3, Nov 26, 1938
   New Republic 97:100, Nov 30, 1938
   New York Times IX, page 3, Oct 23, 1938
             page 32, Nov 10, 1938
             IX, page 1, Nov 20, 1938
             IX, page 3, Nov 20, 1938
             IX, page 1, Sep 10, 1939
             page 20, Sep 16, 1929
             page 27, Jan 18, 1940
   Newsweek 12:24, Nov 21, 1938
   North American Review 247 no2:369, (Jun) 1939
   Stage 16:10-11, Nov 1938
      16:12-15, Dec 1938
   Theatre Arts 23:6+, Jan 1939
   Time 32:39, Nov 7, 1938
      32:66, Nov 21, 1938

Lew Leslie's Blackbirds of 1939 (9 performances)
assembled by: Lew Leslie
music: Ruble Bloom and others
lyrics: Johnny Mercer and others
staging: Lew Leslie
sets: Mabel A. Buell
costumes: Frances Feist
opened: February 11, 1939
   New York Times IX, page 2, Nov 13, 1938
             page 12, Feb 13, 1939

One for the Money (132 performances)
book: Nancy Hamilton
music: Morgan Lewis
lyrics: Nancy Hamilton
staging: John Murray Anderson

```
sets:             Raoul Pene duBois
choreography:     Robert Alton
opened:           February 4, 1939
   Catholic World 148:730, Mar 1939
   New York Times page 9, Feb 6, 1939
   Stage 16:11-12, Feb 1939
```

Sing for Your Supper (44 performances)
```
compiled by:      Harold Hecht
sketches:         Dave Lesan, Turner Bullock,
                     Charlotte Kent, John Latouche
music:            Lee Wainer and Ned Lehak
lyrics:           Robert Sour
staging:          H. Gordon Graham and Harold Hecht
sets:             Herbert Andrews
costumes:         Mary Merrill
choreography:     Anna Sokolow
opened:           April 24, 1939
   Catholic World 149:345-6, Jun 1939
   New York Times page 18, Apr 25, 1939
   Newsweek 13:22, May 8, 1939
   Theatre Arts 23:404, Jun 1939
```

Sing Out the News (105 performances)
```
book:             Harold Rome and Charles Friedman
music:            Will Irwin
lyrics:           Harold Rome
staging:          Charles Friedman
sets:             Jo Mielziner
costumes:         John Hambleton
choreography:     Ned McGurn, Dave Gould, Charles
                     Walters
opened:           September 24, 1938
   Catholic World 148:214-15, Nov 1938
   Commonweal 28:615, Oct 7, 1938
   New Republic 96:271, Oct 12, 1938
   New York Times page 12, Sep 26, 1938
                     IX, page 1, Oct 2, 1938
   Stage 16:6+, Oct 1938
   Theatre Arts 22:784, Nov 1938
   Time 32:30, Oct 3, 1938
```

Stars in Your Eyes (Swing to the Left) (127 perform-

ances)
book: J. P. McEvoy
music: Arthur Schwartz
lyrics: Dorothy Fields
staging: Joshua Logan
sets: Jo Mielziner
costumes: John Hambleton
choreography: Carl Randall
opened: February 9, 1939
    Life 6:66-9, Feb 27, 1939
    Catholic World 149:88-9, Apr 1939
    Commonweal 29:525, Mar 3, 1939
    New York Times page 18, Feb 10, 1939
                    X, page 1, Mar 5, 1939
    Nation 148:245, Feb 25, 1939
    New Republic 98:102-3, Mar 1, 1939
    Stage 16:4+, Feb 1939
    Theatre Arts 23:242-3, Apr 1939
    Time 33:54-5, Feb 20, 1939

Susanna, Don't You Cry (4 performances)
book: Sarah Newmeyer and Clarence Loomis
music: Melodies of Stephen Foster; special
                    music by Haus Spialek
lyrics: Sarah Newmeyer and Clarence Loomis
staging: Jose Ruben
sets: Robert Edmund Jones
opened: May 22, 1939
    Musical Courier 119: 7, Jun 1, 1939
    New York Times X, page 7, Apr 16, 1939
                    page 27, May 23, 1939
    Newsweek 13:34, Jun 5, 1939

You Never Know (78 performances)
book: Rowland Leigh, adapted from the
                    original by Robert Katscher,
                    Siegfried Geyer, Karl Farkas
music: Cole Porter
lyrics: Cole Porter
staging: Rowland Leigh
sets: Watson Barratt and Albert Johnson
choreography: Robert Alton
opened: September 21, 1938

Catholic World 148:215, Nov 1938
New York Times page 16, Mar 4, 1938
               page 26, Sep 22, 1938
Theatre Arts 22:783, Nov 1938
Time 31:38, Apr 11, 1938

Season of 1939-1940

DuBarry Was A Lady (408 performances)
book: B. G. DeSylva and Herbert Fields
music: Cole Porter
lyrics: Cole Porter
staging: Edgar McGregor
sets: Raoul Pene duBois
costumes: Raoul Pene duBois
choreography: Robert Alton
opened: December 6, 1939
   Commonweal 31:227, Dec 29, 1939
   Life 7:58-63, Dec 11, 1939
   Nation 149:716, Dec 23, 1939
   New York Theatre Critics' Reviews 1940:439+
   New York Times X, page 3, Nov 19, 1939
               page 34, Dec 7, 1939
               IX, page 1, Dec 24, 1939
               page 29, Apr 10, 1941
               VIII, page 2, Nov 1, 1942
   Newsweek 14:35, Dec 18, 1939
   Theatre Arts 24:39-49, Jan 1940
                24:92-3, Feb 1940
   Time 34:45, Dec 18, 1939

Earl Carroll Vanities (25 performances)
assembled by: Earl Carroll
music: Charles Rosoff and Peter deRose
lyrics: Dorcas Cochran and Mitchell Parrish
staging: Earl Carroll
sets: Jean LeSeyeux
costumes: Jean LeSeyeux
choreography: Eddie Prinz
opened: January 13, 1940
   New York Theatre Critics' Reviews 1940:418+
   New York Times page 1, Jan 15, 1940

From Vienna (79 performances)
sketches: Lothar Metzl, Werner Michel, Hans
                 Weigel, Jura Soyfer, Peter Hammer-
                 schlag, David Gregory; adaptations
                 by John LaTouche, Eva Frankin,
                 Hugo Hauff
music: Werner Michel, Walter Drix, Otto
                 Andreas, Jimmy Berg
lyrics: Lothar Metzl, Werner Michel, Hans
                 Weigel, Jura Soyfer, Peter Hammer-
                 schlag, David Gregory; adaptations
                 by John LaTouche, Eva Frankin,
                 Hugo Hauff
staging: Herbert Berghof
sets: Donald Oenslager
costumes: Irene Sharaff
opened: June 20, 1939
   Life 7:32-3, Jul 17, 1939
   Nation 149:109, Jul 22, 1939
   New York Times page 26, Jun 21, 1939
                      IX, page 1, Jun 25, 1939
                      IX, page 1, Jul 2, 1939
   Newsweek 14:24, Jul 19, 1939
   Time 34:43, Jul 3, 1939

George White's Scandals (120 performances)
sketches: Matt Brooks, Eddie Davis, George
                 White
music: Sammy Fain
lyrics: Jack Yellen
staging: George White
sets: Albert Johnson
costumes: Charles LeMaire
opened: August 28, 1939
   New York Times IX, page 2, Aug 20, 1939
                     page 17, Aug 29, 1939
                     IX, page 1, Sep 3, 1939
   Newsweek 14:40-1, Sep 11, 1939
   Time 34:55, Sep 11, 1939

Higher and Higher (84 performances)
book: Gladys Hurlbut and Joshua Logan,
                 based on an idea by Irvin Pincus

108

music: Richard Rodgers
lyrics: Lorenz Hart
staging: Joshua Logan
sets: Jo Mielziner
costumes: Lucinda Ballard
choreography: Robert Alton
opened: April 4, 1940
   Life 8:42+, Apr 15, 1940
   New York Theatre Critics' Reviews 1940:337+
   New York Times X, page 2, Mar 17, 1940
                  page 24, Apr 5, 1940
                  page 15, Aug 6, 1940
                  IX, page 1, Aug 11, 1940
   Time 35:76, Apr 15, 1940

John Henry (7 performances)
book: Roark Bradford
music: Jaques Wolfe
lyrics: Roark Bradford
staging: Anthony Brown and Charles Friedman
sets: Albert Johnson
costumes: John Hambleton
opened: January 10, 1940
   Catholic World 150:598-9, Feb 1940
   Collier's 105:15+, Jan 13, 1940
   New York Theatre Critics' Reviews 1940:421+
   New York Times IX, page 1, Jan 7, 1940
                  page 18, Jan 11, 1940
   Newsweek 15:33, Jan 22, 1940
   Theatre Arts 24:166-7, Mar 1940
   Time 35:49, Jan 22, 1940

Keep Off the Grass (44 performances)
book: Mort Lewis, Parke Levy, Alan
                Lipscott, S. J. Kaufman, Reginald
                Beckwith, Panama and Frank
music: James McHugh
lyrics: Al Dubin and Howard Dietz
staging: Fred deCordova
sets: Nat Carson
costumes: Nat Carson
choreography: George Balanchine
opened: May 23, 1940

Catholic World 151:471-2, Jul 1940
Commonweal 32:212, Jun 18, 1940
Life 9:52-4, Jul 8, 1940
Nation 150:716, Jun 8, 1940
New York Theatre Critics' Reviews 1940:302+
New York Times X, page 1, May 5, 1940
                  page 22, May 24, 1940
                  IX, page 1, Jun 16, 1940
Newsweek 15:44, Jun 3, 1940
Time 35:52, Jun 3, 1940

Louisiana Purchase (444 performances)

book:	Morrie Ryskind, based on a story by B. G. DeSylva
music:	Irving Berlin
lyrics:	Irving Berlin
staging:	Edgar MacGregor
sets:	Tom Lee
costumes:	Tom Lee
choreography:	George Balanchine and Carl Randall
opened:	May 28, 1940

   Catholic World 151:471, Jul 1940
   Commonweal 32:191-2, Jun 21, 1940
   Life 8:100-3, Jun 10, 1940
   Nation 150:716, Jun 8, 1940
   New York Theatre Critics' Reviews 1940:296+
                                  1941:484+
   New York Times page 19, May 29, 1940
                IX, page 1, Jun 16, 1940
   New Yorker 16:38, Jun 8, 1940
   Newsweek 15:43, Jun 10, 1940
   Theatre Arts 24:774+, Nov 1940
   Time 35:63, Jun 10, 1940

Reunion in New York (89 performances)

conceived by:	Lothar Metzl and Werner Michel
sketches:	Carl Don, Richard Alma, Richard Holden, Hans Lefebre
music:	André Singer, Bert Silving, Berenece Kazouneff, M. Cooper Paul
lyrics:	David Gregory, Peter Barry, Stewart Arthur
staging:	Herbert Berghof and Ezra Stone

```
sets:            Harry Horner
costumes:        Lester Polakov
choreography:    Lotte Gosler
opened:          February 21, 1940
   New York Theatre Critics' Reviews 1940:388+
   New York Times page 28, Feb 22, 1940
                    X, page 1, Mar 3, 1940
   Theatre Arts 24:237, Apr 1940
   Time 35:34, Mar 4, 1940
```

Scandals (1939) (see George White's Scandals)

The Straw Hat Revue (75 performances)
```
conceived by:    Max Liebman
assembled by:    Max Liebman
sketches:        Max Liebman and Samuel Locke
music:           Sylvia Fine and James Shelton; special
                    music by Glenn Bacon
lyrics:          Sylvia Fine and James Shelton
staging:         Max Liebman
sets:            Edward Gilbert
choreography:    Jerome Andrews
opened:          September 29, 1939
   Catholic World 150:216, Nov 1939
   Commonweal 30.569, Oct 13, 1939
   New York Times page 10, Sep 30, 1939
                    IX, page 3, Oct 29, 1939
                    IX, page 8, Nov 12, 1939
   Theatre Arts 23:860-2, Dec 1939
   Time 34:49, Oct 9, 1939
```

Streets of Paris (274 performances)
```
sketches:        Charles Sherman, Tom McKnight,
                    Mitchell Hodges, S. Jay Kaufman,
                    Edward Duryea Dowling, James
                    LaVer, Frank Eyton, Lee Brody
music:           James McHugh
lyrics:          Harold J. Rome and Al Dubin
staging:         Edward Duryea Dowling and Dennis
                    Murray
sets:            Lawrence L. Goldwasser
costumes:        Irene Sharaff
choreography:    Robert Alton
```

111

opened: June 19, 1939
   Commonweal 30:278, Jul 7, 1939
   Life 7:32+, Jul 17, 1939
   Nation 149:110, Jul 22, 1939
   New York Theatre Critics' Reviews 1940:484+
   New York Times page 25, Jun 20, 1939
                         IX, page 1, Jun 25, 1939
                         IX, page 4, Dec 17, 1939
   Newsweek 14:28, Jul 3, 1939
   Time 34:42, Jul 3, 1939

Swingin' the Dream (13 performances)
book: Gilbert Seldes and Erik Charell, based
                on Shakespeare's A Midsummer
                Night's Dream
music: Jimmy Van Heusen
lyrics: Eddie deLange
staging: Erik Charell
sets: Herbert Andrews and Walter Jageman,
                based on Walt Disney cartoons
choreography: Agnes deMille and Herbert White
opened: November 29, 1939
   Catholic World 150:471, Jan 1940
   New York Times page 24, Nov 30, 1939
                  page 66, Dec 10, 1939
   Theatre Arts 24:93, Feb 1940
   Time 34:50, Dec 11, 1939

Too Many Girls (249 performances)
book: George Marion, Jr.
music: Richard Rodgers
lyrics: Lorenz Hart
staging: George Abbott
sets: Jo Mielziner
costumes: Raoul Pene duBois
choreography: Robert Alton
opened: October 18, 1939
   Catholic World 150:338, Dec 1939
   Commonweal 31:96, Nov 17, 1939
   Life 7:78-80, Oct 23, 1939
   New Republic 101:16, Nov 8, 1939
   New York Theatre Critics' Reviews 1940:467+
   New York Times page 26, Oct 19, 1939

112

Theatre Arts 23:861, Dec 1939
Time 34:42, Oct 30, 1939

Two for the Show (124 performances)
sketches: Nancy Hamilton
music: Morgan Lewis
lyrics: Nancy Hamilton
staging: John Murray Anderson
sets: Raoul Pene duBois
costumes: Raoul Pene duBois
choreography: Robert Alton
opened: February 8, 1940
   Catholic World 150:731-2, Mar 1940
   Commonweal 31:386, Feb 23, 1940
   New York Theatre Critics' Reviews 1940:394+
   New York Times page 14, Feb 9, 1940
                  IX, page 1, Feb 18, 1940
                  IX, page 2, Feb 18, 1940
   Theatre Arts 24:237-8, Apr 1940

Vanities (1940) (see Earl Carroll's Vanities)

Very Warm for May (59 performances)
book: Oscar Hammerstein II
music: Jerome Kern
lyrics: Oscar Hammerstein II
staging: Oscar Hammerstein II and Vincente
                  Minnelli
sets: Vincente Minnelli
choreography: Albertina Rasch
opened: November 17, 1939
   Catholic World 150:470, Jan 1940
   Commonweal 31:137, Dec 1, 1939
   New York Times IX, page 2, Nov 12, 1939
                  page 23, Nov 18, 1939
   Theatre Arts 24:19, Jan 1940
   Time 34:60, Nov 27, 1939

Walk With Music (55 performances)
book: Guy Bolton, Parke Levy, Alan
                  Lipscott, based on Stephen Powys'
                  Three Blind Mice

113

music: Hoagy Carmichael
lyrics: Johnny Mercer
staging: R. H. Burnside
sets: Watson Barratt
costumes: Tom Lee
choreography: Anton Dolin and Herbert Harper
opened: June 4, 1940
    Catholic World 151:472, Jul 1940
    New York Theatre Critics' Reviews 1940:290+
    New York Times page 33, Jun 5, 1940

Yokel Boy (208 performances)
book: Lew Brown and Charles Tobias
music: Sam Stept
lyrics: Lew Brown and Charles Tobias
staging: Lew Brown
sets: Walter Jagemann
costumes: Frances Feist and Veronica
choreography: Gene Snyder
opened: July 6, 1939
    New York Theatre Critics' Reviews 1940:481+
    New York Times page 12, Jul 12, 1939
                    page 16, Aug 17, 1939
    Time 34:66, Jul 17, 1939

                    Season of 1940-1941

All in Fun (3 performances)
book: Virginia Faulkner and Everett Marcy
music and
 lyrics: Baldwin Bergerson, June Sillman,
                        John Rox, Irvin Graham, Will Irwin,
                        Pembroke Davenport, S. K. Russell
staging: Leonard Sillman
sets: Edward Gilbert
costumes: Irene Sharaff
choreography: Marjorie Fielding
opened: December 27, 1940
    New York Theatre Critics' Reviews 1940:167+
    New York Times page 26, Nov 22, 1940
                    page 11, Dec 28, 1940
    Stage 1:6, Dec 1940

                        114

Boys and Girls Together (191 performances)
book: Ed Wynn and Pat C. Flick
music: Sammy Fain
lyrics: Jack Yellen and Irving Kahal
staging: Ed Wynn
sets: William Oden Waller
costumes: Irene Sharaff and Veronica
choreography: Albertina Rasch
opened: October 1, 1940
   Catholic World 152:218-19, Nov 1940
   Life 9:57-8+, Oct 7, 1940
   Nation 151:345, Oct 12, 1940
   New Republic 103:526, Oct 14, 1940
   New York Theatre Critics' Reviews 1940:266,
                                      1941:475+
   New York Times page 28, Sep 5, 1940
                   IX, page 1, Sep 15, 1940
                   page 19, Oct 2, 1940
                   IX, page 1, Oct 13, 1940
   Newsweek 16:74, Oct 14, 1940
   Stage 1:8, Nov 1940
         1:42-3, Nov 1940
         1:7, Dec 1940
   Theatre Arts 24:773-4, Nov 1940
   Time 36:62, Oct 4, 1940

Cabin in the Sky (156 performances)
book: Lynn Root
music: Vernon Duke
lyrics: John La Touche
staging: George Balanchine
sets: Boris Aronson
costumes: Boris Aronson
opened: October 25, 1940
   America 110:239, Feb 15, 1964
   Catholic World 152:333-4, Dec 1940
   Commonweal 33:80, Nov 8, 1940
   Life 9:63+, Dec 9, 1940
   Nation 151:458, Nov 9, 1940
   New Republic 103:661, Nov 11, 1940
   New York Theatre Critics' Reviews 1940:242+
                                      1941:463+
   New York Times page 19, Oct 26, 1940

115

IX, page 3, Nov 10, 1940
Newsweek 16:62, Nov 4, 1940
Stage 1:24-5, Dec 1940
Theatre Arts 24:841-2+, Dec 1940
Time 36:51, Nov 4, 1940

Crazy with the Heat (99 performances)
sketches: Sam E. Werris, Arthur Sheekman,
                Mack Davis, Max Liebman, Don
                Herold
music: Irvin Graham, Dana Suesse, Rudi
                Revil
lyrics: Irvin Graham, Dana Suesse, Rudi
                Revil
staging: Kurt Kasznar
sets: Albert Johnson
costumes: Lester Polakov and Marie Humans
choreography: Catherine Littlefield
opened: January 14, 1941
  Catholic World 152:728, Mar 1941
  Nation 152:137, Feb 1, 1941
  New York Theatre Critics' Reviews 1941:410+
  New York Times page 18, Jan 15, 1941
                page 25, Jan 16, 1941
                page 15, Jan 31, 1941
  Theatre Arts 25:257+, Apr 1941

Hold On to Your Hats (158 performances)
book: Guy Bolton, Matt Brooks, Eddie Davis
music: Burton Lane
lyrics: E. Y. Harburg
staging: Edgar MacGregor
sets: Raoul Pene duBois
choreography: Catherine Littlefield
opened: September 11, 1940
  Catholic World 152:218-19, Nov 1940
  Life 9:60-2, Jul 29, 1940
  Nation 151:281, Sep 28, 1940
  New York Theatre Critics' Reviews 1940:278+
                                   1941:481+
  New York Times page 25, Jul 17, 1940
                IX, page 1, Jul 21, 1940
                page 30, Sep 12, 1940

116

IX, page 3, Oct 20, 1940
Stage 1:12, Nov 1940
     1:12, Dec 1940
Theatre Arts 24:770-1+, Nov 1940
Time 36:41, Sep 23, 1940

Lady in the Dark (162 performances)
book: Moss Hart
music: Kurt Weill
lyrics: Ira Gershwin
staging: Hassard Short and Moss Hart
sets: Harry Horner
costumes: Irene Sharaff and Hattie Carnegie
choreography: Albertina Rasch
opened: January 23, 1941
   Catholic World 152:726-7, Mar 1941
   Commonweal 33:401, Feb 7, 1941
                  37:542, Mar 19, 1943
   Life 10:43, Feb 17, 1941
   Nation 152:164, Feb 8, 1941
   New Republic 104:179, Feb 10, 1941
   New York Theatre Critics' Reviews 1941:400+
   New York Times page 18, Dec 31, 1940
                  IX, page 1, Jan 5, 1941
                  page 14, Jan 24, 1941
                  IX, page 1, Feb 2, 1941
                  IX, page 3, Apr 6, 1941
                  page 26, Sep 3, 1941
                  IX, page 1, Sep 7, 1941
                  page 14, Mar 1, 1943
                  II, page 1, Mar 7, 1943
   New Yorker 16:27, Feb 1, 1941
   Newsweek 17:59, Feb 3, 1941
   Stage 1:26-7, Feb 1941
   Theatre Arts 25:177-8+, Mar 1941
                25:265-75, Apr 1941
   Time 37:53-4, Feb 3, 1941
   Vogue 97:72-3, May 15, 1941

Meet the People (160 performances)
assembled: Henry Myers
sketches: Ben and Sol Barzman, Mortimer
                  Offner, Edward Eliscu, Danny Dare,

117

                    Henry Blankfort, Bert Lawrence,
                    Sid Kuller, Ray Golden, Milt Gross,
                    Mike Quin, Arthur Ross
music: Jay Gorney and George Bassman
staging: Danny Dare
sets: Frederick Stover
costumes: Gerda Vanderneers and Kate Lawson
opened: December 25, 1940
    Catholic World 152:598, Feb 1941
    Collier's 107:24-5+, Mar 22, 1941
    Life 8:39-41, Feb 26, 1940
    New York Theatre Critics' Reviews 1940:170+
                                        1941:440+
    New York Times IX, page 3, Oct 20, 1940
                    page 22, Dec 26, 1940
                    IX, page 3, Jan 5, 1941
                    IX, page 1, Jan 12, 1941
                    II, page 1, Aug 22, 1943
    Theatre Arts 25:184, Mar 1941
                 28:123, Feb 1944
                 39:93, Jun 1955
    Time 35:36, Jan 29, 1941

Night of Love (7 performances)
book: Rowland Leigh, based on Lili
                    Hatvany's Tonight or Never
music: Robert Stolz
lyrics: Rowland Leigh
staging: Barrie O'Daniels
sets: Watson Barratt
costumes: Ernest Schraps
opened: January 7, 1941
    New York Theatre Critics' Reviews 1941:421+
    New York Times page 14, Jan 8, 1941

Pal Joey (374 performances)
book: John O'Hara
music: Richard Rodgers
lyrics: Lorenz Hart
staging: George Abbott
sets: Jo Mielziner
costumes: John Koenig
choreography: Robert Alton

                    118

opened: December 25, 1940
    Catholic World 152:598, Feb 1941
                   174:391, Feb 1952
    Commonweal 55:398-9, Jan 25, 1952
                   74:379-80, Jul 7, 1961
    Dance Magazine 35:21, Jul 1961
    Life 10:44, Feb 17, 1941
        32:67-8+, Jan 21, 1952
    Nation 152:81, Jan 18, 1941
    New Republic 126:23, Jan 21, 1952
    New York Theatre Critics' Reviews 1940:172+
                                      1941:442+
                                      1952:398+
    New York Times page 22, Dec 26, 1940
                   IX, page 8, Jun 8, 1941
                   page 17, Mar 7, 1949
                   II, page 1, Dec 30, 1951
                   page 17, Jan 4, 1952
                   II, page 1, Jan 13, 1952
                   II, page 13, Feb 17, 1952
                   page 23, Jun 17, 1952
                   II, page 3, Nov 23, 1952
                   page 40, Apr 1, 1954
                   II, page 2, Apr 11, 1954
                   page 32, Jun 1, 1961
                   page 21, May 30, 1963
    New Yorker 27:38, Jan 12, 1952
    Newsweek 17:42, Jan 6, 1941
                   39:73, Jan 14, 1952
    Saturday Review 35:28-9, Feb 2, 1952
    School and Society 76:404, Dec 20, 1952
    Stage 1:17, Dec 1940
        1:22-3, Feb 1941
    Theatre Arts 25:95, Feb 1941
    Time 37:41, Jan 6, 1941
        59:62, Jan 14, 1952

Panama Hattie (501 performances)
book: Herbert Fields and B. G. DeSylva
music: Cole Porter
lyrics: Cole Porter
staging: Edgar MacGregor
sets: Raoul Pene duBois

119

costumes: Raoul Pene du Bois
choreography: Robert Alton
opened: October 30, 1940
    Catholic World 152:335, Dec 1940
    Commonweal 33:103, Nov 15, 1940
    Life 9:67-8, Oct 28, 1940
    Nation 151:513, Nov 23, 1940
    New York Theatre Critics' Reviews 1940:233+
                                    1941:460+
    New York Times page 28, Oct 4, 1940
                    page 28, Oct 31, 1940
                    IX, page 1, Nov 10, 1940
                    II, page 5, Dec 5, 1943
    Newsweek 16:60, Nov 11, 1940
    Stage 1:40-41, Nov 1940
    Theatre Arts 25:12-13, Jan 1941
    Time 36:65, Oct 28, 1940

'Tis of Thee (1 performance)
assembled: Alfred Hayes
sketches: Sam Locke
music: Alex North and Al Moss, additional
                    music and lyrics by Peter Barry,
                    David Gregory, Richard Levine
staging: Nat Lichtman
sets: Carl Kent
choreography: Esther Junger
opened: October 26, 1940
    New York Theatre Critics' Reviews 1940:240+
    New York Times page 21, Oct 28, 1940
    Stage 1:20, Nov 1940

                Season of 1941-1942

Banjo Eyes (126 performances)
book: Joe Quillan and Izzy Elinson from
                    John Cecil Holm and George Abbott's
                    Three Men On A Horse
music: Vernon Duke
lyrics: John La Touche and Harold Adamson
staging: Hassard Short
sets: Harry Horner ·
costumes: Irene Sharaff

                        120

choreography: Charles Walters
opened: December 25, 1941
   Catholic World 154:731, Mar 1942
   Life 12:62-3, Feb 23, 1942
   New York Theatre Critics' Reviews 1941:164+
   New York Times page 10, Nov 8, 1941
                        page 20, Dec 26, 1941
                        page 17, Apr 16, 1942
   New Yorker 17:28, Jan 3, 1942
   Theatre Arts 26:155, Mar 1942
   Time 39:47, Jan 5, 1942

Best Food Forward (326 performances)
book: John Cecil Holm
music: Hugh Martin and Ralph Blane
lyrics: Hugh Martin and Ralph Blane
staging: George Abbott
sets: Jo Mielziner
costumes: Miles White
choreography: Gene Kelly
opened: October 1, 1941
   America 108:594, Apr 20, 1963
   Catholic World 154:213, Nov 1941
   Life 11:91-2+, Oct 12, 1941
         12:63, Feb 23, 1942
   New York Theatre Critics' Reviews 1941:286+
   New York Times page 24, Sep 12, 1941
                        page 28, Oct 2, 1941
                        IX, page 1, Oct 26, 1941
                        page 43, Apr 3, 1963
                        VI, page 104, May 5, 1963
   New Yorker 17:44, Oct 11, 1941
              39:140, Apr 13, 1963
   Newsweek 18:68, Oct 13, 1941
   Players Magazine 18:14, Feb 1942
   Theatre Arts 25:868+, Dec 1941
               26:18, Jan 1942
               47:12-13+, Jun 1963
   Time 38:67, Oct 13, 1941

By Jupiter (427 performances)
book: Richard Rodgers and Lorenz Hart,
                  based on Julian F. Thompson's The

121

Warrior's Husband

music: Richard Rodgers
lyrics: Lorenz Hart
staging: Joshua Logan
sets: Jo Mielziner
costumes: Irene Sharaff
choreography: Robert Alton
opened: June 3, 1942
   Catholic World 155:472-3, Jul 1942
   Commonweal 36:255-6, Jul 3, 1942
   Independent Woman 22:155, May 1943
   Life 12:82-5, Jun 1, 1942
   Nation 154:693, Jun 13, 1942
   New York Theatre Critics' Reviews 1942:274+
   New York Times page 22, Jun 4, 1942
               VIII, page 1, Aug 30, 1942
   New Yorker 18:36, Jun 13, 1942
   Newsweek 19:70-1, Jun 15, 1942
   Theatre Arts 26:607, Oct 1942
   Time 39:66, Jun 15, 1942

High Kickers (171 performances)

book: George Jessel, from a suggestion by
                Sid Silvers
music: Harry Ruby
lyrics: Bert Dalmar
staging: Edward Sobel
sets: Nat Karson
choreography: Carl Randall
opened: October 31, 1941
   New York Theatre Critics' Reviews 1941:246+
   New York Times page 54, Oct 12, 1941
               page 21, Nov 1, 1941
   Theatre Arts 26-8, Jan 1942
   Time 38:55, Nov 10, 1941

The Lady Comes Across (3 performances)

book: Fred Thompson and Dawn Powell
music: Vernon Duke
lyrics: John LaTouche
staging: Romney Brent
sets: Stewart Chaney
costumes: Stewart Chaney

choreography: George Balanchine
opened: January 9, 1942
  New York Theatre Critics' Reviews 1942:388+
  New York Times page 10, Jan 10, 1942
               IX, page 3, Jan 11, 1942

Let's Face It (547 performances)
book: Herbert and Dorothy Fields, based on
               Russell Medcraft and Norma
               Mitchell's play The Cradle Snatchers
music: Cole Porter
lyrics: Cole Porter
staging: Edgar MacGregor
sets: Harry Horner
costumes: John Harkrider
choreography: Charles Walters
opened: October 29, 1941
  Catholic World 154:601-2, Feb 1942
  Cosmopolitan 115:98, Nov 1943
  Harper's Bazaar 75:77, Nov 1941
  Life 11:114-16+, Nov 10, 1941
  New York Theatre Critics' Reviews 1941:249+
  New York Times page 27, Oct 10, 1941
              page 26, Oct 30, 1941
              IX, page 1, Nov 16, 1941
              page 11, Feb 15, 1943
              page 23, Mar 2, 1943
  New Yorker 17:36, Nov 8, 1941
  Theatre Arts 26:6-8, Jan 1942
  Time 38:54, Nov 10, 1941
  Vogue 98:90, Dec 1, 1941

Sons O'Fun (742 performances)
book: Ole Olsen, Chic Johnson, Hal Block
songs: Jack Yellen and Sam E. Fain
staging: Edward D. Dowling
sets: Raoul Pene duBois
choreography: Robert Alton
opened: December 1, 1941
  Catholic World 154:474, Jan 1942
  Life 11:44-5, Nov 17, 1941
  Nation 153:621, Dec 13, 1941
  New York Theatre Critics' Reviews 1941:193+

New York Times page 20, Nov 1, 1941
                  page 28, Dec 2, 1941
    Time 38:73, Dec 15, 1941

Sunny River (36 performances)
book: Oscar Hammerstein, II
music: Sigmund Romberg
lyrics: Oscar Hammerstein, II
staging: Oscar Hammerstein, II
sets: Stewart Chaney
costumes: Irene Sharaff
choreography: Carl Randall
opened: December 4, 1941
    Catholic World 154:474, Jan 1942
    New York Theatre Critics' Reviews 1941:186+
    New York Times page 28, Dec 5, 1941
    Newsweek 18:72, Dec 15, 1941

Viva O'Brien (20 performances)
book: William K. and Eleanor Wells
music: Marie Grever
lyrics: Raymond Leveen
staging: Robert Milton
sets: Clark Robinson
costumes: John N. Booth, Jr.
choreography: Chester Hale
opened: October 9, 1941
    New York Theatre Critics' Reviews 1941:271+
    New York Times page 27, Oct 10, 1941

Season of 1942-1943

Beat the Band (68 performances)
book: George Marion, Jr. and George Abbott
music: Johnny Green
lyrics: George Marion, Jr. and George Abbott
staging: George Abbott
sets: Sam Leve
costumes: Freddy Wittop
choreography: David Lichine
opened: October 14, 1942
    Catholic World 156:337, Dec 1942
    Nation 155:458, Oct 31, 1942

New York Theatre Critics' Reviews 1942:204+
New York Times VIII, page 8, Oct 4, 1942
                  page 26, Oct 15, 1942
Newsweek 20:87, Oct 26, 1942
Theatre Arts 26:742, Dec 1942
Time 40:54, Oct 26, 1942

Count Me In (61 performances)
book: Walter Kerr, Leo Brady, Nancy
                 Hamilton
music: Ann Ronell and Will Irwin
lyrics: Walter Kerr, Leo Brady, Nancy
                 Hamilton
staging: Robert Ross
sets: Howard Bay
costumes: Irene Sharaff
choreography: Robert Alton
opened: October 8, 1942
   New York Theatre Critics' Reviews 1942:214+
   New York Times page 24, Oct 9, 1942
   Newsweek 20:76, Oct 19, 1942
   Theatre Arts 26:742, Dec 1942

Follies (1943) (see Ziegfeld Follies (1943)

Let Freedom Sing (8 performances)
book: Sam Locke
music and
 lyrics: Harold Rome, Earl Robinson, Marc
                 Blitzstein, Lou Cooper, Roslyn
                 Harvey Walter Kent, John Latouche,
                 Hy Zaret, Lewis Allan
staging: Joseph Pevney and Robert H. Gordon
sets: Herbert Andrews
costumes: Paul DuPont
choreography: Dan Eckley
opened: October 5, 1942
   New York Theatre Critics' Reviews 1942:216+
   New York Times page 18, Oct 6, 1942

New Faces of 1943 (94 performances)
sketches: John Lund, additional sketches by
                 June Carroll and J. B. Rosenberg

music: John Lund
lyrics: John Lund, additional lyrics by June
                Carroll and J. B. Rosenberg
staging: Leonard Sillman
choreography: Charles Weidman
opened: December 22, 1942
    New York Theatre Critics' Reviews 1942:140+
    New York Times page 22, Dec 23, 1942

Oklahoma (2,248 performances)
book: Oscar Hammerstein II, based on Lynn
                Riggs' play Green Grow the Lilacs
music: Richard Rodgers
lyrics: Oscar Hammerstein II
staging: Rouben Mamoulian
sets: Lemuel Ayers
costumes: Miles White
choreography: Agnes de Mille
opened: March 31, 1943
    America 89:609+, Sep 19, 1953
    Catholic World 157:186-7, May 1943
                173:308, Jul 1951
                178:67, Oct 1953
    Commonweal 54:285, Jun 29, 1951
    Cosmopolitan 134:24-7, May 1953
    Dance Magazine 32:17, May 1958
                37:32-4, Mar 1963
    Holiday 20:75+, Oct 1956
    Independent Woman 22:144, May 1943
    Life 14:56-8+, May 24, 1943
        16:82-5, Mar 6, 1944
    Look 17:4, Apr 7, 1953
    Mademoiselle 41:125+, May 1955
    Nation 156:572, Apr 17, 1943
    New Republic 108:508-9, Apr 19, 1943
    New York Theatre Critics' Reviews 1943:341+
                                      1951:257+
                                      1953:294+
    New York Times page 27, Apr 1, 1943
                II, page 1, Apr 11, 1943
                II, page 6, May 9, 1943
                II, page 5, Jun 6, 1943
                VI, page 10, Jul 25, 1943

II, page 1, Aug 1, 1943
II, page 2, Sep 5, 1943
VI, page 39, Jan 21, 1945
II, page 5, Feb 4, 1945
VI, page 18, Mar 25, 1945
page 14, Jul 13, 1945
II, page 1, Mar 31, 1946
page 19, Oct 5, 1946
II, page 1, Mar 30, 1947
page 35, May 1, 1947
II, page 3, May 11, 1947
page 18, Jun 20, 1947
page 31, May 19, 1948
II, page 1, Jun 6, 1948
page 35, Mar 29, 1950
page 23, Sep 5, 1950
page 78, Oct 22, 1950
page 15, May 30, 1951
page 38, Sep 13, 1951
II, page 3, Sep 23, 1951
page 79, Feb 15, 1953
II, page 1, Mar 29, 1953
page 22, Aug 31, 1953
page 19, Sep 1, 1953
II, page 1, Sep 6, 1953
page 19, Aug 15, 1955
page 15, Mar 8, 1958
page 32, Mar 20, 1958
page 8, Feb 28, 1963
VI, pages 30-31, May 12, 1963
page 40, May 16, 1963
New York Times Magazine pages 18-19, Mar 25,
1945
pages 30-1, May 12,
1963
New Yorker 19:61, May 29, 1943
Newsweek 61:86, Mar 11, 1963
Saturday Review 26:14, Sep 4, 1943
School and Society 67:475, Jun 26, 1948
Theatre Arts 27:329-31, Jun 1943
35:5, Sep 1951
37:17, Nov 1953
Time 51:75, Apr 12, 1948

Oy Is Dus A Leben! (139 performances)
book: Jacob Kalich
music: Joseph Rumshinsky
lyrics: Molly Picon
staging: Jacob Kalich
sets: Harry Gordon Bennett
choreography: David Lubritzky and Lillian Shapero
opened: October 12, 1942
    New York Times page 19, Oct 13, 1942

Something for the Boys (422 performances)
book: Herbert and Dorothy Fields
music: Cole Porter
lyrics: Cole Porter
staging: Hassard Short
sets: Howard Bay
costumes: Billy Livingston
choreography: Jack Cole
opened: January 7, 1943
    Catholic World 156:601, Feb 1943
    Life 14:79+, Feb 8, 1943
    New York Theatre Critics' Reviews 1943:398+
    New York Times page 24, Jan 8, 1943
                 VIII, page 1, Jan 17, 1943
                 II, page 1, Apr 30, 1944
    New Yorker 18:32, Jan 16, 1943
    Theatre Arts 27:138-9, Mar 1943
    Time 41:58, Jan 18, 1943

Star and Garter (609 performances)
assembled: Michael Todd
music and
 lyrics: Irving Berlin, Al Dubin, Will Irwin,
                 Harold Rome, Lester Lee, Irving
                 Gordon, Alan Roberts, Harold
                 Arlen, Frank McCue, Doris Tauber,
                 Dorival Caymmi, Jerry Seelen,
                 Jerome Brainin, Johnny Mercer,
                 Sis Wilner, Al Stillman
staging: Hassard Short
sets: Harry Horner
costumes: Irene Sharaff
opened: June 24, 1942

128

Life 13:60+, Jul 27, 1942
Nation 155:18, Jul 4, 1942
New York Theatre Critics' Reviews 1942:262+
New York Times page 26, Jun 25, 1942
                VIII, page 1, Sep 13, 1942
Newsweek 20:60, Jul 6, 1942
Time 40:54, Jul 6, 1942

This Is the Army (113 performances)
sketches: James McColl, based on the musical
                show Yip, Yip, Yaphank
music: Irving Berlin
lyrics: Irving Berlin
staging: Ezra Stone
sets: John Koenig
costumes: John Koenig
choreography: Robert Sidney and Nelson Barclift
opened: July 4, 1942
    American Mercury 55:450-1, Oct 1942
    Catholic World 155:726, Sep 1942
    Collier's 110:14-15+, Oct 17, 1942
    Commonweal 36:303-4, Jul 17, 1942
    Life 13:72-5, Jul 20, 1942
    New York Theatre Critics' Reviews 1942:256
    New York Times VIII, page 1, Jun 14, 1942
                    page 28, Jul 5, 1942
                    VII, page 1, Jul 12, 1942
                    VII, page 6, Jul 12, 1942
                    VIII, page 1, Aug 16, 1942
                    VIII, page 8, Sep 13, 1942
    New York Times Magazine pages 6-7, Jul 12, 1942
                    page 20, Nov 21, 1943
    Newsweek 20:52+, Jul 13, 1942
    Theatre Arts 26:546, Sep 1942
                26:608+, Oct 1942
    Time 40:36, Jul 13, 1942

The Time, The Place, and The Girl (13 performances)
book: Will Morrissey, John Neff, William B.
                Friedlander, based on the musical by
                Will M. Hough, Frank R. Adams,
                and Joe Howard, originally produced
                in Chicago in 1906

129

music: Joe Howard
lyrics: Will Morrissey, John Neff, William B.
                Friedlander, based on the musical
                by Will M. Hough, Frank R. Adams,
                and Joe Howard, originally produced
                in Chicago in 1906
staging: William B. Friedlander
sets: Karl Amend
costumes: Paul DuPont
choreography: Carl Randall
opened: October 21, 1942
    New York Theatre Critics' Reviews 1942:198+
    New York Times page 24, Oct 22, 1942

You'll See Stars (4 performances)
book: Herman Timberg
music: Leo Edwards
lyrics: Herman Timberg
staging: Herman Timberg and Dave Kramer
choreography: Eric Victor
opened: December 29, 1942
    New York Theatre Critics' Reviews 1942:122+
    New York Times page 26, Jan 1, 1943

Ziegfeld Follies (553 performances)
sketches: Lester Lee, Jerry Seelen, Bud
                Pearson, Les White, Joseph Erens,
                Charles Sherman, Harry Young,
                Lester Lawrence, Baldwin Bergersen,
                Ray Golden, Sid Kuller, William
                Wells, Harold Rome
music: Ray Henderson and Dan White
lyrics: Jack Yellen and Buddy Burston
staging: John Murray Anderson
sets: Watson Barratt
costumes: Miles White
choreography: Robert Alton
opened: April 1, 1943
    New York Theatre Critics' Reviews 1943:338+
    New York Times page 16, Apr 2, 1943
                II, page 1, Apr 11, 1943
    Newsweek 21:84, Apr 12, 1943
    Theatre Arts 27:331, Jun 1943

Allah Be Praised! (20 performances)
book: George Marion, Jr.
music: Don Walker and Baldwin Bergersen
lyrics: George Marion, Jr.
staging: Robert H. Gordon and Jack Small
sets: George Jenkins
costumes: Miles White
choreography: Jack Cole
opened: April 20, 1944
    New York Theatre Critics' Reviews 1944:207+
    New York Times page 14, Apr 21, 1944
    New Yorker 20:46, Apr 29, 1944
    Newsweek 23:78, May 1, 1944
    Time 43:58, May 1, 1944

Artists and Models (28 performances)
assembled: Lou Walters
dialogue: Lou Walters, Don Ross, Frank Luther
music: Dan Shapiro, Milton Pascal, Phil
                    Charig
lyrics: Dan Shapiro, Milton Pascal, Phil
                    Charig
staging: Lou Walters
sets: Watson Barratt
costumes: Kathryn Kuhn
choreography: Natalie Kamarova and Laurette
                    Jefferson
opened: November 5, 1943
    New York Theatre Critics' Reviews 1943:239+
    New York Times page 16, Nov 6, 1943
                II, page 1, Nov 21, 1943

Bright Lights of 1944 (4 performances)
book: Norman Anthony and Charles Sherman
                    (additional dialogue by Joseph
                    Erens)
music: Jerry Livingston
lyrics: Mack David
staging: Dan Eckley
sets: Perry Watkins
costumes: Perry Watkins

131

choreography: Truly McGee
opened: September 16, 1943
   New York Theatre Critics' Reviews 1943:276+
   New York Times page 27, Sep 17, 1943
                   II, page 1, Sep 26, 1943
   Theatre Arts 27:647-8, Nov 1943

Carmen Jones (503 performances)
book: Oscar Hammerstein II, based on
               Meilhac and Halevy's adaptation of
               Prosper Merimee's Carmen (Georges
               Bizet and Prosper Merimee)
music: Georges Bizet, arranged by Robert
               Russell
lyrics: Oscar Hammerstein II
staging: Hassard Short
sets: Howard Bay
costumes: Raoul Pene du Bois
choreography: Eugene Loring
opened: December 2, 1943
   America 95:290-2, Jun 16, 1956
   Catholic World 158:394, Jan 1944
                  183:311, Jul 1956
   Collier's 113:14-15+, Jan 15, 1944
   Commonweal 39:231-2, Dec 17, 1943
   Life 15:111-12+, Dec 20, 1943
        16:70-4, May 8, 1944
   Nation 157:740, Dec 18, 1943
   New Republic 109:885, Dec 20, 1943
   New York Theatre Critics' Reviews 1943:207+
   New York Times page 17, Oct 20, 1943
                   page 29, Oct 28, 1943
                   II, page 1, Nov 28, 1943
                   page 26, Dec 3, 1943
                   II, page 3, Dec 12, 1943
                   II, page 9, Dec 19, 1943
                   II, page 1, Jun 18, 1944
                   II, page 1, Apr 7, 1946
                   page 32, Apr 8, 1946
                   page 8, Sep 22, 1951
                   page 28, Jun 1, 1956
                   II, page 1, Jun 10, 1956
                   page 25, Aug 18, 1959

Newsweek 22:91-2, Dec 13, 1943
Theatre Arts 28:69-73, Feb 1944
        28:154-63, Mar 1944
        40:19, Aug 1956
Time 42:44, Dec 13, 1943
Vogue 103:80-1, Mar 15, 1944

Dream with Music (28 performances)
book: Sidney Sheldon, Dorothy Kilgallen, Ben
                  Roberts
music: Clay Warnick
lyrics: Edward Eager
staging: Richard Kollmar
sets: Stewart Chaney
costumes: Miles White
choreography: George Balanchine and Henry LeTang
opened: May 18, 1944
   Commonweal 40:156, Jun 2, 1944
   Nation 158:688, Jun 10, 1944
   New York Theatre Critics' Reviews 1944:188+
   New York Times page 15, May 19, 1944
   New Yorker 20:40, May 27, 1944
   Newsweek 23:91, May 29, 1944

Early to Bed (382 performances)
book: George Marion, Jr.
music: Thomas Waller
lyrics: George Marion, Jr.
staging: Alfred Bloomingdale
sets: George Jenkins
costumes: Miles White
choreography: Robert Alton
opened: June 17, 1943
   Catholic World 157:522, Aug 1943
   Commonweal 38:274, Jul 2, 1943
   Life 15:54, Aug 30, 1943
   New York Theatre Critics' Reviews 1943:314+
   New York Times page 16, Jun 18, 1943
   New Yorker 19:33, Jun 26, 1943
   Newsweek 21:108+, Jun 28, 1943
   Theatre Arts 27:573, Oct 1943
   Time 41:94, Jun 28, 1943

Follow the Girls (882 performances)
book: Guy Bolton and Eddie Davis, with
                  dialogue by Fred Thompson
music: Dan Shapiro, Milton Pascal, Phil
                  Charig
lyrics: Dan Shapiro, Milton Pascal, Phil
                  Charig
staging: Harry Delmar
sets: Howard Bay
costumes: Lou Eisele
choreography: Catherine Littlefield
opened: April 8, 1944
    Commonweal 40:38-9, Apr 28, 1944
    Life 16:115-18+, Apr 24, 1944
    New York Theatre Critics' Reviews 1944:222+
    New York Times page 15, Apr 10, 1944
                II, page 1, Apr 16, 1944
    Newsweek 23:106, Apr 17, 1944

Jackpot (69 performances)
book: Guy Bolton, Sidney Sheldon, Ben
                  Roberts
music: Vernon Duke
lyrics: Howard Dietz
staging: Roy Hargrave
sets: Raymond Sovey and Robert Edmund
                  Jones
costumes: Kiviette
choreography: Lauretta Jefferson and Charles Weid-
                  man
opened: January 13, 1944
    New York Theatre Critics' Reviews 1944:284+
    New York Times page 15, Jan 14, 1944
                II, page 1, Jan 30, 1944
    New Yorker 19:34+, Jan 22, 1944
    Theatre Arts 28:142, Mar 1944

Mexican Hayride (481 performances)
book: Herbert and Dorothy Fields
music: Cole Porter
lyrics: Cole Porter
staging: Hassard Short
sets: George Jenkins

costumes: Mary Grant
choreography: Paul Haakon
opened: January 28, 1944
  Catholic World 158:586, Mar 1944
  Collier's 113:18-21, Feb 5, 1944
  Commonweal 39:446, Feb 18, 1944
  Life 16:83-4+, Feb 21, 1944
  Nation 158:197, Feb 12, 1944
  New York Theatre Critics' Reviews 1944:271+
  New York Times page 9, Jan 29, 1944
            II, page 1, Feb 6, 1944
            II, page 8, Mar 26, 1944
            II, page 1, Jul 2, 1944
  Saturday Review 27:18, Feb 19, 1944
  Theatre Arts 28:202+, Apr 1944
  Time 43:94, Feb 7, 1944

My Dear Public (45 performances)
book: Irving Caesar and Chuno Gottesfeld
songs: Irving Caesar, Sam Lerner, Gerald
            Marks
staging: Edgar MacGregor
sets: Albert Johnson
costumes: Lucinda Ballard
choreography: Felicia Sorel and Henry LeTang
opened: September 9, 1943
  Commonweal 38:562, Sep 24, 1943
  New York Theatre Critics' Reviews 1943:281+
  New York Times page 28, Sep 10, 1943
            page 10, Oct 18, 1943
  Theatre Arts 27:645-6, Nov 1943

One Touch of Venus (567 performances)
book: S. J. Perelman and Ogden Nash,
            suggested by "The Tinted Venus"
            by F. Anstey (Thomas Anstey
            Guthrie)
music: Kurt Weill
lyrics: Ogden Nash
staging: Elia Kazan
sets: Howard Bay
costumes: Paul Du Pont, Kermit Love,
            Mainbocher

choreography: Agnes de Mille
opened: October 7, 1943
   Catholic World 158:185-7, Nov 1943
   Commonweal 39:14-15, Oct 22, 1943
   Life 15:61-4, Oct 25, 1943
   Nation 157:479, Oct 23, 1943
   New York Theatre Critics' Reviews 1943:264+
   New York Times page 14, Oct 8, 1943
                  II, page 1, Oct 17, 1943
                  II, page 1, Feb 20, 1944
   New Yorker 19:41, Oct 16, 1943
   Newsweek 22:86+, Oct 18, 1943
   Theatre Arts 27:703-7, Dec 1943
   Time 42:50, Oct 18, 1943
   Vogue 102:60-1, Nov 1, 1943

What's Up (63 performances)
book: Alan Jay Lerner and Arthur Pierson
music: Frederick Loewe
lyrics: Alan Jay Lerner and Arthur Pierson
staging: George Balanchine and Robert H.
                Gordon
sets: Boris Aronson
costumes: Grace Houston
opened: November 11, 1943
   Catholic World 158:395, Jan 1944
   Commonweal 39:144, Nov 26, 1943
   New York Theatre Critics' Reviews 1943:229+
   New York Times page 24, Nov 12, 1943
                  II, page 1, Nov 21, 1943

                  Season of 1944-1945

Bloomer Girl (654 performances)
book: Sig Herzig and Fred Saidy, based on
                a play by Lilith and Dan James
music: Harold Arlen
lyrics: E. Y. Harburg
staging: E. Y. Harburg
sets: Lemuel Ayers
costumes: Miles White
choreography: Agnes de Mille
opened: October 5, 1944

Catholic World 160:168, Nov 1944
            164:455, Feb 1947
Collier's 114:12-13+, Dec 9, 1944
Commonweal 41:37, Oct 27, 1944
Harpers 78:81, Dec 1944
Life 17:67-70, Nov 6, 1944
Nation 159:483, Oct 21, 1944
New Republic 111:521, Oct 23, 1944
New York Theatre Critics' Reviews 1944:118+
New York Times VI, page 16, Sep 24, 1944
            page 18, Oct 6, 1944
            II, page 1, Oct 8, 1944
            VI, page 52, Nov 19, 1944
            II, page 6, Dec 17, 1944
            II, page 1, Feb 24, 1946
            II, page 3, Jan 5, 1947
            page 33, Jan 7, 1947
            page 19, Feb 15, 1947
New York Times Magazine pages 16-17, Sep 24,
            1944
New Yorker 20:41, Oct 14, 1944
Newsweek 24:85-6, Oct 16, 1944
Theatre Arts 28:643-5, Nov 1944
            29:78, Feb 1945
            29:652, Nov 1945
Time 44:52, Oct 16, 1944

Carousel (890 performances)
book: Benjamin F. Glazer and Oscar
                Hammerstein II, adapted from
                Ferenc Molnar's play Liliom
music: Richard Rodgers
lyrics: Oscar Hammerstein II
staging: Rouben Mamoulian
sets: Jo Mielziner
costumes: Miles White
choreography: Agnes de Mille
opened: April 19, 1945
  America 91:367, Jul 3, 1954
            98:27, Oct 5, 1957
          113:266-7, Sep 11, 1965
  Catholic World 161:260, Jun 1945
            168:481, Mar 1949

179:308, Jul 1954
Christian Science Monitor Magazine page 7, Jun
24, 1950
Collier's 115:18-19+, May 26, 1945
Commonweal 42:70, May 4, 1945
Dance Magazine 39:16-17, Oct 1965
Life 18:67-70+, May 14, 1945
Nation 160:525, May 5, 1945
178:550, Jun 26, 1954
New Republic 112:644, May 7, 1945
New York Theatre Critics' Reviews 1945:226+
New York Times II, page 1, Apr 15, 1945
page 24, Apr 20, 1945
II, page 1, Apr 29, 1945
II, page 1, May 6, 1945
II, page 1, Apr 7, 1946
II, page 11, Dec 29, 1946
page 28, Jan 26, 1949
page 14, Jan 31, 1949
II, page 1, Feb 6, 1949
page 37, Jun 8, 1950
page 85, Oct 14, 1951
page 38, May 6, 1953
II, page 3, May 30, 1954
page 32, Jun 3, 1954
II, page 1, Jun 13, 1954
page 38, Sep 12, 1957
page 39, Aug 11, 1965
New Yorker 21:38, Apr 28, 1945
24:52, Feb 5, 1949
Newsweek 25:87, Apr 30, 1945
Saturday Review 28:18-19, May 5, 1945
Theatre Arts 29:328-30, Jun 1945
30:41, Jan 1946
41:18-19, Nov 1957
Time 45:56, Apr 30, 1945

The Firebrand of Florence (43 performances)
book: Edwin Justus Mayer and Ira Gershwin,
                based on The Firebrand by Edwin
                Justus Mayer
music: Kurt Weill
lyrics: Edwin Justus Mayer and Ira Gershwin

138

staging: John Murray Anderson
sets: Jo Mielziner
costumes: Raoul Pene du Bois
choreography: Catherine Littlefield
opened: March 22, 1945
   Catholic World 161:167, May 1945
   New York Theatre Critics' Reviews 1945:241+
   New York Times page 13, Mar 23, 1945
   New Yorker 21:42, Mar 3, 1945
   Newsweek 25:84, Apr 2, 1945
   Theatre Arts 29:271, May 1945
   Time 45:60, Apr 2, 1945

Hollywood Pinafore (53 performances)
book: George S. Kaufman, based on Gilbert
              and Sullivan's H. M. S. Pinafore
music: Original Sullivan score
lyrics: George S. Kaufman
staging: George S. Kaufman
sets: Jo Mielziner
costumes: Kathryn Kuhn and Mary Percy Schenck
choreography: Antony Tudor and Douglas Coudy
opened: May 31, 1945
   Catholic World 161:351, Jul 1945
   Commonweal 42:213, Jun 15, 1945
   Nation 160:705, Jun 23, 1945
   New York Theatre Critics' Reviews 1945:203+
   New York Times page 20, Jun 1, 1945
                  II, page 1, Jun 10, 1945
                  II, page 4, Jun 17, 1945
                  page 14, Jul 9, 1945
   New Yorker 21:38, Jun 9, 1945
   Newsweek 25:93, Jun 11, 1945
   Saturday Review 28:24-5, Jun 16, 1945
   Theatre Arts 29:389, Jul 1945
   Time 45:58, Jun 11, 1945

A Lady Says Yes (87 performances)
book: Clayton Ashley (Dr. Maxwell Maltz)
              and Stanley Adams
music: Fred Spielman and Arthur Gershwin
lyrics: Clayton Ashley and Stanley Adams
sets: Watson Barratt

costumes: Lou Eisele
choreography: Boots McKenna and Natalie Kamarova
opened: January 10, 1945
   Nation 160:136, Feb 3, 1945
   New York Theatre Critics' Reviews 1945:294+
   New York Times page 18, Jan 11, 1945
   Time 45:63, Jan 22, 1945

Laffing Room Only (233 performances)
book: Ole Olsen, Chic Johnson, Eugene
               Conrad
music: Burton Lane
lyrics: Burton Lane
staging: John Murray Anderson
sets: Stewart Chaney
costumes: Billy Livingston
choreography: Robert Alton
opened: December 23, 1944
   Life 18:76, Apr 9, 1945
   New York Theatre Critics' Reviews 1944:52+
   New York Times page 15, Dec 25, 1944
               page 31, Sep 20, 1945
   Theatre Arts 29:142+, Mar 1945
   Time 45:67, Jan 8, 1945

Memphis Bound! (36 performances)
book: Albert Barker and Sally Benton, a
               swing version of Gilbert and
               Sullivan's H. M. S. Pinafore
music: Don Walker and Clay Warnick
lyrics: Don Walker and Clay Warnick
staging: Robert Ross
sets: George Jenkins
costumes: Lucinda Ballard
choreography: Al White
opened: May 24, 1945
   Catholic World 161:350, Jul 1945
   Commonweal 42:191, Jun 8, 1945
   Life 18:57-8+, Jun 25, 1945
   Nation 160:705, Jun 23, 1945
   New York Theatre Critics' Reviews 1945:207+
   New York Times page 23, May 25, 1945
               II, page 1, Jun 10, 1945

140

New Yorker 21:36+, Jun 2, 1945
Newsweek 25:90, Jun 4, 1945
Theatre Arts 29:389, Jul 1945
Time 45:85, Jun 4, 1945

On the Town (463 performances)
book: Betty Comden and Adolph Green,
                  based on an idea by Jerome Robbins
music: Leonard Bernstein
lyrics: Betty Comden and Adolph Green
staging: George Abbott
sets: Oliver Smith
costumes: Alvin Colt
choreography: Jerome Robbins
opened: December 28, 1944
  Catholic World 160:453, Feb 1945
  Commonweal 41:332, Jan 12, 1945
  Dance Magazine 33:22-3, Apr 1959
  Life 18:49-51, Jan 15, 1945
  Nation 160:48, Jan 13, 1945
  New Republic 112:85, Jan 15, 1945
  New York Theatre Critics' Reviews 1944:45+
  New York Times page 11, Dec 29, 1944
                    II, page 1, Jan 7, 1945
                    II, page 5, Feb 4, 1945
                    II, page 1, Feb 18, 1945
                    II, page 2, Oct 17, 1945
                    page 36, Jan 16, 1959
                    II, page 1, Jan 25, 1959
                    page 15, Feb 14, 1959
                    page 30, May 31, 1963
  New Yorker 20:40, Jan 6, 1945
  Newsweek 25:72+, Jan 8, 1945
  Saturday Review 28:26-7, Feb 17, 1945
  Theatre Arts 29:133-4, Mar 1945
  Time 45:67-8, Jan 8, 1945

Sadie Thompson (60 performances)
book: Howard Dietz and Rouben Mamoulian,
                  adapted from Rain, a drama by John
                  Colton and Clemence Randolph,
                  based on a story by Somerset
                  Maugham

music: Vernon Duke
lyrics: Howard Dietz and Rouben Mamoulian
staging: Rouben Mamoulian
sets: Boris Aronson
costumes: Motley and Azadia Newman
choreography: Edward Caton
opened: November 16, 1944
   Catholic World 160:357, Jan 1945
   Collier's 115:12-13, Jan 6, 1945
   Commonweal 41:174-5, Dec 1, 1944
   Life 17:43-6+, Dec 11, 1944
   Nation 159:698, Dec 2, 1944
   New York Theatre Critics' Reviews 1944:84+
   New York Times VI, page 28, Nov 12, 1944
                   page 25, Nov 17, 1944
                   II, page 1, Nov 26, 1944
   New Yorker 20:46, Nov 25, 1944
   Newsweek 24:100, Nov 27, 1944
   Theatre Arts 29:12+, Jan 1945
   Time 44:48, Nov 27, 1944

Seven Lively Arts (183 performances)
assembled: Billy Rose
sketches: Moss Hart, George S. Kaufman,
                   Robert Pirosh, Joseph Schrank,
                   Charles Sherman, Ben Hecht
music: Cole Porter and Igor Stravinsky
lyrics: Cole Porter
staging: Hassard Short
sets: Norman Bel Geddes
costumes: Mary Shaw and Valentina
choreography: Anton Dolin
opened: December 7, 1944
   Catholic World 160:356, Jan 1945
   Commonweal 41:253-4, Dec 22, 1944
   Life 17:24-6, Dec 25, 1944
   Nation 159:781, Dec 23, 1944
   New Republic 111:867, Dec 25, 1944
   New York Theatre Critics' Reviews 1944:62+
   New York Times page 26, Dec 8, 1944
                   II, page 5, Dec 10, 1944
                   II, page 3, Dec 17, 1944
   New Yorker 20:42+, Dec 16, 1944

Newsweek 24:76+, Dec 18, 1944
Saturday Review 28:26, Jan 20, 1945
                 28:19-20, Mar 10, 1945
Theatre Arts 29:66+, Feb 1945
Time 44:72+, Dec 18, 1944

Sing Out Sweet Land (102 performances)
book: Walter Kerr
special music: Elie Siegmeister (other music folk and
                       popular)
staging: Leon Leonidoff
sets: Albert Johnson
costumes: Lucinda Ballard
choreography: Doris Humphrey and Charles Weidman
opened: December 27, 1944
   Catholic World 160:452, Feb 1945
   Collier's 115:22-3, Apr 7, 1945
   Commonweal 41:331, Jan 12, 1945
   Nation 160:52, Jan 13, 1945
   New Republic 112:85, Jan 15, 1945
   New York Theatre Critics' Reviews 1944:48+
   New York Times page 24, Nov 10, 1944
                   VI, page 14, Dec 24, 1944
                   page 24, Dec 28, 1944
                   II, page 1, Jan 7, 1945
                   II, page 1, Jan 14, 1945
                   II, page 5, Jan 21, 1945
   New York Times Magazine pages 14-15, Dec 24,
                        1944
   New Yorker 20:40, Jan 6, 1945
   Newsweek 25:72, Jan 8, 1945
   Theatre Arts 29:79, Feb 1945
                29:134-6, Mar 1945
   Time 45:67, Jan 8, 1945

Up in Central Park (504 performances)
book: Herbert and Dorothy Fields
music: Sigmund Romberg
lyrics: Herbert and Dorothy Fields
staging: John Kennedy
sets: Howard Bay
costumes: Grace Houston and Ernest Schraps
choreography: Helen Tamiris

opened: January 27, 1945
   Catholic World 160:549-50, Mar 1945
   Commonweal 41:448, Feb 16, 1945
   Life 18:41-2+, Feb 19, 1945
   New York Theatre Critics' Reviews 1945:280+
   New York Times II, page 1, Jan 21, 1945
                      page 17, Jan 29, 1945
                      II, page 4, Feb 4, 1945
                      II, page 1, May 18, 1947
                      page 29, May 20, 1947
                      II, page 1, May 25, 1947
                      page 31, May 27, 1947
   New Yorker 20:40+, Feb 3, 1945
   Newsweek 25:83, Feb 12, 1945
   Theatre Arts 29:205+, Apr 1945
                29:333, Jan 1945
                29:651, Nov 1945
   Time 45:60, Feb 5, 1945

                  Season of 1945-1946

Annie Get Your Gun (1,147 performances)
book: Herbert Fields and Dorothy Fields
music: Irving Berlin
lyrics: Irving Berlin
staging: Joshua Logan
sets: Jo Mielziner
costumes: Lucinda Ballard
choreography: Helen Tamiris
opened: May 16, 1946
   America 98:677, Mar 8, 1958
   Catholic World 163:359, Jul 1946
                187:146-7, May 1958
   Life 20:89-94, Jun 3, 1946
   Modern Music 23 no. 2:144, Apr 1946
   New York Theatre Critics' Reviews 1946:382+
   New York Times page 18, Mar 29, 1946
                   page 14, May 17, 1946
                   II, page 1, May 26, 1946
                   II, page 1, Jul 21, 1946
                   II, page 1, Sep 29, 1946
                   VI, page 25, Sep 29, 1946

                      144

II, page 3, Dec 15, 1946
page 63, Jun 8, 1947
page 26, Jun 9, 1947
page 10, Oct 4, 1947
page 35, May 11, 1949
page 35, May 3, 1950
page 18, Feb 28, 1957
page 18, Aug 31, 1957
page 15, Mar 9, 1957
page 29, Feb 20, 1958
New Yorker 22:42+, May 25, 1946
Newsweek 27:84-5, May 27, 1946
Saturday Review 29:30-2, Jun 15, 1946
Time 47:66, May 27, 1946

Are You With It? (267 performances)
book: Sam Perrin and George Balzer,
                adapted from George Malcolm-
                Smith's Slightly Perfect
music: Harry Revel
lyrics: Arnold B. Horwitt
staging: Edward Reveaux
sets: George Jenkins
costumes: Raoul Pene du Dois
opened: November 10, 1945
    Catholic World 162:359, Jan 1946
    Collier's 117:14-15, Feb 2, 1946
    Commonweal 43:169, Nov 30, 1945
    Life 19:97-100, Nov 26, 1945
    Nation 161:604, Dec 1, 1945
    New York Theatre Critics' Reviews 1945:113+
    New York Times page 17, Nov 12, 1945
                II, page 1, Feb 3, 1946
                II, page 1, Apr 28, 1946
    New Yorker 21:50+, Nov 24, 1945
    Newsweek 26:96, Nov 26, 1945
    Theatre Arts 30:14, Jan 1946
    Time 46:64, Nov 19, 1945
    Vogue 106:145, Dec 1, 1945

Around the World (75 performances)
book: Orson Welles from Jules Verne's
                Around the World in Eighty Days

145

```
music:         Cole Porter
lyrics:        Cole Porter
staging:       Orson Welles
sets:          Robert Davison
costumes:      Alvin Colt
choreography:  Nelson Barclift
opened:        May 31, 1946
```
 Catholic World 163:359-60, Jul 1946
 Commonweal 44:238, Jun 21, 1946
 Life 20:74-6, Jun 17, 1946
 New York Theatre Critics' Reviews 1946:375+
 New York Times page 9, Jun 1, 1946
     II, page 1, Jun 9, 1946
 New Yorker 22:48+, Jun 8, 1946
 Newsweek 27:87, Jun 10, 1946
 Theatre Arts 30:473, Aug 1946
 Time 47:64, Jun 3, 1946
   47:67, Jun 10, 1946

Billion Dollar Baby (220 performances)

```
book:          Betty Comden and Adolph Green
music:         Morton Gould
lyrics:        Betty Comden and Adolph Green
staging:       George Abbott
sets:          Oliver Smith
costumes:      Irene Sharaff
choreography:  Jerome Robbins
opened:        December 21, 1945
```
 Catholic World 162:458, Feb 1946
 Harpers 80:106, Jan 1946
 Life 20:67+, Jan 21, 1946
 Modern Music 23 no. 2:145, Apr 1946
 New York Theatre Critics' Reviews 1945:61+
 New York Times page 17, Dec 22, 1945
     II, page 1, Dec 30, 1945
     II, page 1, Feb 10, 1946
 New Yorker 21:40, Jan 5, 1946
 Newsweek 26:78, Dec 31, 1945
 Theatre Arts 30:80-1, Feb 1946
 Time 46:64, Dec 31, 1945
 Vogue 107:170-1, Feb 1, 1946

Call Me Mister (734 performances)

book: Arnold Auerbach and Arnold B.
                   Horwitt
music: Harold Rome
lyrics: Harold Rome
staging: Robert H. Gordon
sets: Lester Polokov
costumes: Grace Houston
choreography: John Wray
opened: April 18, 1946
   Catholic World 163:264, Jun 1946
   Collier's 117:22-3, May 18, 1946
   Commonweal 44:72, May 3, 1946
   Forum 105:938-9, Jun 1946
   Life 20:131-2+, May 27, 1946
   Modern Music 23 no.3:223, Jul 1946
   New Republic 114:662, May 6, 1946
   New York Theatre Critics' Reviews 1946:403+
   New York Times VI, page 26, Apr 7, 1946
                   page 26, Apr 19, 1946
                   II, page 1, Apr 14, 1946
                   II, page 1, Apr 18, 1946
                   II, page 1, Aug 4, 1946
                   II, page 3, Apr 13, 1947
                   II, page 1, Jun 29, 1947
                   II, page 1, Oct 12, 1947
                   II, page 3, Dec 14, 1947
   New York Times Magazine pages 26-7, Apr 7, 1946
   New Yorker 22:42, Apr 27, 1946
   Newsweek 27:80, Apr 29, 1946
   Saturday Review 20:34 6, May 18, 1946
   Theatre Arts 30:322, Jun 1946
   Time 47:68+, Apr 29, 1946
        47:70, May 6, 1946

Carib Song (36 performances)
book: William Archibald
music: Baldwin Bergersen
lyrics: William Archibald
staging: Katherine Dunham and Mary Hunter
sets: Jo Mielziner
costumes: Motley
choreography: Katherine Dunham
opened: September 27, 1945

Catholic World 162:167, Nov 1945
Commonweal 43:17, Oct 19, 1945
New York Theatre Critics' Reviews 1945:157+
New York Times page 17, Sep 28, 1945
New Yorker 21:50, Oct 6, 1945
Theatre Arts page 29:624+, Nov 1945
Time 46:78, Oct 8, 1945

The Day Before Spring (165 performances)
book: Alan Jay Lerner
music: Frederick Loewe
lyrics: Alan Jay Lerner
staging: John C. Wilson
sets: Robert Davison
costumes: Miles White
choreography: Antony Tudor
opened: November 22, 1945
   Catholic World 162:360, Jan 1946
   Commonweal 43:238, Dec 14, 1945
   Harpers 79:128, Dec 1945
   Life 19:85-6+, Dec 17, 1945
   New York Theatre Critics' Reviews 1945:92+
   New York Times page 27, Nov 23, 1945
                  II, page 1, Dec 2, 1945
   New Yorker 21:52, Dec 1, 1945
   Newsweek 26:92, Dec 3, 1945
   Theatre Arts 30:14, Jan 1946
   Time 46:68, Dec 3, 1945

The Duchess Misbehaves (5 performances)
book: Gladys Shelly
music: Frank Black
lyrics: Gladys Shelly
staging: Martin Manulis
sets: A. A. Ostrander
costumes: Willa Kim
choreography: George Tapps
opened: February 13, 1946
   New York Theatre Critics' Reviews 1946:456+
   New York Times page 32, Feb 14, 1946
                  page 10, Feb 16, 1946
   New Yorker 22:44+, Feb 23, 1946

The Girl from Nantucket (12 performances)
book: Paul Stamford and Harold M. Sherman
                 from a story by Fred Thompson
                 and Berne Giler
music: Jacques Belasco
lyrics: Kay Twomey
staging: Edward Clarke Lilley
sets: Albert Johnson
costumes: Lou Eisele
choreography: Val Raset and Van Grona
opened: November 8, 1945
    New York Theatre Critics' Reviews 1945:121+
    New York Times page 17, Nov 9, 1945
    Time 46:64, Nov 19, 1945

Lute Song (142 performances)
book: Sidney Howard and Will Irwin from a
                 Chinese classic
music: Raymond Scott
lyrics: Bernard Hanighen
staging: John Houseman
sets: Robert Edmund Jones
costumes: Robert Edmund Jones
choreography;   Yeichi Nimura
opened: February 6, 1946
    American Mercury 62:587-90, May 1946
    Catholic World 162:553, Mar 1946
                 189:159, May 1959
    Commonweal 43:479, Feb 22, 1946
    Dance Magazine 33:23, Apr 1959
    Life 20:53-6, Mar 4, 1946
    Modern Music 23no. 2:145, Apr 1946
    Nation 162:240, Feb 23, 1946
    New Republic 114:254, Feb 18, 1946
    New York Theatre Critics' Reviews 1946:459+
    New York Times page 29, Feb 7, 1946
                 II, page 1, Feb 17, 1946
                 page 32, Oct 12, 1948
                 page 24, Mar 13, 1959
    New Yorker 22:48+, Feb 16, 1946
    Newsweek 27:92, Feb 18, 1946
    Saturday Review 29:28-9, May 2, 1946
    Theatre Arts 30:199-200, Apr 1946

32:67, Feb 1948
43:67-8, May 1959
Time 47:49, Feb 18, 1946

Markina (165 performances)
book: George Marion, Jr. and Karl Farkas
music: Emmerick Kalman
lyrics: George Marion, Jr. and Karl Farkas
staging: Hassard Short
sets: Howard Bay
costumes: Mary Grant
choreography: Albertina Rasch
opened: July 18, 1945
   Catholic World 161:509-10, Sep 1945
   Commonweal 42:381, Aug 3, 1945
   New York Theatre Critics' Reviews 1945:186+
   New York Times page 19, Jul 1945
                  II, page 1, Sep 16, 1945
   New Yorker 21:40, Jul 28, 1945
   Newsweek 26:65, Jul 30, 1945
   Saturday Review 28:22-3, Sep 29, 1945
   Theatre Arts 29:551, Oct 1945
   Time 46:72, Jul 30, 1945

Mr. Strauss Goes to Boston (12 performances)
book: Leonard L. Levenson from a story
                  by Alfred Greenwald and Geza
                  Herczeg
music: Robert Stolz
lyrics: Robert Sour
staging: Felix Brentano
sets: Stewart Chaney
costumes: Walter Florell
choreography: George Balanchine
opened: September 6, 1945
   Catholic World 162:70, Oct 1945
   New York Theatre Critics' Reviews 1945:180+
   New York Times page 20, Sep 7, 1945
                  II, page 1, Sep 16, 1945
   New Yorker 21:46, Sep 15, 1945
   Newsweek 26:103, Sep 17, 1945
   Time 46:74, Sep 17, 1945

150

Nellie Bly (16 performances)
book: Joseph Quillan based on a story by
                 Jack Emmanuel
music: James Van Heusen
lyrics: Johnny Burke
staging: Edgar McGregor
sets: Nat Karson
choreography: Lee Sherman
opened: January 21, 1946
   New York Theatre Critics' Reviews 1946:481+
   New York Times page 32, Jan 22, 1946
                  II, page 1, Jan 27, 1946
   Newsweek 27:80, Feb 4, 1946
   Theatre Arts 30:137, Mar 1946
   Time 47:63, Feb 4, 1946

Polonaise (113 performances)
book: Gottfried Reinhardt and Anthony
                 Veiller
music: Frederic Chopin (Adaptations by
                 Bronislaw Kaper)
lyrics: John Latouche
staging: Stella Adler
sets: Howard Bay
costumes: Mary Grant
choreography: David Lichine
opened: October 6, 1945
   Catholic World 162:167, Nov 1945
   New York Theatre Critics' Reviews 1945:149+
   New York Times page 20, Oct 8, 1945
                  II, page 1, Oct 14, 1945
   New Yorker 21:50, Oct 13, 1945
   Newsweek 26:94, Oct 15, 1945
   Theatre Arts 29:687, Dec 1945
   Time 46:66, Oct 15, 1945

The Red Mill (531 performances)
book: Henry Blossom
music: Victor Herbert
lyrics: Henry Blossom
additional
 lyrics: Forman Brown
staging: Billy Gilbert

151

sets: Arthur Lonergan
costumes: Walter Israel and Emile Santiago
choreography: Aida Broadbent
opened: October 16, 1945 (originally produced
                 in 1906)
    Catholic World 162:262, Dec 1945
    Life 19:75-8+, Nov 12, 1945
    Nation 161:441, Oct 27, 1945
    New York Theatre Critics' Reviews 1945:141+
    New York Times page 16, Oct 17, 1945
                    II, page 1, Oct 28, 1945
                    II, page 1, Aug 11, 1946
                    VI, page 23, Dec 8, 1946
    New Yorker 21:42+, Oct 27, 1945
    Newsweek 26:90, Oct 29, 1945
    Theatre Arts 29:687, Dec 1945
    Time 46:62, Oct 29, 1945

St. Louis Woman (113 performances)
book: Arna Bontemps and Countee Cullen
                 based on Arna Bontemps' God Sends
                 Sunday
music: Harold Arlen
lyrics: Johnny Mercer
staging: Rouben Mamoulian
sets: Lemuel Ayers
costumes: Lemuel Ayers
choreography: Charles Walters
opened: March 30, 1946
    Catholic World 163:170, May 1946
    Commonweal 44:14, Apr 19, 1946
    Forum 105:937-8, Jun 1946
    Life 20:63-4, Apr 29, 1946
    Modern Music 23 no2:146, Apr 1946
    New York Theatre Critics' Reviews 1946:415+
    New York Times page 22, Apr 1, 1946
                    page 20, Jul 3, 1946
    New Yorker 22:46+, Apr 6, 1946
    Newsweek 27:84, Apr 15, 1946
    Saturday Review 29:24, Apr 27, 1946
    Time 47:47, Apr 8, 1946

Three to Make Ready (327 performances)

152

book: Nancy Hamilton
music: Morgan Lewis
lyrics: Nancy Hamilton
staging: John Murray Anderson
sets: Donald Oenslager
costumes: Andre
choreography: Robert Sidney
opened: March 7, 1946
   Catholic World 163:72-3, Apr 1946
   Commonweal 43:572-3, Mar 22, 1946
   Life 20:67-70, Mar 25, 1946
   Musical Courier 133:14, Apr 15, 1946
   New York Theatre Critics' Reviews 1946:434+
   New York Times page 16, Mar 8, 1946
                    II, page 1, Mar 17, 1946
                    II, page 1, May 19, 1946
                    II, page 2, Oct 27, 1946
   New Yorker 22:44+, Mar 16, 1946
   Newsweek 27:92, Mar 18, 1946
   Theatre Arts 30:261-2, May 1946
   Time 47:56, Mar 18, 1946

                 Season of 1946-1947

Barefoot Boy with Cheek (108 performances)
book: Max Shulman, from his novel Bare-
                 foot Boy with Cheek
music: Sidney Lippman
lyrics: Sylvia Dee
staging: George Abbott
sets: Jo Mielziner
costumes: Alvin Colt
choreography: Richard Barstow
opened: April 3, 1947
   Catholic World 165:169, May 1947
   Commonweal 46:16, Apr 18, 1947
   New Republic 116:37, Apr 21, 1947
   New York Theatre Critics' Reviews 1947:402+
   New York Times page 20, Apr 4, 1947
                    II, page 1, May 4, 1947
   New Yorker 23:46, Apr 12, 1947
   Newsweek 29:86, Apr 14, 1947
   Theatre Arts 31:41, Jun 1947

Time 49:70, Apr 14, 1947

Beggar's Holiday (108 performances)
book: John Latouche, adapted from John
                Gay's The Beggar's Opera
music: Duke Ellington
lyrics: John Latouche
staging: Nicholas Ray
sets: Oliver Smith
costumes: Walter Florell
choreography: Valerie Bettis
opened: December 26, 1936
    Catholic World 164:455-6, Feb 1947
    Commonweal 45:351-2, Jan 17, 1947
    Life 22:75, Feb 24, 1947
    New York Theatre Critics' Reviews 1946:204+
    New York Times II, page 3, Dec 22, 1946
                    page 13, Dec 27, 1946
                    II, page 1, Jan 26, 1947
                    II, page 3, Feb 2, 1947
    New Yorker 22:46-7, Jan 4, 1947
    Newsweek 29:64, Jan 6, 1947
    School and Society 65:252, Apr 5, 1947
    Theatre Arts 31:16-17, Mar 1947
                 31:27, Mar 1947
    Time 49:57, Jan 6, 1947

Brigadoon (581 performances)
book: Alan Jay Lerner
music: Frederick Loewe
lyrics: Alan Jay Lerner
staging: Robert Lewis
sets: Oliver Smith
costumes: David Ffolkes
choreography: Agnes de Mille
opened: March 13, 1947
    Catholic World 165:73, Apr 1947
                 185:227, Jun 1957
    Commonweal 45:593, Mar 28, 1947
              66:128, May 3, 1957
    Harpers 81:174, May 1947
    Life 23:57-60, Jul 21, 1947
    New Republic 116:38, Mar 31, 1947

154

New York Theatre Critics' Reviews 1947:427+
                                    1957:305+
New York Times II, page 1, Mar 9, 1947
                  VI, page 32, Mar 9, 1947
                  page 28, Mar 14, 1947
                  II, page 1, Mar 23, 1947
                  II, page 1, Apr 6, 1947
                  II, page 1, Jun 22, 1947
                  page 11, Apr 16, 1949
                  page 36, May 3, 1950
                  II, page 3, May 21, 1950
                  II, page 1, Dec 31, 1950
                  page 37, Mar 28, 1957
                  II, page 1, Apr 7, 1957
                  page 21, May 31, 1962
                  page 6, Feb 1, 1963
                  page 9, Dec 24, 1964
New Yorker 23:54+, Mar 22, 1947
Newsweek 29:84, Mar 24, 1947
Saturday Review 30:24-6, Apr 5, 1947
School and Society 66:245-7, Sep 27, 1947
                     68:386, Dec 4, 1948
Theatre Arts 31:21, May 1947
             31:41, Jun 1947
             41:18, Jun 1957
             46:58-9, Aug 1962
             47:64-5, Mar 1963
Time 49:66, Mar 24, 1947

Finian's Rainbow (725 performances)
book: E. Y. Harburg and Fred Saidy
music: Burton Lane
lyrics: E. Y. Harburg
staging: Bretaigne Windust
sets: Jo Mielziner
costumes: Eleanor Goldsmith
choreography: Michael Kidd
opened: January 10, 1947
  Catholic World 164:453-4, Feb 1947
                 181:308, Jul 1955
  Collier's 120:14-15, Aug 2, 1947
  Commonweal 45:446, Feb 14, 1947
  Harpers 81:174, May 1947

155

Life 22:76-7, Feb 24, 1947
New Republic 116:43, Feb 3, 1947
New York Theatre Critics' Reviews 1947:486+
1960:279+
New York Times VI, page 28, Jan 5, 1947
page 23, Jan 11, 1947
II, page 1, Jan 26, 1947
II, page 3, Feb 2, 1947
II, page 1, Apr 6, 1947
II, page 1, Jul 13, 1947
II, page 1, Aug 17, 1947
page 38, Oct 22, 1947
II, page 3, Nov 9, 1947
II, page 1, Aug 29, 1948
page 36, Oct 19, 1949
page 13, Mar 17, 1953
page 25, May 17, 1955
page 31, Apr 28, 1960
New York Times Magazine pages 28-9, Jan 5, 1947
New Yorker 22:46+, Jan 18, 1947
Newsweek 29:84, Jan 20, 1947
30:78, Nov 3, 1947
Saturday Review 30:28-30, Feb 15, 1947
Theatre Arts 31:8, 15, 23, Mar 1947
32:49, Feb 1948
Time 49:69, Jan 20, 1947
Vogue 109:148, Feb 15, 1947

If the Shoe Fits (21 performances)
book: June Carroll and Robert Duke
music: David Raksin
lyrics: June Carroll and Robert Duke
staging: Eugene Bryden
sets: Edward Gilbert
costumes: Kathryn Kuhn
choreography: Charles Weidman
opened: December 5, 1946
   New York Theatre Critics' Reviews 1946:226+
   New York Times II, page 1, Dec 1, 1946
                page 29, Dec 6, 1946
   New Yorker 22:64, Dec 14, 1946

Park Avenue (72 performances)

book:	Nunnally Johnson and George S. Kaufman, based on the story "Holy Matrimony"
music:	Arthur Schwartz
lyrics:	Ira Gershwin
staging:	George S. Kaufman
sets:	Donald Oenslager
choreography:	Helen Tamiris
opened:	November 4, 1946

Catholic World 164:361, Jan 1946
Nation 163:629, Nov 30, 1946
New York Theatre Critics' Reviews 1946:275+
New York Times VI, page 26, Sep 22, 1946
                 page 31, Nov 5, 1946
                 II, page 3, Dec 15, 1946
New Yorker 22:59, Nov 16, 1946
Newsweek 28:98, Nov 18, 1946
Time 48:64+, Nov 18, 1946
Vogue 108:196, Nov 15, 1946

Street Scene (148 performances)

book:	Elmer Rice, based on his nonmusical play Street Scene
music:	Kurt Weill
lyrics:	Langston Hughes
staging:	Charles Friedman
sets:	Jo Mielziner
costumes:	Lucinda Ballard
choreography:	Anna Sokolow
opened:	January 0, 1947

Catholic World 164:453, Feb 1947
Commonweal 45:397, Jan 31, 1947
Life 22:78, Feb 24, 1947
Musical Courier 135:52, Feb 1, 1947
Musical America 79:3+, May 1959
                79:29-30, Oct 1959
New Republic 116:40, Feb 10, 1947
New York Theatre Critics' Reviews 1947:490+
New York Times II, page 3, Jan 5, 1947
                page 17, Jan 10, 1947
                II, page 2, Jan 19, 1947
                II, page 7, Jan 26, 1947
                II, page 3, Feb 2, 1947

VI, page 28, Feb 2, 1947
II, page 1, May 4, 1947
page 24, May 12, 1947
New Yorker 22:44+, Jan 18, 1947
Newsweek 29:84, Jan 20, 1947
Saturday Review 30:24-6, Feb 1, 1947
Theatre Arts 31:12-13+, Mar 1947
Time 49:69, Jan 20, 1947

Toplitzky of Notre Dame (60 performances)
book: George Marion, Jr.
music: Sammy Fain
lyrics: Jack Barnett
staging: Jose Ruben
sets: Edward Gilbert
costumes: Kenn Barr
choreography: Robert Sidney
opened: December 26, 1946
   Catholic World 164:455, Feb 1947
   New York Theatre Critics' Reviews 1946:201+
   New York Times II, page 4, Dec 22, 1946
                 page 13, Dec 27, 1946
                 page 19, Feb 16, 1947
   New Yorker 22:48+, Jan 11, 1947
   Newsweek 29:64, Jan 6, 1947
   Theatre Arts 31:17, Mar 1947
   Time 49:56, Jan 6, 1947

Season of 1947-1948

Allegro (315 performances)
book: Oscar Hammerstein II
music: Richard Rodgers
lyrics: Oscar Hammerstein II
staging: Lawrence Langner and Theresa
                  Helburn
sets: Jo Mielziner
costumes: Lucinda Ballard
choreography: Agnes de Mille
opened: October 10, 1947
   Catholic World 166:167, Nov 1947
   Collier's 120:20-1+, Oct 25, 1947
   Commonweal 47:70-1, Oct 31, 1947

Forum 109:23-4, Jan 1948
Life 23:70-2, Oct 13, 1947
Nation 165:567-8, Nov 22, 1947
New Republic 117:35, Oct 27, 1947
New York Theatre Critics' Reviews 1947:300+
New York Times II, page 2, Oct 5, 1947
              page 10, Oct 11, 1947
              II, page 1, Nov 2, 1947
              II, page 6, Nov 9, 1947
              II, page 1, Nov 16, 1947
              II, page 3, Jan 18, 1948
              page 36, Sep 18, 1952
New Yorker 23:55-6, Oct 18, 1947
Newsweek 30:86, Oct 20, 1947
Saturday Review 30:30-3, Nov 8, 1947
              30:59, Nov 29, 1947
School and Society 67:476, Jun 26, 1948
Theatre Arts 31:23, Oct 1947
              31:13-15, Nov 1947
Time 50:66-8+, Oct 20, 1947
Vogue 110:191, Nov 15, 1947

Angel in the Wings (300 performances)
sketches: Ted Luce, Hank Ladd, Grace
               Hartman, Paul Hartman
music: Carl Sigman
lyrics: Bob Hilliard
staging: John Kennedy
sets: Donald Oenslager
costumes: Julia Sze
choreography: Edward Noll
opened: December 11, 1947
    Catholic World 166:456, Feb 1948
    Commonweal 47:277, Dec 26, 1947
    Forum 109:155, Mar 1948
    Life 24:35-7, Jan 5, 1948
    New Republic 117:37, Dec 29, 1947
    New York Theatre Critics' Reviews 1947:238+
    New York Times page 36, Dec 12, 1947
              II, page 3, Dec 21, 1947
              II, page 2, Feb 8, 1948
              II, page 1, Aug 29, 1948
    New Yorker 23:48, Dec 20, 1947

Newsweek 30:76, Dec 22, 1947
Time 50:72, Dec 22, 1947
Vogue 111:151+, Apr 1, 1948

Caribbean Carnival (11 performances)
book: Samuel L. Manning and Adolph
                 Thenstead
music: Samuel L. Manning and Adolph
                 Thenstead
lyrics: Samuel L. Manning and Adolph
                 Thenstead
staging: Samuel L. Manning and John Hirshman
costumes: Lou Eisele
choreography: Pearl Primus and Claude Marchant
opened: December 5, 1947
   New York Theatre Critics' Reviews 1947:246+
   New York Times page 12, Dec 6, 1947
                page 34, Dec 15, 1947

High Button Shoes (727 performances)
book: Stephen Longstreet, adapted from his
                 novel The Sisters Liked Them Hand-
                 some
music: Jule Styne
lyrics: Sammy Cahn
staging: George Abbott
sets: Oliver Smith
costumes: Miles White
choreography: Jerome Robbins
opened: October 9, 1947
   Catholic World 166:172, Nov 1947
   Commonweal 47:71, Oct 31, 1947
   Life 23:102-4, Nov 10, 1947
   New Republic 117:35, Oct 27, 1947
   New York Theatre Critics' Reviews 1947:304+
   New York Times II, page 3, Oct 5, 1947
                page 32, Oct 10, 1947
                II, page 6, Nov 9, 1947
                II, page 3, Nov 30, 1947
                II, page 1, Nov 23, 1947
                page 23, Dec 23, 1948
                page 10, Mar 12, 1955
   New Yorker 23:56+, Oct 18, 1947

Newsweek 30:86+, Oct 20, 1947
Theatre Arts 31:15-16, Nov 1947
Time 50:73, Oct 20, 1947
Vogue 110:190, Nov 15, 1947

Hold It! (46 performances)
book: Matt Brooks and Art Arthur
music: Gerald Marks
lyrics: Sam Lerner
staging: Robert E. Perry
sets: Edward Gilbert
costumes: Julia Sze
choreography: Irma Jurist
opened: May 5, 1948
  New York Theatre Critics' Reviews 1948:274+
  New York Times page 31, May 6, 1948
  New Yorker 24:48, May 15, 1948
  Newsweek 31:89, May 17, 1948
  Theatre Arts 32:14+, Jun 1948

Inside U.S.A. (399 performances)
sketches: Arnold Auerbach, Moss Hart, Arnold
                  B. Horwitt, suggested by John
                  Gunther's book
music: Arthur Schwartz
lyrics: Howard Dietz
staging: Victor Samrock
sets: Lemuel Ayers
costumes: Eleanor Goldsmith and Castillo
choreography: Helen Tamiris
opened: April 30, 1948
  Catholic World 167:265, Jun 1948
  Collier's 121:24-5+, May 15, 1948
  Commonweal 48:100, May 14, 1948
  Harper 196:478-80, May 1948
  Life 24:135-6+, May 17, 1948
  New Republic 118:35-6, May 17, 1948
  New York Theatre Critics' Reviews 1948:279+
  New York Times page 27, Mar 30, 1948
                  page 19, May 1, 1948
                  II, page 1, May 23, 1948
                  II, page 6, Jun 13, 1948
                  II, page 1, Aug 29, 1948

161

page 34, Jun 9, 1949
New Yorker 24:52+, May 8, 1948
Newsweek 31:76, May 10, 1948
Saturday Review 31:25, May 22, 1948
Theatre Arts 32:14-15+, Jun 1948
Time 51:80, May 10, 1948
Vogue 111:137, May 1, 1948

Look, Ma, I'm Dancin' (188 performances)
book: Jerome Lawrence and Robert E. Lee
music: Hugh Martin
lyrics: Hugh Martin
staging: George Abbott and Jerome Robbins
sets: Oliver Smith
costumes: John Pratt
choreography: Trude Rittman
opened: January 29, 1948
   Catholic World 166:553, Mar 1948
   Commonweal 47:447, Feb 13, 1948
   Forum 109:155, Mar 1948
   New Republic 118:32, Feb 16, 1948
   New York Theatre Critics' Reviews 1948:364+
   New York Times page 20, Jan 30, 1948
                  II, page 1, Feb 8, 1948
                  II, page 2, Feb 8, 1948
   New Yorker 23:40, Feb 7, 1948
   Newsweek 31:70, Feb 9, 1948
   Saturday Review 31:26-7, Feb 21, 1948
   Time 51:55, Feb 9, 1948

Louisiana Lady (4 performances)
book: Isaac Green, Jr. and Eugene Berton
music: Monte Carlo and Alma Sanders
lyrics: Monte Carlo and Alma Sanders
staging: Edgar MacGregor
sets: Watson Barratt
choreography: Felicia Sorel
opened: June 2, 1947
   New York Theatre Critics' Reviews 1947:362+
   New York Times II, page 1, Jun 1, 1947
                  page 35, Jun 3, 1947

Make Mine Manhattan (429 performances)

book:	Arnold B. Horwitt
music:	Richard Lewine
lyrics:	Arnold B. Horwitt
staging:	Hassard Short
sets:	Frederick Fox
costumes:	Morton Haack
choreography:	Lee Sherman
opened:	January 15, 1948

Catholic World 166:553-4, Mar 1948
Commonweal 47:399, Jan 30, 1948
Forum 109:155, Mar 1948
Life 24:121-1+, Feb 9, 1948
Look 12:50-51, Mar 30, 1948
New Republic 118:34, Feb 9, 1948
New York Theatre Critics' Reviews 1948:382+
New York Times page 26, Jan 16, 1948
          II, page 2, Feb 8, 1948
New Yorker 23:40, Jan 24, 1948
Newsweek 31:81, Jan 26, 1948
Time 51:62, Jan 26, 1948

Music in My Heart (125 performances)

book:	Patsy Ruth Miller, based on the life of Tchaikowsky
music:	Franz Steininger, adapted from Tchaikovsky
lyrics:	Forman Brown
staging:	Hassard Short
sets:	Alvin Colt
costumes:	Alvin Colt
choreography:	Ruth Page
opened:	October 2, 1947

Catholic World 166:171, Nov 1947
New York Theatre Critics' Reviews 1947:324+
New York Times II, page 1, Sep 28, 1947
          page 30, Oct 3, 1947
          II, page 6, Nov 9, 1947
          II, page 4, Dec 21, 1947
New Yorker 23:54, Oct 11, 1947
Newsweek 30:81, Oct 13, 1947
School and Society 66:508-9, Dec 27, 1947
Theatre Arts 31:16, Nov 1947

Under the Counter (27 performances)
book: Arthur Macrae
music: Manning Sherwin
lyrics: Harold Purcell
staging: Jack Hulbert
sets: Clifford Pember
costumes: Clifford Pember
choreography: Jack Hulbert
opened: October 3, 1947
    Catholic World 166:172, Nov 1947
    Nation 165:481, Nov 1, 1947
    New York Theatre Critics' Reviews 1947:320+
    New York Times II, page 3, Sep 28, 1947
                    page 10, Oct 4, 1947
    New Yorker 23:52, Oct 11, 1947
    Newsweek 30:81, Oct 13, 1947

Season of 1948-1949

All for Love (141 performances)
sketches: Max Shulman and others
music: Allan Roberts and Lester Lee
lyrics: Allan Roberts and Lester Lee
staging: Edward Reveaux
sets: Edward Gilbert
costumes: Billy Livingston
choreography: Eric Victor
opened: January 22, 1949
    Commonweal 49:447, Feb 11, 1949
    New York Theatre Critics' Reviews 1949:377+
    New York Times page 16, Jan 24, 1949
    New Yorker 24:42, Jan 29, 1949
    Newsweek 33:71, Jan 31, 1949
    Time 53:44, Jan 31, 1949
         53:63-4, May 2, 1949

Along Fifth Avenue (180 performances)
sketches: Charles Sherman and Nat Hiken
music: Gordon Jenkins
lyrics: Tom Adair
additional
  music and
  lyrics: Richard Stutz, Milton Pascal, Nat Hiken
sets: Oliver Smith

164

costumes: David Ffolkes
choreography: Robert Sidney
opened: January 13, 1949
   Catholic World 168:481, Mar 1949
   New Republic 120:29, Jan 31, 1949
   New York Theatre Critics' Reviews 1949:392+
   New York Times page 28, Jan 14, 1949
   New Yorker 24:44, Jan 22, 1949
   Newsweek 33:70, Jan 24, 1949
   Time 53:52, Jan 24, 1949
   Theatre Arts 33:16-17+, Mar 1949

As the Girls Go (420 performances)
book: William Roos
music: Jimmy McHugh
lyrics: Harold Adamson
staging: Howard Bay
sets: Howard Bay
costumes: Oleg Cassini
choreography: Hermes Pan
opened: November 13, 1948
   Catholic World 168:324, Jan 1949
   Commonweal 49:231, Dec 10, 1948
   Life 25:89-90+, Nov 29, 1948
   New Republic 119:37, Dec 6, 1948
   New York Theatre Critics' Reviews 1948:159+
   New York Times page 21, Nov 15, 1948
               II, page 2, Jan 2, 1949
   New Yorker 24:58, Nov 20, 1948
   Newsweek 32:80, Nov 22, 1948
   Theatre Arts 33:18, Jan 1949
   Time 52:85, Nov 22, 1948
   Vogue 113:114, Jan 1949

Heaven On Earth (12 performances)
book: Barry Trivers
music: Jay Gorney
lyrics: Barry Trivers
staging: John Murray Anderson
sets: Raoul Pene du Bois
costumes: Raoul Pene du Bois
choreography: Nick Castle
opened: September 16, 1948

New York Theatre Critics' Reviews 1948:240+
New York Times page 29, Sep 17, 1948
                    II, page 1, Sep 26, 1948
New Yorker 24:53, Sep 25, 1948
Newsweek 32:79, Sep 27, 1948
Time 52:63, Sep 27, 1948

Hilarities (14 performances)
sketches: Sidney Zelinka, Howard Harris,
                    Morey Amsterdam
music: Buddy Kaye, Carl Lampl
lyrics: Stanley Arnold
opened: September 9, 1948
    New Republic 119:38, Sep 27, 1948
    New York Theatre Critics' Reviews 1948:250+
    New York Times page 20, Sep 10, 1948

Kiss Me, Kate (1,070 performances)
book: Bella Spewack and Samuel Spewack,
                    based on Shakespeare's The Taming
                    of the Shrew
music: Cole Porter
lyrics: Cole Porter
staging: John C. Wilson
sets: Lemuel Ayers
costumes: Lemuel Ayers
choreography: Hanya Holm
opened: December 30, 1948
    America 95:252, Jun 2, 1956
    Catholic World 168:402-3, Feb 1949
                    193:311, Jul 1956
    Commonweal 49:376, Jan 21, 1949
    Good Housekeeping 139:4+, Dec 1949
    Life 26:99-100+, Feb 7, 1949
    New Republic 120:25, Jan 24, 1949
    New York Theatre Critics' Reviews 1948:91+
    New York Times page 10, Dec 31, 1948
                    II, page 1, Jan 9, 1949
                    II, page 1, Jan 16, 1949
                    VI, page 20, Jan 16, 1949
                    II, page 6, Jan 30, 1949
                    page 30, Mar 9, 1951
                    II, page 3, Apr 15, 1951

```
                    page 31, Jul 17, 1951
                    page 24, Jan 9, 1952
                    page 13, Mar 27, 1954
                    page 19, Dec 17, 1955
                    page 27, Feb 15, 1956
                    page 94, Feb 19, 1956
                    page 27, May 10, 1956
                    page 24, Aug 10, 1959
                    page 184, Dec 1, 1963
                    page 31, May 13, 1965
New Yorker 24:50-2, Jan 8, 1949
           41:130+, Jun 12, 1965

Newsweek 33:72, Jan 10, 1949
Saturday Review 32:34-5, Jan 22, 1949
                39:24, May 26, 1956
Theatre Arts 33:17+, Mar 1949
             39:32, Jan 1955
             40:78-80+, Jun 1956
             40:21, Jul 1956
Time 53:36+, Jan 10, 1949
     53:40-4, Jan 31, 1949
     67:47, Mar 5, 1956
```

Lend An Ear (400 performances)

sketches:	Charles Gaynor, additional sketches by Joseph Stein and Will Glickman
music:	Charles Gaynor
lyrics:	Charles Gaynor
staging:	Gower Champion
sets:	Raoul Pene du Bois
costumes:	Raoul Pene du Bois
choreography:	Gower Champion
opened:	December 16, 1948

Catholic World 168:403, Feb 1949
Commonweal 49:306, Dec 31, 1948
Life 26:79-80+, Feb 28, 1949
Nation 168:25, Jan 1, 1949
New Republic 120:29-31, Jan 3, 1949
New York Theatre Critics' Reviews 1948:122+
New York Times page 38, Dec 17, 1948
              II, page 3, Sep 20, 1959
New Yorker 24:32, Dec 25, 1948

Newsweek 32:65, Dec 27, 1948
Theatre Arts 32:22, Aug 1948
            33:56, Mar 1949
Time 52:46, Dec 27, 1948
Vogue 113:214, Feb 1, 1949
            113:90, Feb 15, 1949

Love Life (252 performances)
book: Alan Jay Lerner
music: Kurl Weill
lyrics: Alan Jay Lerner
staging: Eliz Kazan
sets: Boris Aronson
costumes: Lucinda Ballard
choreography: Michael Kidd
opened: October 7, 1948
    Catholic World 168:161, Nov 1948
    Commonweal 49:94, Nov 5, 1948
    Forum 111:32-3, Jan 1949
    Harper 198:110, Jan 1949
    Musical Courier 138:4, Nov 15, 1948
    New Republic 119:28, Nov 1, 1948
    New York Theatre Critics' Reviews 1948:201+
    New York Times II, page 3, Oct 3, 1948
                    page 31, Oct 8, 1948
    New Yorker 24:52, Oct 16, 1948
    Newsweek 32:89, Oct 18, 1948
    School and Society 68:385-6, Dec 4, 1948
    Theatre Arts 33:18, Jan 1949
    Time 52:82, Oct 18, 1948

Magdalena (88 performances)
book: Frederick Hazlitt Brennan and Homer
                    Curran
music: Heitor Villa-Lobos
lyrics: Robert Wright and George Forrest
staging: Jules Dassin
sets: Howard Bay
costumes: Irene Sharaff
choreography: Jack Cole
opened: September 20, 1948
    Catholic World 168:158-9, Nov 1948
    Collier's 122:24-5, Nov 20, 1948

Commonweal 48:618, Oct 8, 1948
Life 25:106-7, Oct 25, 1948
New Republic 119:29, Oct 11, 1948
New York Theatre Critics' Reviews 1948:235+
New York Times page 27, Jul 28, 1948
             page 31, Sep 20, 1948
             II, page 1, Sep 26, 1948
             II, page 7, Sep 26, 1948
             II, page 6, Nov 7, 1948
New Yorker 24:50, Oct 2, 1948
Newsweek 32:76, Oct 4, 1948
School and Society 68:301-2, Oct 30, 1948
Theatre Arts 33:18, Jan 1949
Time 52:59, Oct 4, 1948
Vogue 112:183, Dec 1948

My Romance (95 performances)
book: Rowland Leigh, based on Edward
                 Sheldon's Romance
music: Sigmund Romberg
lyrics: Rowland Leigh
staging: Rowland Leigh
sets: Watson Barratt
costumes: Lou Eisele
choreography: Fredric N. Kelly
opened: October 19, 1948
   Catholic World 168:242, Dec 1948
   New Republic 119:26, Nov 8, 1948
   New York Theatre Critics' Reviews 1948:186+
   New York Times page 30, Oct 20, 1948
   New Yorker 24:44, Oct 30, 1948
   Time 52:52, Nov 1, 1948
   Vogue 112:154+, Dec 1948

Sleepy Hollow (12 performances)
book: Russell Maloney and Miriam Battista,
                 based on Washington Irving's "The
                 Legend of Sleepy Hollow"
music: George Lessner
lyrics: Russell Maloney and Miriam Battista
staging: John O'Shaughnessy and Marc Connelly
sets: Jo Mielziner
costumes: David Ffolkes

choreography: Anna Sokolow
opened: June 3, 1948
   New Republic 118:29, Jun 21, 1948
   New York Theatre Critics' Reviews 1948:258+
   New York Times page 26, Jun 4, 1948
   New Yorker 24:44, Jun 12, 1948
   Newsweek 31:86, Jun 14, 1948
   Time 51:64, Jun 14, 1948

Small Wonder (134 performances)
sketches: Charles Spalding, Max Wilk, George
                Axelrod, Louis Laun
music: Baldwin Bergersen and Albert Selden
lyrics: Phyllis McGinley and Billings Brown
staging: Burt Shevelove
sets: Ralph Alswang
costumes: John Derro
choreography: Gower Champion
opened: September 15, 1948
   Catholic World 168:160, Nov 1948
   New Republic 119:26-7, Oct 4, 1948
   New York Theatre Critics' Reviews 1948:244+
   New York Times page 33, Sep 16, 1948
                II, page 1, Sep 26, 1948
   New York Times Magazine pages 40-1, Sep 12,
                1948
   New Yorker 24:53, Sep 25, 1948
   Newsweek 32:79, Sep 27, 1948
   School and Society 68:302, Oct 30, 1948
   Theatre Arts 33:17, Jan 1949
   Time 52:63, Sep 27, 1948

South Pacific (1,925 performances)
book: Oscar Hammerstein II and Joshua
                Logan, based on James A. Michener's
                Tales of the South Pacific
music: Richard Rodgers
lyrics: Oscar Hammerstein II
staging: Joshua Logan
sets: Jo Mielziner
costumes: Motley
choreography: Joshua Logan
opened: April 7, 1949

America 93:221+, May 21, 1955
      105:355, May 20, 1961
American Mercury 73:114-18, Dec 1951
Business World pages 96-8+, Jun 18, 1949
Catholic World 169:145-6, May 1949
Commonweal 50:69, Apr 29, 1949
Coronet 26:10-11, Jul 1949
      29:44-52, Mar 1951
Good Housekeeping 129:4+, Dec 1949
Harper's Bazaar 83:83, Jun 1949
Life 26:93-6, Apr 18, 1949
    30:63-5, Jan 29, 1951
Musical America 69:13, May 1949
Nation 168:480, Apr 23, 1949
New Republic 120:27-8, Apr 25, 1949
New York Theatre Critics' Reviews 1949:312+
New York Times II, page 1, Apr 3, 1949
           page 30, Apr 8, 1949
           II, page 1, Apr 17, 1949
           II, page 1, May 1, 1949
           II, page 1, Jun 5, 1949
           II, page 1, Jul 3, 1949
           page 26, Apr 25, 1950
           page 36, Apr 26, 1950
           page 1, May 2, 1950
           page 32, Oct 24, 1950
           page 30, Jul 10, 1951
           II, page 1, Sep 2, 1951
           II, page 3, Nov 11, 1951
           page 17, Jan 29, 1952
           page 9, Jan 31, 1952
           page 16, Sep 15, 1952
           II, page 3, Nov 2, 1952
           page 41, Dec 11, 1953
           page 83, Jan 17, 1954
           page 39, May 5, 1955
           II, page 1, Sep 23, 1956
           page 35, Apr 25, 1957
           page 26, Apr 27, 1961
           page 25, Jun 3, 1965
New York Times Magazine pages 22-3, Mar 27,
                1949
            page 56+, Nov 27, 1949

New Yorker 25:54+, Apr 16, 1949
             41:130+, Jun 12, 1965
Newsweek 33:78-9, Apr 11, 1949
Saturday Review 32:47-8, Mar 26, 1949
                 32:28-30, Apr 30, 1949
                 33:4, Jan 14, 1950
Theatre Arts 33:15, Jun 1949
              34:42-3, Jun 1950
              41:16, Jul 1957
Time 53:77, Apr 18, 1949
      65:91, Mar 28, 1955

Where's Charley? (792 performances)
book: George Abbott, based on Brandon
                 Thomas's Charley's Aunt
music: Frank Loesser
lyrics: Frank Loesser
staging: George Abbott
sets: David Ffolkes
costumes: David Ffolkes
choreography: George Balanchine and Fred Danielli
opened: October 11, 1948
   Catholic World 168:242, Dec 1948
   Collier's 122:26-7, Dec 11, 1948
   Commonweal 49:94, Nov 5, 1948
   Life 25:85-8, Nov 8, 1949
   Nation 167:503, Oct 30, 1948
   New Republic 119:28, Nov 1, 1948
   New York Theatre Critics' Reviews 1948:197+
   New York Times II, page 1, Oct 10, 1948
                     page 33, Oct 12, 1948
                   II, page 1, Oct 24, 1948
                   II, page 2, Apr 3, 1949
                   II, page 3, Nov 20, 1949
                   II, page 1, Aug 20, 1950
   New Yorker 24:52, Oct 23, 1948
   Newsweek 32:87, Oct 25, 1948
   Saturday Review 31:26-7, Nov 6, 1948
   Theatre Arts 33:17, Jan 1949
   Time 52:63, Oct 25, 1948
   Vogue 112:154, Dec 1948

172

Alive and Kicking (46 performances)

sketches:	Ray Golden, I. A. Diamond, Henry Morgan, Jerome Chodorov, Joseph Stein, Will Glickman, Mike Stuart
music:	Hal Borne, Irma Jurist and Sammy Fain
lyrics:	Paul Francis Webster and Ray Golden
additional music and lyrics:	Sonny Burke, Leonard Gershe, Billy Kyle, Sid Kuller
special music and lyrics:	Harold Rome
staging:	Robert H. Gordon
sets:	Raoul Pene du Bois
costumes:	Raoul Pene du Bois
choreography:	Jack Cole
opened:	January 17, 1950

New York Theatre Critics' Reviews 1950:390+
New York Times page 25, Jan 18, 1950
Newsweek 35:66, Jan 30, 1950
Theatre Arts 34:16, Mar 1950
Time 55:40, Jan 30, 1950

Arms and the Girl (134 performances)

book:	Herbert and Dorothy Fields, Rouben Mamoulian, based on Lawrence Langner and Armina Marshall's play The Pursuit of Happiness
music:	Morton Gould
lyrics:	Dorothy Fields
staging:	Rouben Mamoulian
sets:	Horace Armistead
costumes:	Audre
opened:	February 2, 1950

Catholic World 171:67, Apr 1950
New York Theatre Critics' Reviews 1950:356+
New York Times II, page 1, Jan 28, 1950
                    page 28, Feb 3, 1950
New Yorker 25:46-7, Feb 11, 1950
Newsweek 35:80, Feb 13, 1950

173

Theatre Arts 34:17, Apr 1950
Time 55:53-4, Feb 13, 1950

Blackouts of 1949 (see Ken Murray's Blackouts of 1949)

The Consul (269 performances)
book: Gian-Carlo Menotti
music: Gian-Carlo Menotti
lyrics: Gian-Carlo Menotti
staging: Gian-Carlo Menotti
sets: Horace Armistead
costumes: Grace Houston
choreography: John Butler
opened: March 15, 1950
   Catholic World 171:148, May 1950
   Christian Science Monitor Magazine page 5, Mar
                                    25, 1950
   Commonweal 51:677, Apr 7, 1950
   Life 28:61-3, Apr 10, 1950
   Musical America 70:7, Mar 1950
                   71:90, Apr 1951
                   71:6, Oct 1951
                   72:12, Jul 1952
   Musical Quarterly 36:447-50, Jul 1950
   Nation 170:305, Apr 1, 1950
          170:557-8, Jun 3, 1950
   New Republic 122:21-2, Apr 10, 1950
   New York Theatre Critics' Reviews 1950:329+
   New York Times page 32, Mar 2, 1950
                   II, page 1, Mar 12, 1950
                   page 41, Mar 16, 1950
                   II, page 1, Mar 26, 1950
                   II, page 7, Apr 2, 1950
                   II, page 1, May 21, 1950
                   page 24, Jan 23, 1951
                   II, page 7, Jan 28, 1951
                   page 26, Feb 8, 1951
                   page 9, Sep 8, 1951
                   page 40, Oct 9, 1952
                   page 41, Oct 30, 1952
                   page 30, Apr 17, 1953
   New Yorker 26:54+, Mar 25, 1950
              28:149, Oct 18, 1952

Saturday Review 33:28-30, Apr 22, 1950
School and Society 72:183, Sep 16, 1950
Theatre Arts 34:28-9, Mar 1950
        34:17, May 1950

Dance Me A Song (35 performances)

sketches:	Jimmy Kirkwood and Lee Goodman, George Oppenheimer and Vincente Minnelli, Marya Mannes, Robert Anderson, James Shelton and Wally Cox
songs:	James Shelton, Herman Hupfeld, Albert Hague, Maurice Valency and Bud Gregg
staging:	James Shelton
sets:	Jo Mielziner
costumes:	Irene Sharaff
choreography:	Robert Sidney
opened:	January 20, 1950

New York Theatre Critics' Reviews 1950:380+
New York Times page 10, Jan 21, 1950
New Yorker 25:48, Jan 28, 1950
Newsweek 35:66, Jan 30, 1950
Theatre Arts 34:19, Mar 1950
Time 55:40, Jan 30, 1950

Gentlemen Prefer Blondes (740 performances)

book:	Joseph Fields and Anita Loos, based on a collection of stories by Anita Loos
music:	Jule Styne
lyrics:	Leo Robin
staging:	John C. Wilson
sets:	Oliver Smith
costumes:	Miles White
choreography:	Agnes De Mille
opened:	December 8, 1949

Catholic World 170:387, Feb 1950
Commonweal 51:342, Dec 30, 1949
Life 27:68-71, Dec 26, 1949
Nation 169:629, Dec 24, 1949
New Republic 122:21, Jan 2, 1950
New York Theatre Critics' Reviews 1949:198+

New York Times II, page 5, Dec 4, 1949
                page 35, Dec 9, 1949
                II, page 3, Dec 18, 1949
                II, page 3, Jan 8, 1950
New Yorker 25:50+, Dec 17, 1949
Newsweek 34:72, Dec 19, 1949
Saturday Review 32:28-9, Dec 31, 1949
Theatre Arts 34:13, Feb 1950
Time 54:62, Dec 19, 1949
        55:50-2+, Jan 9, 1950

Great to Be Alive (52 performances)
book: Walter Bullock and Sylvia Regan
music: Abraham Ellstein
lyrics: Walter Bullock
staging: Mary Hunter
sets: Stewart Chaney
costumes: Stewart Chaney
choreography: Helen Tamiris
opened: March 23, 1950
    Catholic World 171:149, May 1950
    New York Theatre Critics' Reviews 1950:324+
    New York Times page 28, Mar 24, 1950
    New Yorker 26:46+, Apr 1, 1950
    Newsweek 35:73, Apr 3, 1950
    Theatre Arts 34:18, May 1950
    Time 55:51, Apr 3, 1950

Happy As Larry (3 performances)
book: Donagh Mac Donagh
music: Mescha and Wesley Portnoff
lyrics: Donagh Mac Donagh
staging: Burgess Meredith
sets: Motley
costumes: Motley
choreography: Anna Sokolow
opened: January 6, 1950
    New York Theatre Critics' Reviews 1950:394+
    New York Times page 11, Jan 7, 1950
    New Yorker 25:48, Jan 14, 1950
    Newsweek 35:74, Jan 16, 1950
    Theatre Arts 34:14, Mar 1950
    Time 55:45, Jan 16, 1950

Ken Murray's Blackouts of 1949 (51 performances)
music: Charles Henderson and Ray Foster
lyrics: Charles Henderson and Ray Foster
sets: Ben Tipton
opened: September 6, 1949
    Life 27:12-13, Oct 3, 1949
    New Republic 121:29, Sep 26, 1949
    New York Theatre Critics' Reviews 1949:273+
    New York Times page 39, Sep 7, 1949
    New Yorker 25:56, Sep 17, 1949
    Newsweek 34:79, Sep 19, 1949
    Saturday Evening Post 222:38-9+, Sep 10, 1949
    Theatre Arts 33:8, Oct 1949
    Time 54:70, Sep 19, 1949

The Liar (12 performances)
book: Edward Eager and Alfred Drake,
                     based on the Carlo Goldoni play
music: John Mundy
lyrics: Edward Eager
staging: Alfred Drake
sets: Donald Oenslager
costumes: Motley
choreography: Hanya Holm
opened: May 18, 1950
    Christian Science Monitor Magazine page 6, May
                                        27, 1950
    New York Theatre Critics' Reviews 1950:296+
    New York Times page 30, May 19, 1950
    New Yorker 26:49, May 27, 1950
    Newsweek 35:69, May 29, 1950
    Theatre Arts 34:17, Jul 1950

Lost in the Stars (273 performances)
book: Maxwell Anderson, based on Alan
                     Paton's Cry, the Beloved Country
music: Kurt Weill
lyrics: Maxwell Anderson
staging: Rouben Mamoulian
sets: George Jenkins
costumes: Anna Hill Johnstone
opened: October 30, 1949
    American Mercury 70:170-2, Feb 1950

177

Catholic World 170:226, Dec 1949
Commonweal 51:212, Nov 25, 1949
Forum 112:340, Dec 1949
Life 27:143-6+, Nov 14, 1949
Musical America 69:9, Nov 15, 1949
Nation 169:478, Nov 12, 1949
       186:398-9, May 3, 1958
New Republic 121:19, Nov 21, 1949
New York Theatre Critics' Reviews 1949:241+
New York Times II, page 3, Oct 30, 1949
            page 21, Oct 31, 1949
            II, page 1, Nov 6, 1949
            VI, page 14, Dec 11, 1949
            page 21, Apr 11, 1958
            page 26, May 5, 1958
New Yorker 25:64, Nov 5, 1949
       25:58, Nov 12, 1949
       34:138, Apr 19, 1958
Newsweek 34:80, Nov 7, 1949
       51:84, Apr 21, 1958
Saturday Review 32:31-2, Nov 26, 1949
       32:43, Dec 31, 1949
Theatre Arts 34:11, Jan 1950
Time 54:80, Nov 7, 1949

Miss Liberty (308 performances)
book: Robert E. Sherwood
music: Irving Berlin
lyrics: Irving Berlin
staging: Moss Hart
sets: Oliver Smith
costumes: Motley
choreography: Jerome Robbins
opened: July 15, 1949
   Catholic World 170:67-8, Oct 1949
   Commonweal 50:414, Aug 5, 1949
   Good Housekeeping 129:121, Dec 1949
   Holiday 6:16-17+, Nov 1949
   Life 27:56-8, Jul 4, 1949
   New Republic 121:27-8, Aug 1, 1949
   New York Theatre Critics' Reviews 1949:279+
   New York Times page 23, Feb 13, 1949
                VI, page 16, May 29, 1949

```
                page 26, Jun 14, 1949
                page 39, Jun 15, 1949
                page 6, Jul 16, 1949
                II, page 6, Aug 7, 1949
New York Times Magazine pages 16-17, May 29,
                            1949
                         pages 22-3, Jun 26,
                            1949
New Yorker 25:18, Jun 25, 1949
           25:44, Jul 23, 1949
Newsweek 34:70-1, Jul 25, 1949
Saturday Review 32:28-9, Aug 13, 1949
Theatre Arts 33:10, Sep 1949
Time 54:66, Jul 25, 1949
```

Regina (56 performances)

book:	Marc Blitzstein, based on Lillian Hellman's The Little Foxes
music:	Marc Blitzstein
lyrics:	Marc Blitzstein
staging:	Robert Lewis
sets:	Horace Armistead
costumes:	Aline Bernstein
choreography:	Anna Abravanel
opened:	October 31, 1949

```
American Mercury 70:172-3, Feb 1950
Catholic World 170:228-9, Dec 1949
Commonweal 51:238, Dec 2, 1949
Musical America 69:9, Dec 1, 1949
                 73:5, Apr 15, 1953
Nation 169:478, Nov 12, 1949
       177:118-19, Aug 8, 1953
       186:399, May 3, 1958
New Republic 121:22, Dec 5, 1949
New York Theatre Critics' Reviews 1949:237+
New York Times II, page 1, Oct 30, 1949
                page 32, Nov 1, 1949
                II, page 1, Nov 13, 1949
                VI, page 14, Dec 11, 1949
                page 25, Jun 2, 1952
                page 18, Apr 3, 1953
                II, page 7, Apr 12, 1953
                page 12, Oct 10, 1953
```

                    page 19, Apr 19, 1958
                    page 10, May 3, 1958
                    page 36, Apr 20, 1959
New Yorker 25:56-8, Nov 12, 1949
           28:103-5, Jun 14, 1952
           29:113, Oct 17, 1953
           34:80, Apr 26, 1958
Newsweek 34:84-5, Nov 14, 1949
         41:96, Apr 13, 1953
Reporter 8:36-7, Jun 23, 1953
Saturday Review 32:54-5, Nov 19, 1949
                36:41-2, Apr 4, 1953
                36:33, Apr 18, 1953
School and Society 71:24-5, Jan 14, 1950
Theatre Arts 34:12, Jan 1950
Time 54:46, Nov 14, 1949
     61:79, Apr 13, 1953

Texas, Li'l Darlin' (221 performances)
book: John Whedon and Sam Moore
music: Robert Edmund Dolan
lyrics: Johnny Mercer
staging: Paul Crabtree
sets: Theodore Cooper
costumes: Eleanor Goldsmith
choreography: Al White, Jr.
opened: November 25, 1949
   Catholic World 170:309, Jan 1950
   Commonweal 51:293, Dec 16, 1949
   New York Theatre Critics' Reviews 1949:214+
   New York Times page 10, Nov 26, 1949
                 page 19, Jul 11, 1951
   New Yorker 25:70-1, Dec 3, 1949
   Newsweek 34:84, Dec 5, 1949
   Theatre Arts 34:9, Feb 1950
   Time 54:66, Dec 5, 1949

Tickets, Please! (245 performances)
sketches: Harry Herrmann, Edmund Rice,
               Jack Roche, Ted Luce
music and
  lyrics: Lyn Duddy, Joan Edwards, Mel
               Tolkin, Lucille Kallen, Clay Warnick

180

staging: Mervyn Nelson
sets: Ralph Alswang
costumes: Peggy Morrison
choreography: Joan Mann
opened: April 27, 1950
     Catholic World 171:227, Jun 1950
     New Republic 122:20, May 15, 1950
     New York Theatre Critics' Reviews 1950:300+
     New York Times page 25, Apr 28, 1950
                 II, page 1, May 7, 1950
                 II, page 1, Aug 6, 1950
     New Yorker 26:52, May 6, 1950
     Newsweek 35:80, May 8, 1950
     Theatre Arts 34:16, Jul 1950
     Time 55:48, May 8, 1950

Touch and Go (176 performances)
sketches: Jean Kerr and Walter Kerr
music: Jay Gorney
lyrics: Jean Kerr and Walter Kerr
staging: Walter Kerr
sets: John Robert Lloyd
choreography: Helen Tamiris
opened;   October 13, 1949
     Catholic World 170:228, Dec 194
     Commonweal 51:159, Nov 11, 1949
     Life 27:52, Oct 24, 1949
     New York Theatre Critics' Reviews 1949:250+
     New York Times page 34, Oct 14, 1949
                 II, page 1, Oct 30, 1949
                 II, page 1, Nov 6, 1949
                 page 9, May 20, 1950
     New Yorker 25:60+, Oct 22, 1949
     Newsweek 34:84, Oct 24, 1949
     Saturday Review 33:4-5, Jan 14, 1950
     Theatre Arts 33:13, Dec 1949
     Time 54:57, Oct 24, 1949

Season of 1950-1951

The Barrier (4 performances)
book: Langston Hughes
music: Jan Meyerowitz

lyrics: Langston Hughes
staging: Doris Humphrey
sets: H. A. Condell
choreography: Charles Weidman and Doris Humphrey
opened: November 2, 1950
　　Christian Science Monitor Magazine page 8, Nov
　　　　　　　　　　　　　　　　　　　11, 1950
　　Commonweal 53:172, Nov 24, 1950
　　Musical America 70:244, Feb 1950
　　New York Theatre Critics' Reviews 1950:218+
　　New York Times page 34, Jan 19, 1950
　　　　　　　　　　page 32, Nov 3, 1950
　　　　　　　　　　page 24, Mar 9, 1953
　　New Yorker 25:71, Jan 28, 1950
　　　　　　　　26:79-81, Nov 11, 1950
　　Newsweek 35:68, Jan 30, 1950
　　School and Society 71:120, Feb 25, 1950
　　Theatre Arts 35:12, Jan 1951
　　Time 55:68+, Jan 30, 1950

Bless You All (84 performances)
sketches: Arnold Auerbach
music: Harold Rome
lyrics: Harold Rome
staging: John C. Wilson
sets: Oliver Smith
costumes: Miles White
choreography: Helen Tamiris
opened: December 14, 1950
　　Catholic World 172:387, Feb 1951
　　Christian Science Monitor Magazine page 7, Dec
　　　　　　　　　　　　　　　　　　　23, 1950
　　Commonweal 53:327, Jan 5, 1951
　　Life 30:58+, Jan 22, 1951
　　Nation 171:709, Dec 30, 1950
　　New Republic 124:22, Jan 8, 1951
　　New York Theatre Critics' Reviews 1950:170+
　　New York Times VI, page 62, Dec 10, 1950
　　　　　　　　　　page 42, Dec 15, 1950
　　New Yorker 26:40, Dec 23, 1950
　　Newsweek 36:59, Dec 25, 1950
　　Theatre Arts 35:18, Feb 1951
　　Time 56:47, Dec 25, 1950

182

Call Me Madam (644 performances)
book: Howard Lindsay and Russel Crouse
music: Irving Berlin
lyrics: Irving Berlin
staging: George Abbott
sets: Raoul Pene du Bois
costumes: Raoul Pene du Bois
choreography: Jerome Robbins
opened: October 12, 1950
   Catholic World 172:225, Dec 1950
   Christian Science Monitor Magazine page 6, Oct
                                          21, 1950
   Collier's 126:22-3+, Oct 21, 1950
   Commonweal 53:94, Nov 3, 1950
   Life 29:117-18+, Oct 30, 1950
   Nation 171:370, Oct 21, 1950
   New Republic 123:23, Nov 6, 1950
   New York Theatre Critics' Reviews 1950:243+
   New York Times II, page 1, Sep 3, 1950
                  VI, page 24, Oct 1, 1950
                  II, page 1, Oct 8, 1950
                  page 25, Oct 13, 1950
                  II, page 1, Oct 22, 1950
                  II, page 1, Apr 29, 1951
                  page 84, Mar 16, 1952
                  page 17, Mar 17, 1952
                  II, page 3, Apr 13, 1952
                  page 35, May 6, 1952
                  page 44, Dec 16, 1952
   New Yorker 26:55, Oct 21, 1950
   Newsweek 36:84, Oct 23, 1950
   Saturday Review 33:49-50, Sep 30, 1950
                   33:42-4, Oct 28, 1950
   Theatre Arts 34:16-17, Nov 1950
                34:15, Dec 1950
   Time 56:58, Oct 23, 1950

Flahooley (40 performances)
book: E. Y. Harburg and Fred Saidy
music: Sammy Fain
lyrics: E. Y. Harburg
staging: E. Y. Harburg and Fred Saidy
sets: Howard Bay

183

costumes: David Ffolkes
choreography: Helen Tamiris
opened: May 14, 1951
    Catholic World 173:307, Jul 1951
    Commonweal 54:189, Jun 1, 1951
    New York Theatre Critics' Reviews 1951:264+
    New York Times II, page 1, May 13, 1951
                    page 39, May 15, 1951
                    II, page 1, May 20, 1951
                    page 17, Aug 13, 1952
    New Yorker 27:48+, May 26, 1951
    Newsweek 37:58, May 28, 1951
    Theatre Arts 35:5, Sep 1951
    Time 57:78, May 28, 1951

Guys and Dolls (1,200 performances)
book: Jo Swerling and Abe Burrows, based
               on a story and characters of Damon
               Runyon
music: Frank Loesser
lyrics: Frank Loesser
staging: George S. Kaufman
sets: Jo Mielziner
costumes: Alvin Colt
choreography: Michael Kidd
opened: November 24, 1950
    America 93:192, May 14, 1955
    Catholic World 172:309, Jan 1951
                    181:228, Jun 1955
    Christian Science Monitor Magazine page 13, Dec
                                            2, 1950
    Commonweal 53:252, Dec 15, 1950
    Holiday 20:75+, Oct 1956
    Life 29:64-5, Dec 25, 1950
    Nation 171:515, Dec 2, 1950
    New Republic 123:22, Dec 25, 1950
                    132:22, May 2, 1955
    New York Theatre Critics' Reviews 1950:185+
    New York Times page 32, Oct 24, 1950
                    II, page 1, Nov 12, 1950
                    page 11, Nov 25, 1950
                    II, page 1, Dec 3, 1950
                    VI, page 63, Dec 10, 1950

```
                    II, page 1, Dec 17, 1950
                    page 20, Mar 26, 1951
                    page 34, Apr 4, 1951
                    II, page 1, Oct 7, 1951
                    page 17, May 29, 1953
                    II, page 1, Jun 7, 1953
                    page 32, Apr 21, 1955
                    page 22, Jul 22, 1959
                    page 39, Apr 29, 1965
```
New Yorker 26:77, Dec 2, 1950
Newsweek 36:75, Dec 4, 1950
Saturday Review 33:27-8, Dec 23, 1950
                    33:38+, Dec 30, 1950
Theatre Arts 35:131, Feb 1951
             35:32+, Jul 1951
             39:88, Jul 1955
Time 56:63, Dec 4, 1950

The King and I (1,246 performances)
book: Oscar Hammerstein II, based on
                 Margaret Landon's novel Anna and
                 the King of Siam
music: Richard Rodgers
lyrics: Oscar Hammerstein II
staging: John Van Druten
sets: Jo Mielziner
costumes: Irene Sharaff
choreography: Jerome Robbins
opened: March 29, 1951
America 95:147, May 5, 1056
        111:143-4, Aug 8, 1964
Catholic World 173:145-6, May 1951
               183:229, Jun 1956
               183:311, Jul 1956
Colliers 127:24-5+, Apr 7, 1951
Commonweal 54:12, Apr 13, 1951
           64:299, Jun 22, 1956
Harper 203:99-100, Sep 1951
Life 30:79-80+, Apr 23, 1951
Nation 172:353, Apr 14, 1951
New Republic 124:29, Apr 16, 1951
New York Theatre Critics' Reviews 1951:304+
                                  1960:267+

                    185

New York Times II, page 1, Mar 25, 1951
                page 26, Mar 30, 1951
                II, page 1, Apr 8, 1951
                II, page 1, Oct 5, 1952
                page 33, Oct 9, 1953
                II, page 3, Oct 18, 1953
                page 33, May 17, 1955
                page 35, Apr 19, 1956
                page 40, May 12, 1960
                II, page 1, May 22, 1960
                I, page 22, Mar 19, 1961
                page 30, Jun 13, 1963
                page 20, Jul 6, 1964
                page 26, Jul 7, 1964
                page 39, Jul 8, 1964
                page 27, Jul 9, 1964
New Yorker 27:70+, Apr 7, 1951
Newsweek 37:78, Apr 9, 1951
Saturday Review 34:32, Mar 31, 1951
                34:44-6, Apr 14, 1951
                47:18, Jul 25, 1964
Theatre Arts 35:30-1, Jul 1951
                40:19, Jun 1956
Time 57:78, Apr 9, 1951

Make A Wish (103 performances)
book: Preston Sturges, based on Ferenc
                Molnar's The Good Fairy
music: Hugh Martin
lyrics: Hugh Martin
staging: John C. Wilson
sets: Raoul Pene du Bois
costumes: Raoul Pene du Bois
choreography: Gower Champion
opened: April 18, 1951
    Catholic World 173:228, Jun 1951
    Commonweal 54:88, May 4, 1951
    Life 30:137-8, May 14, 1951
    Musical America 71:7+, Jul 1951
    Nation 172:403, Apr 28, 1951
    New York Theatre Critics' Reviews 1951:294+
    New York Times page 38, Apr 19, 1951
    New Yorker 27:58, Apr 28, 1951

186

Newsweek 37:53, Apr 30, 1951
Theatre Arts 35:14, Jun 1951
Time 57:89, Apr 30, 1951

Michael Todd's Peep Show (278 performances)
sketches: Bobby Clark, H. I. Phillips, William
                 Roos, Billy K. Wells
music and
  lyrics: Bhumibal and Chakraband, Sammy
                 Fain and Herb Magidson, Harold
                 Rome, Raymond Scott, Sammy
                 Stept and Dan Shapiro, Jule Styne
                 and Bob Hilliard
staging: Hassard Short
sets: Howard Bay
costumes: Irene Sharaff
choreography: James Starbuck
opened: June 28, 1950
    Life 29:67-70, Jul 10, 1950
    New Republic 123:21, Jul 17, 1950
    New York Theatre Critics' Reviews 1950:285+
    New York Times page 34, Jun 7, 1950
                     VI, page 28, Jun 18, 1950
                     VI, page 29, Jun 18, 1950
                     II, page 2, Jun 25, 1950
                     page 37, Jun 29, 1950
                     II, page 1, Jul 9, 1950
    New York Times Magazine pages 28-9, Jun 18,
                                             1950
    New Yorker 26:111, Jul 8, 1950
    Newsweek 36:77, Jul 10, 1950
    Theatre Arts 34:26-31+, Jul 1950
                 34:9, Sep 1950
    Time 56:58, Jul 10, 1950
         56:59-60, Jul 17, 1950

Out of this World (157 performances)
book: Dwight Taylor and Reginald Lawrence
music: Cole Porter
lyrics: Cole Porter
staging: Agnes de Mille
sets: Lemuel Ayers
costumes: Lemuel Ayers

choreography: Hanya Holm
opened: December 21, 1950
   Catholic World 173:69, Apr 1951
   Christian Science Monitor Magazine page 9, Dec
                      30, 1950
   Commonweal 53:349, Jan 12, 1951
   New York Theatre Critics' Reviews 1950:166+
   New York Times VI, page 62, Dec 10, 1950
              II, page 3, Dec 17, 1950
              page 17, Dec 22, 1950
              II, page 8, Jan 14, 1951
              page 35, Oct 13, 1955
              page 44, Nov 10, 1955
   New Yorker 26:44, Dec 30, 1950
   Newsweek 37:35, Jan 1, 1951
   Theatre Arts 35:19, Feb 1951
   Time 57:42, Jan 1, 1951

Pardon Our French (100 performances)
sketches: Ole Olsen and Chic Johnson
music: Victor Young
lyrics: Edward Heyman
sets: Albert Johnson
costumes: Jack Mosser
opened: October 5, 1950
   Catholic World 172:228, Dec 1950
   Commonweal 53:62, Oct 27, 1950
   New York Theatre Critics' Reviews 1950:254+
   New York Times page 22, Oct 6, 1950
   New Yorker 26:52+, Oct 14, 1950
   Newsweek 36:86, Oct 16, 1950
   Theatre Arts 34:12, Dec 1950
   Time 56:54, Oct 16, 1950

Razzle Dazzle (8 performances)
sketches: Mike Stewart
music: Leo Schumer, Shelley Mowell, James
              Reed Lawlor, Bernice Kroll, Irma
              Jurist
lyrics: Mike Stewart
sets: William Riva
choreography: Nelle Fischer
opened: February 19, 1951

Commonweal 53:542, Mar 9, 1951
New York Theatre Critics' Reviews 1951:339+
New York Times page 21, Feb 20, 1951
Newsweek 37:83, Mar 5, 1951
Theatre Arts 35:21, Apr 1951

A Tree Grows in Brooklyn (270 performances)
book: Betty Smith and George Abbott, based
                on Betty Smith's novel
music: Arthur Schwartz
lyrics: Dorothy Fields
staging: George Abbott
sets: Jo Mielziner
choreography: Herbert Ross
opened: April 19, 1951
   Catholic World 173:229, Jun 1951
   Commonweal 54:88, May 4, 1951
   Life 30:97-8+, May 7, 1951
   Musical America 71:34, Jul 1951
   Nation 172:403, Apr 28, 1951
   New Republic 124:20, May 14, 1951
   New York Theatre Critics' Reviews 1951:291+
   New York Times II, page 3, Apr 15, 1951
                    page 24, Apr 20, 1951
                 II, page 1, Apr 29, 1951
   New Yorker 27:56+, Apr 28, 1951
   Newsweek 37:53, Apr 30, 1951
   Saturday Review 34:23-4, May 5, 1951
   Time 57:89, Apr 30, 1951

Season of 1951-1952

Courtin' Time (37 performances)
book: William Roos, based on Eden Phill-
                pott's play The Farmer's Wife
music: Don Walker
lyrics: Jack Lawrence
staging: Alfred Drake
sets: Ralph Alswang
costumes: Saul Bolsani
choreography: George Balanchine
opened: June 13, 1951
   Catholic World 173:386-7, Aug 1951

189

Commonweal 54:285, Jun 29, 1951
Nation 172:594, Jun 23, 1951
New York Theatre Critics' Reviews 1951:254+
New York Times page 30, Jun 14, 1951
              II, page 1, Jun 17, 1951
              II, page 1, Jul 1, 1951
              II, page 9, Jul 1, 1951
New Yorker 27:45, Jun 23, 1951
Newsweek 37:72, Jun 25, 1951
Theatre Arts 35:6, Sep 1951
Time 57:73, Jun 25, 1951

New Faces of 1952 (365 performances)
sketches: not credited
music: Francis Lemarque, Sheldon Harnick,
               Murray Grand, Elisse Boyd, Arthur
               Siegel, Ronald Graham, Michael
               Brown
lyrics: Francis Lemarque, Sheldon Harnick,
               Murray Grand, Elisse Boyd, June
               Carroll, Ronald Graham, Michael
               Brown
staging: John Murray Anderson
sets: Raoul Pene du Bois
costumes: Thomas Becher
choreography: Richard Barstow
opened: May 16, 1952
   Catholic World 175:310, Jul 1952
   Commonweal 56:224, Jun 6, 1952
   Life 32:91-2, Jun 2, 1952
   New York Theatre Critics' Reviews 1952:278+
   New York Times page 23, May 17, 1952
                  II, page 1, May 25, 1952
                  II, page 2, Nov 2, 1952
   New Yorker 28:88, May 24, 1952
   Newsweek 39:84, May 26, 1952
   Saturday Review 35:26, May 31, 1952
   Theatre Arts 36:82, Jul 1952
                 36:18-21, Aug 1952
   Time 59:56, May 26, 1952

Paint Your Wagon (289 performances)
book: Alan Jay Lerner

```
music:          Frederick Loewe
lyrics:         Alan Jay Lerner
staging:        Daniel Mann
sets:           Oliver Smith
costumes:       Motley
choreography:   Agnes de Mille
opened:         November 12, 1951
```
Catholic World 174:308, Jan 1952
Commonweal 55:199, Nov 30, 1951
Nation 173:484-5, Dec 1, 1951
New Republic 126:22, Jan 7, 1952
New York Theatre Critics' Reviews 1951:172+
New York Times II, page 1, Nov 11, 1951
                 page 32, Nov 13, 1951
                 II, page 1, Nov 18, 1951
New Yorker 27:67, Nov 24, 1951
Newsweek 38:84, Nov 26, 1951
Saturday Review 35:27, Jul 5, 1952
School and Society 75:246, Apr 19, 1952
Theatre Arts 36:72, Feb 1952
                 36:33-5, Dec, 1952
Time 58:87, Nov 26, 1951

Seventeen (182 performances)
```
book:           Sally Benson, based on Booth Tarking-
                ton's novel
music:          Walter Kent
lyrics:         Kim Gannon
staging:        Hassard Short
sets:           Stewart Chaney
costumes:       David Ffolkes
choreography:   Dania Krupska
opened:         June 21, 1951
```
Catholic World 173:386, Aug 1951
Commonweal 54:309, Jul 6, 1951
Life 31:57-8, Jul 23, 1951
Musical America 71:34, Jul 1951
New York Theatre Critics' Reviews 1951:250+
New York Times II, page 2, Jun 10, 1951
                 page 16, Jun 22, 1951
                 II, page 1, Jul 1, 1951
                 II, page 9, Jul 1, 1951
New Yorker 27:39, Jun 30, 1951

Newsweek 38:74, Jul 2, 1951
Theatre Arts 35:6-7, Sep 1951
Time 58:55, Jul 2, 1951

Three Wishes for Jamie (91 performances)
book: Charles O'Neal and Abe Burrows,
                based on Charles O'Neal's novel
music: Ralph Blane
lyrics: Ralph Blane
staging: Abe Burrows
sets: George Jenkins
costumes: Miles White
choreography: Ted Cappy, Herbert Ross, Eugene
                Loring
opened: March 21, 1952
    Catholic World 175:148, May 1952
    Commonweal 56:14, Apr 11, 1952
    Life 32:119+, Apr 14, 1952
    New York Theatre Critics' Reviews 1952:332+
    New York Times page 9, Mar 22, 1952
    New Yorker 28:62, Mar 29, 1952
    Newsweek 39:84, Mar 31, 1952
    Saturday Review 35:27, Apr 5, 1952
    Theatre Arts 36:91, May 1952
    Time 59:69, Mar 31, 1952

Top Banana (350 performances)
book: Hy Kraft
music: Johnny Mercer
lyrics: Johnny Mercer
staging: Jack Donohue
sets: Jo Mielziner
costumes: Alvin Colt
choreography: Ron Fletcher
opened: November 1, 1951
    Catholic World 174:228, Dec 1951
    Commonweal 55:173-4, Nov 23, 1951
    Life 31:75-6+, Dec 3, 1951
    New York Theatre Critics' Reviews 1951:180+
    New York Times page 19, Nov 2, 1951
                II, page 1, Nov 18, 1951
    New Yorker 27:64+, Nov 10, 1951
    Newsweek 38:92, Nov 12, 1951

Theatre Arts 35:3, Dec 1951
36:81, Jan 1952
Time 58:59, Nov 12, 1951

Two On the Aisle (281 performances)
sketches: Betty Comden, Adolph Green, Nat
                 Hiken, William Friedberg
music: Jule Styne
lyrics: Betty Comden, Adolph Green, Nat
                 Hiken, William Friedberg
staging: Abe Burrows
sets: Howard Bay
costumes: Joan Personette
choreography: Genevieve Pitot
opened: July 19, 1951
    Catholic World 173:469-70, Sep 1951
    Commonweal 54:405-6, Aug 3, 1951
    Harper 203:100-1, Sep 1951
    Life 31:111-12, Sep 10, 1951
    Nation 173:78, Jul 28, 1951
    New Republic 125:21, Sep 17, 1951
    New York Theatre Critics' Reviews 1951:246+
    New York Times page 13, Jul 20, 1951
                    II, page 1, Jul 29, 1951
                    VI, page 14, Aug 5, 1951
    New York Times Magazine page 14, Aug 5, 1951
    New Yorker 27:48+, Jul 28, 1951
    Newsweek 38:47, Jul 30, 1951
    Theatre Arts 35:6, 22-3+, Sep 1951
    Time 58:47, Jul 30, 1951

                Season of 1952-1953

Buttrio Square (7 performances)
book: Billy Gilbert and Gen Genovese, based
                 on a play by Hal Cranton from an
                 original story by Gen Genovese
music: Arthur Jones and Fred Stamer
lyrics: Gen Genovese
staging: Eugene Loring
sets: Samuel Leve
costumes: Sal Anthony
choreography: Eugene Loring

                      193

opened: October 14, 1952
   New York Theatre Critics' Reviews 1952:238+
   New York Times page 40, Oct 15, 1952
   New Yorker 28:30, Oct 25, 1952
   Time 60:76, Oct 27, 1952

Can-Can (892 performances)
book: Abe Burrows
music: Cole Porter
lyrics: Cole Porter
staging: Abe Burrows
sets: Jo Mielziner
costumes: Motley
choreography: Michael Kidd
opened: May 7, 1953
   America 89:228, May 23, 1953
           107:361, Jun 2, 1962
   Catholic World 177:308-9, Jul 1953
   Commonweal 58:200, May 29, 1953
   Life 34:59-60+, Jun 1, 1953
   Look 17:36-8, May 19, 1953
   Nation 176:441-2, May 23, 1953
   New York Theatre Critics' Reviews 1953:304+
   New York Times VI, page 68, Apr 26, 1953
                    page 28, May 8, 1953
                    II, page 1, May 17, 1953
                    II, page 3, Oct 24, 1954
                    page 32, May 17, 1962
   New York Times Magazine pages 68-9, Apr 26,
                    1953
   New Yorker 29:59, May 16, 1953
   Newsweek 42:60, Dec 21, 1953
   Saturday Review 36:28, May 23, 1953
   Theatre Arts 37:14, Jul 1953
   Time 61:69, May 18, 1953
   Vogue 121:86-7, Apr 15, 1953

Hazel Flagg (190 performances)
book: Ben Hecht, based on a story by
                  James Street and the film Nothing
                  Sacred
music: Jule Styne
lyrics: Bob Hilliard

194

staging: David Alexander
sets: Harry Horner
costumes: Miles White
choreography: Robert Alton
opened: February 11, 1953
   America 88:661, Mar 14, 1953
   Catholic World 177:70, Apr 1953
   Commonweal 57:552, Mar 6, 1953
   Dance Magazine 27:12-15+, Mar 1953
   Life 34:102-4+, Mar 9, 1953
   Look 17:20, Mar 24, 1953
   Nation 176:193, Feb 28, 1953
   New York Theatre Critics' Reviews 1953:362+
   New York Times page 22, Feb 12, 1953
                   II, page 3, Sep 13, 1953
   New Yorker 29:58, Feb 21, 1953
   Newsweek 41:62, Feb 23, 1953
   Saturday Review 36:38, Feb 28, 1953
   Theatre Arts 37:14-15, Feb 1953
                   37:15, May 1953
   Time 61:86, Feb 23, 1953

Maggie (5 performances)
book: Hugh Thomas, based on Sir James M.
                   Barrie's play What Every Woman
                   Knows
music: Hugh Thomas
lyrics: Hugh Thomas
staging: Michael Gordon
sets: Raoul Pene du Bois
costumes: Raoul Pene du Bois
choreography: June Graham
opened: February 18, 1953
   Commonweal 57:577, Mar 13, 1953
   New York Theatre Critics' Reviews 1953:351+
   New York Times page 20, Feb 19, 1953
   New Yorker 29:65, Feb 28, 1953
   Newsweek 41:84, Mar 2, 1953
   Saturday Review 36:35, Mar 7, 1953
   Theatre Arts 37:14, Jan 1953
                   37:15, May 1953
   Time 61:77, Mar 2, 1953

195

<u>Me and Juliet</u> (358 performances)
book: Oscar Hammerstein II
music: Richard Rodgers
lyrics: Oscar Hammerstein II
staging: George Abbott
sets: Jo Mielziner
costumes: Irene Scharaff
choreography: Robert Alton
opened: May 28, 1953
    America 89:305, Jun 13, 1953
    Catholic World 177:308, Jul 1953
    Commonweal 58:273, Jun 19, 1953
    Life 34:89-90+, Jun 15, 1953
    Look 17:34-6, Jun 16, 1953
    Nation 176:530, Jun 20, 1953
    New York Theatre Critics' Reviews 1953:298+
    New York Times page 33, Apr 21, 1953
                    II, page 1, May 24, 1953
                    VI, page 28, May 24, 1953
                    page 17, May 29, 1953
                    II, page 1, Jun 7, 1953
    New York Times Magazine pages 28-9, May 24,
                    1953
    New Yorker 29:64+, Jun 6, 1953
    Newsweek 42:60, Dec 21, 1953
                41:72, Jun 8, 1953
    Saturday Review 36:37, Jul 11, 1953
                    36:26-7, Jun 13, 1953
    Theatre Arts 37:15-16, Aug 1953
                 37:28-9, Sep 1953
    Time 61:93, Jun 8, 1953
    Vogue 121:90-1, Jun 1953

<u>My Darlin' Aida</u> (89 performances)
book: Charles Friedman, based on Verdi's
                opera
music: Giuseppe Verdi
staging: Charles Friedman
sets: Lemuel Ayers
costumes: Lemuel Ayers
choreography: Hanya Holm
opened: October 27, 1952
    Catholic World 176:228, Dec 1952

196

Commonweal 57:164, Nov 21, 1952
Musical America 72:9, Dec 15, 1952
New York Theatre Critics' Reviews 1952:218+
New York Times II, page 1, Oct 26, 1952
        page 36, Oct 28, 1952
        II, page 7, Nov 9, 1952
        II, page 1, Nov 9, 1952
New Yorker 28:86+, Nov 8, 1952
Newsweek 40:94-5, Nov 10, 1952
Theatre Arts 37:24-5, Jan 1953
Time 60:72, Nov 10, 1952

Two's Company (90 performances)
sketches: Charles Sherman and Peter De Vries
music: Vernon Duke
lyrics: Ogden Nash and Sammy Cahn
staging: John Murray Anderson
sets: Ralph Alswang
costumes: Miles White
choreography: Jerome Robbins
opened: December 15, 1952
    Catholic World 176:389, Feb 1953
    Colliers 130:20-1, Nov 29, 1952
    Commonweal 57:376-7, Jan 16, 1953
    Life 33:24, Dec 29, 1952
    Nation 175:613, Dec 27, 1952
    New York Theatre Critics' Reviews 1952:157+
    New York Times page 43, Dec 16, 1952
                II, page 3, Dec 21, 1952
    New Yorker 28:44, Dec 27, 1952
    Newsweek 40:40. Dec 29, 1952
    Saturday Review 36:52, Jan 3, 1953
    Time 60:54, Dec 29, 1952

Wish You Were Here (598 performances)
book: Arthur Kober and Joshua Logan, based
                 on Arthur Kober's play Having
                 Wonderful Time
music: Harold Rome
lyrics: Harold Rome
staging: Joshua Logan
sets: Jo Mielziner
costumes: Robert Mackintosh

197

choreography: Joshua Logan
opened: June 25, 1952
   Catholic World 175:388, Aug 1952
   Commonweal 56:366-7, Jul 18, 1952
   Life 33:79-80, Jul 21, 1952
   Nation 175:18, Jul 5, 1952
   New York Theatre Critics' Reviews 1952:266+
   New York Times VI, page 22, Jun 15, 1952
               II, page 1, Jun 22, 1952
               page 26, Jun 26, 1952
               II, page 1, Aug 31, 1952
               II, page 1, Feb 22, 1953
               II, page 1, Jul 12, 1953
               page 83, Oct 11, 1953
               II, page 3, Oct 18, 1953
   New Yorker 28:45, Jul 5, 1952
              28:56, Dec 20, 1952
   Newsweek 40:70, Jul 7, 1952
   Saturday Review 35:24, Jul 12, 1952
              35:5, Aug 16, 1952
   Theatre Arts 36:14, Jul 1952
              36:28-9, Aug 1952
   Time 60:60, Jul 7, 1952

Wonderful Town (559 performances)
book: Joseph Fields and Jerome Chodorov,
                 based on the play My Sister Eileen
                 by Joseph Fields and Jerome
                 Chodorov and the stories of Ruth
                 McKenney
music: Leonard Bernstein
lyrics: Betty Comden and Adolph Green
staging: George Abbott
sets: Raoul Pene du Bois
costumes: Raoul Pene du Bois
choreography: Donald Saddler
opened: February 25, 1953
   America 88:661, Mar 14, 1953
   Catholic World 177:67-8, Apr 1953
   Commonweal 57:603-4, Mar 20, 1953
   Dance Magazine 32:15, Apr 1958
   Life 34:134-5, Mar 16, 1953
   Look 17:84-5, Mar 10, 1953

Nation 176:232, Mar 14, 1953
New York Theatre Critics' Reviews 1953:344+
New York Times II, page 1, Feb 22, 1953
                page 22, Feb 26, 1953
                II, page 1, Mar 8, 1953
                II, page 1, Apr 5, 1953
                II, page 7, May 10, 1953
                II, page 1, May 9, 1954
                page 33, May 17, 1955
                page 32, Mar 6, 1958
                page 10, Feb 15, 1963
New Yorker 29:59, Mar 7, 1953
Newsweek 41:59, Mar 9, 1953
Saturday Review 36:36, Mar 14, 1953
                36:6, May 9, 1953
Theatre Arts 37:16-17, May 1953
                37:18-21, Aug 1953
Time 61:96+, Mar 9, 1953
        61:40-2+, Mar 30, 1953

Season of 1953-1954

Almanac (1953) (see John Murray Anderson's Almanac)

By the Beautiful Sea (270 performances)
book: Herbert and Dorothy Fields
music: Arthur Schwartz
lyrics: Dorothy Fields
staging: Marshall Jamison
sets: Jo Mielziner
costumes: Irene Sharaff
choreography: Helen Tamiris
opened: April 8, 1954
   America 91:171-2, May 8, 1954
   Catholic World 179:225, Jun 1954
   Commonweal 60:95-6, Apr 30, 1954
   Life 36:109-10, May 17, 1954
   Mademoiselle 38:125, Apr 1954
   Nation 178:370, Apr 24, 1954
   New York Theatre Critics' Reviews 1954:335+
   New York Times page 20, Apr 9, 1954
                II, page 1, Apr 18, 1954
   New Yorker 30:64-6, Apr 17, 1954

Newsweek 43:66, Apr 19, 1954
Saturday Review 37:32, May 1, 1954
Theatre Arts 38:18-19, Jun 1954
Time 63:85, Apr 19, 1954

Carnival in Flanders (6 performances)
book: Preston Sturges, based on La Kermesse
               Heroique by C. Spaak, J. Feyder
               and B. Zimmer
music: James Van Heusen
lyrics: Johnny Burke
staging: Preston Sturges
sets: Oliver Smith
costumes: Lucinda Ballard
choreography: Helen Tamiris
opened: September 8, 1953
   America 89:629, Sep 26, 1953
   Commonweal 58:634, Oct 2, 1953
   New York Theatre Critics' Reviews 1953:286+
   New York Times page 38, Sep 9, 1953
   New Yorker 29: 74, Sep 19, 1953
   Theatre Arts 37:18, Nov 1953

The Girl in Pink Tights (115 performances)
book: Jerome Chodorov and Joseph Fields
music: Sigmund Romberg
lyrics: Leo Robin
staging: Shepard Traube
sets: Eldon Elder
costumes: Miles White
choreography: Agnes de Mille
opened: March 5, 1954
   America 91:79, Apr 17, 1954
   Catholic World 179:149, May 1954
   Commonweal 60:95-6, Apr 30, 1954
   Life 36:67-8+, Mar 29, 1954
   Mademoiselle 38:124, Apr 1954
   Musical America 74:7, Jun 1954
   Nation 178:246, Mar 20, 1954
   New York Theatre Critics' Reviews 1954:354+
   New York Times II, page 1, Feb 21, 1954
                page 13, Mar 6, 1954
   New Yorker 30:71, Mar 13, 1954

Newsweek 43:63, Mar 15, 1954
Theatre Arts 38:24-5, Apr 1954
          38:16-17, May 1954
Time 63:87, Mar 15, 1954

The Golden Apple (125 performances)
book: John Latouche
music: Jerome Moross
lyrics: John Latouche
staging: Norman Lloyd
sets: William and Jean Eckart
costumes: Alvin Colt
choreography: Hanya Holm
opened: March 11, 1954
    America 91:24-5+, Apr 3, 1954
    Catholic World 179:148, May 1954
    Commonweal 60:95, Apr 30, 1954
              76:210, May 18, 1962
    Harper 208:91-2, May 1954
    Life 36:163-4+, Apr 12, 1954
    Musical America 74:7, Jun 1954
    Nation 178:265-6, Mar 27, 1954
    New York Theatre Critics' Reviews 1954:346+
    New York Times page 15, Mar 12, 1954
              II, page 1, Mar 21, 1954
              page 38, Feb 13, 1962
              page 47, May 9, 1962
    New Yorker 30:60+, Mar 20, 1954
    Saturday Review 37:23, Mar 27, 1954
    Theatre Arts 38:80, May 1954
              38:23, Jun 1954
              38:22-5, Aug 1954
              46:59-61, Apr 1962
    Time 63:96+, Mar 22, 1954

John Murray Anderson's Almanac (229 performances)
sketches: Jean Kerr, Summer Locke-Elliot,
               Arthur Macrae, Herbert Farjeon,
               Lauri Wylie, Billy K. Wells
music and
lyrics: Richard Adler, Jerry Ross, Cy Cole-
               man, Michael Grace, Joseph Mc-
               Carthy, Jr., Henry Sullivan, John

                    Rox, Bart Howard
staging: John Murray Anderson
sets: Raoul Pene du Bois
costumes: Thomas Becher
choreography: Donald Saddler
opened: December 10, 1953
    America 90:366, Jan 2, 1954
    Catholic World 178:390, Feb 1954
    Commonweal 59:353, Jan 8, 1954
    Life 35:72-3, Dec 28, 1953
    Nation 177:574, Dec 26, 1953
    News Republic 130:21, Jan 4, 1954
    New York Theatre Critics' Reviews 1953:191+
    New York Times page 42, Dec 11, 1953
                    page 51, Dec 14, 1953
                    II, page 1, Jan 3, 1954
    New Yorker 29:75, Dec 19, 1953
    Newsweek 42:60, Dec 21, 1953
    Saturday Review 37:30, Jan 9, 1954
    Theatre Arts 38:76-8, Jan 1954
                    38:22-3, Feb 1954
    Time 62:57, Dec 21, 1953

Kismet (583 performances)
book: Charles Lederer and Luther Davis,
                    based on the play by Edward
                    Knoblock
music: Alexander Borodin, adapted by Robert
                    Wright and George Forrest
lyrics: Robert Wright and George Forrest
staging: Albert Marre
sets: Lemuel Ayers
costumes: Lemuel Ayers
choreography: Jack Cole
opened: December 3, 1953
    America 90:366, Jan 2, 1954
            113:122, Jul 31, 1965
    Catholic World 178:388, Feb 1954
    Colliers 133:78-9, Jan 8, 1954
    Commonweal 59:353, Jan 8, 1954
    Dance Magazine 39:24, Aug 1965
    Life 35:25-8, Dec 21, 1953
    Nation 177:555, Dec 19, 1953

                    202

New York Theatre Critics' Reviews 1953:198+
New York Times page 2, Dec 4, 1953
                   page 51, Dec 14, 1953
                   II, page 1, Jun 20, 1965
                   page 45, Jun 23, 1965
New Yorker 29:85-7, Dec 12, 1953
Newsweek 42:61, Dec 14, 1953
           42:60, Dec 21, 1953
Saturday Review 36:28-9, Dec 26, 1953
Theatre Arts 38:18-19, Feb 1954
Time 62:94, Dec 14, 1953

The Pajama Game (1,063 performances)
book: George Abbott and Richard Bissell,
               based on Bissell's novel 7-1/2 Cents
music: Richard Adler and Jerry Ross
lyrics: Richard Adler and Jerry Ross
staging: George Abbott and Jerome Robbins
sets: Lemuel Ayers
costumes: Lemuel Ayers
choreography: Bob Fosse
opened: May 13, 1954
   America 91:306, Jun 12, 1954
   Business Week page 76+, Jun 5, 1954
   Catholic World 179:307-8, Jul 1954
   Life 36:125-6+, Jun 7, 1954
   Nation 178:470, May 29, 1954
   New York Theatre Critics' Reviews 1954:324+
   New York Times page 20, May 14, 1954
                     II, page 1, May 30, 1954
                     page 87, Jan 30, 1955
                     II, page 3, May 8, 1955
                     page 27, May 16, 1957
                     II, page 1, May 26, 1957
   New Yorker 30:68+, May 22, 1954
   Newsweek 43:64, May 24, 1954
   Saturday Review 37:24-5, Jun 12, 1954
                   39:12, Sep 15, 1956
   Theatre Arts 38:14, Sep 1954
                38:18-19, Jul 1954
                41:17, Jul 1957
   Time 63:66, May 24, 1954

Season of 1954-1955

Ankles Aweigh (176 performances)
book: Guy Bolton and Eddie Davis
music: Sammy Fain
lyrics: Dan Shapiro
staging: Fred F. Finklehoffe
sets: George Jenkins
costumes: Miles White
choreography: Tony Charmoli
opened: April 18, 1955
   Catholic World 181:228, Jun 1955
   Commonweal 62:330, Jul 1, 1955
   New York Theatre Critics' Reviews 1955:329+
   New York Times page 27, Apr 19, 1955
   New Yorker 31:71-2, Apr 30, 1955
   Theatre Arts 39:16, 88, Jul 1955
   Time 65:78, May 2, 1955

The Boy Friend (485 performances)
book: Sandy Wilson
music: Sandy Wilson
lyrics: Sandy Wilson
staging: Vida Hope
sets: Reginald Woolley
costumes: Reginald Woolley
choreography: John Heawood
opened: September 30, 1954
   America 92:138, Oct 30, 1954
   Catholic World 180:226, Dec 1954
   Commonweal 61:93, Oct 29, 1954
   Dance Magazine 32:17, May 1958
   Life 37:113-14+, Oct 25, 1954
   Mademoiselle 40:142, Nov 1954
   Nation 179:349, Oct 16, 1954
   New Republic 131:23, Nov 1, 1954
   New York Theatre Critics' Reviews 1954:299+
   New York Times II, page 1, Sep 26, 1954
                    page 20, Oct 1, 1954
                    II, page 1, Oct 10, 1954
                    VI, page 33, Nov 21, 1954
                    II, page 5, Dec 23, 1956
   New Yorker 29:69, Feb 6, 1954

204

               30:58+, Oct 9, 1954
    Newsweek 44:56, Oct 11, 1954
    Saturday Review 37:24, Sep 18, 1954
               37:29, Oct 16, 1954
    Theatre Arts 38:18-19+, Dec 1954
    Time 64:93, Oct 11, 1954
    Vogue 124:125, Oct 1, 1954

Damn Yankees (1,019 performances)
book: George Abbott and Douglass Wallop,
               based on Douglass Wallop's novel
               The Year the Yankees Lost the
               Pennant
music: Richard Adler and Jerry Ross
lyrics: Richard Adler and Jerry Ross
staging: George Abbott
sets: William and Jean Eckart
costumes: William and Jean Eckart
choreography: Bob Fosse
opened: May 5, 1955
    America 93:278, Jun 4, 1955
    Catholic World 181:307, Jul 1955
    Commonweal 62:329, Jul 1, 1955
    Life 38:163-71, May 16, 1955
    Look 19:64+, Jul 12, 1955
    Nation 180:449, May 21, 1955
    New York Theatre Critics' Reviews 1955:310+
    New York Times VI, page 67, Apr 17, 1955
               II, page 1, May 1, 1955
               page 17, May 6, 1955
               II, page 1, Apr 1, 1956
               II, page 1, May 13, 1956
               page 15, Mar 29, 1957
    New York Times Magazine page 67, Apr 17, 1955
    New Yorker 31:132+, May 14, 1955
    Newsweek 45:96, May 16, 1955
    Saturday Review 38:44, May 21, 1955
               39:12, Sep 15, 1956
    Theatre Arts 39:20-2, Jul 1955
    Time 65:104, May 16, 1955
    Vogue 125:77, May 15, 1955

Fanny (888 performances)

book:	S. N. Behrman and Joshua Logan, based on Marcel Pagnol's "Marius," "Fanny," and "Cesar."
music:	Harold Rome
lyrics:	Harold Rome
staging:	Joshua Logan
sets:	Jo Mielziner
costumes:	Alvin Colt
choreography:	Helen Tamiris
opened:	November 4, 1954

America 92:305, Dec 11, 1954
Catholic World 180:307-8, Jan 1955
Commonweal 61:288, Dec 10, 1954
Life 37:117-20, Nov 29, 1954
Look 18:56-60, Nov 16, 1954
Mademoiselle 40:142, Nov 1954
Nation 179:451, Nov 20, 1954
New Republic 131:22-3, Nov 29, 1954
New York Theatre Critics' Reviews 1954:256+
New York Times VI, page 64, Oct 31, 1954
    page 16, Nov 5, 1954
    II, page 1, Nov 21, 1954
    VI, page 23, Jan 16, 1955
    II, page 1, Oct 30, 1955
    page 19, Dec 17, 1955
    page 17, Nov 17, 1956
    II, page 3, Dec 2, 1956
New York Times Magazine pages 64-5, Oct 31, 1954
New Yorker 30:104, Nov 13, 1954
Newsweek 44:98, Nov 15, 1954
Saturday Review 37:30, Nov 20, 1954
    38:5, 23, Jan 8, 1955
    38:23, Feb 5, 1955
    39:13, Sep 15, 1956
Theatre Arts 39:17-18, 20-1, Jan 1955
Time 64:62, Nov 15, 1954

<u>Hit the Trail</u> (4 performances)
book:	Frank O'Neill
music:	Frederico Valerio
lyrics:	Elizabeth Miele
staging:	Charles W. Christenberry Jr. and

Byrle Cass
sets: Leo Kerz
costumes: Michi
choreography: Gene Bayliss
opened: December 2, 1954
   New York Theatre Critics' Reviews 1954:228+
   New York Times page 31, Dec 3, 1954
   New Yorker 30:98, Dec 11, 1954
   Theatre Arts 39:16, 92, Feb 1955

House of Flowers (165 performances)
book: Truman Capote
music: Harold Arlen
lyrics: Truman Capote and Harold Arlen
staging: Peter Brook
sets: Oliver Messel
costumes: Oliver Messel
choreography: Herbert Ross
opened: December 30, 1954
   Catholic World 180:469, Mar 1955
   Commonweal 61:454-5, Jan 28, 1955
   Mademoiselle 40:142, Nov 1954
   Nation 180:106, Jan 29, 1955
   New York Theatre Critics' Reviews 1954:189+
   New York Times page 75, Dec 19, 1954
                   page 11, Dec 31, 1954
   New Yorker 30:62, Jan 8, 1955
   Newsweek 45:62, Jan 10, 1955
   Saturday Review 38:31, Jan 15, 1955
   Theatre Arts 39:30-1+, Jan 1955
                 39:20-1+, Mar 1955
   Time 65:34, Jan 10, 1955
   Vogue 125:125, Jan 1955

Peter Pan (152 performances)
book: Richard Halliday, adapted from James
                   M. Barrie's play
music: Mark Charlap and Jule Styne
lyrics: Carolyn Leigh, Betty Comden, Adolph
                   Green
staging: Jerome Robbins
sets: Peter Larkin
costumes: Motley

choreography: Jerome Robbins
opened: October 20, 1954
   America 92:259, Nov 27, 1954
   Catholic World 180:225, Dec 1954
   Commonweal 61:223, Nov 26, 1954
   Dance Magazine 28:24-5, Dec 1954
   Life 37:109-10+, Nov 8, 1954
      38:97-100, Apr 4, 1955
   Look 18:54-5, Dec 14, 1954
   Nation 179:428, Nov 13, 1954
   New Republic 131:23, Nov 1, 1954
   New York Theatre Critics' Reviews 1954:273+
   New York Times page 15, Jul 20, 1954
            II, page 1, Oct 17, 1954
            page 30, Oct 21, 1954
            II, page 1, Oct 31, 1954
   New York Times Magazine page 60, Oct 10, 1954
   New Yorker 30:66+, Oct 30, 1954
   Newsweek 44:60, Nov 1, 1954
   Saturday Review 37:29, Nov 20, 1954
   Theatre Arts 38:18-19+, Nov 1954
      39:12-13+, Jan 1955
   Time 64:80, Nov 1, 1954
   Vogue 124:124, Dec 1954

Phoenix '55 (97 performances)
sketches: Ira Wallach
music: David Baker
lyrics: David Craig
staging: Marc Daniels
sets: Eldon Elder
costumes: Alvin Colt
choreography: Boris Runanin
opened: April 23, 1955
   America 93:191, May 14, 1955
   Catholic World 181:228, Jun 1955
   Life 38:130, May 23, 1955
   Nation 180:430, May 14, 1955
   New York Theatre Critics' Reviews 1955:317+
   New York Times page 20, Apr 25, 1955
   New Yorker 31:67-9, Apr 30, 1955
   Newsweek 46:55, Jul 18, 1955
   Theatre Arts 39:86, 88, Jul 1955

Plain and Fancy (461 performances)
book: Joseph Stein and Will Glickman
music: Albert Hague
lyrics: Arnold B. Horwitt
staging: Morton Da Costa
sets: Raoul Pene du Bois
costumes: Raoul Pene du Bois
choreography: Helen Tamiris
opened: January 27, 1955
   America 92:545+, Feb 19, 1955
   Catholic World 181:67-8, Apr 1955
   Commonweal 61:551, Feb 25, 1955
   Life 38:75-6+, Feb 21, 1955
   New York Theatre Critics' Reviews 1955:382+
   New York Times page 14, Jan 28, 1955
            II, page 1, Feb 6, 1955
            II, page 6, Feb 6, 1955
            II, page 3, Feb 5, 1956
   New Yorker 30:52, Feb 5, 1955
   Newsweek 45:72, Feb 7, 1955
   Saturday Review 38:24, Feb 12, 1955
            39:12-13, Sep 15, 1956
   Theatre Arts 39:18-19+, Apr 1955
   Time 65:50, Feb 7, 1955

The Saint of Bleecker Street (92 performances)
book: Gian-Carlo Menotti
music: Gian-Carlo Menotti
lyrics: Gian-Carlo Menotti
staging: Gian-Carlo Menotti
sets: Robert Randolph
costumes: Robert Randolph
opened: December 27, 1954
   America 92:434, Jan 22, 1955
   Catholic World 180:385, Feb 1955
   Commonweal 61:476-7, Feb 4, 1955
   Life 38:62-3, Feb 14, 1955
   Musical America 75:3+, Jan 15, 1955
   Nation 180:83, Jan 22, 1955
   New York Theatre Critics' Reviews 1954:199+
   New York Times page 21, Dec 28, 1954
            II, page 1, Jan 2, 1955
            II, page 1, Mar 6, 1955

```
                    page 26, May 9, 1955
                    page 76, Sep 18, 1955
                    page 26, Nov 1, 1955
                    page 38, Nov 22, 1955
                    page 78, Jun 10, 1956
                    page 40, Sep 4, 1957
New Yorker 30:74-6, Jan 8, 1955
           30:77, Jun 2, 1955
Newsweek 45:62, Jan 10, 1955
Reporter 12:40, Apr 7, 1955
Saturday Review 38:28, Jan 8, 1955
Theatre Arts 39:17+, Mar 1955
Time 65:42, Jan 10, 1955
```

Seventh Heaven (44 performances)

book:	Victor Wolfson and Stella Unger, based on Austin Strong's play Seventh Heaven
music:	Victor Young
lyrics:	Stella Unger
staging:	John C. Wilson
sets:	Marcel Vertes
costumes:	Marcel Vertes
choreography:	Peter Gennaro
opened:	May 26, 1955

```
America 93:298, Jun 11, 1955
Catholic World 181:307-8, Jul 1955
Commonweal 62:329, Jul 1, 1955
Nation 180:510, Jun 11, 1955
New York Theatre Critics' Reviews 1955:302+
New York Times VI, page 19, May 15, 1955
              II, page 1, May 22, 1955
              page 16, May 27, 1955
New York Times Magazine page 19, May 15, 1955
Saturday Review 38:25, Jun 11, 1955
Theatre Arts 39:18-19, Aug 1955
Time 65:57, Jun 6, 1955
```

Silk Stockings (478 performances)

book:	George S. Kaufman, Leueen MacGrath, and Abe Burrows, suggested by Melchior Lengyel's Ninotchka
music:	Cole Porter

lyrics: Cole Porter
staging: Cy Feuer
sets: Jo Mielziner
costumes: Lucinda Ballard and Robert Mackintosh
choreography: Eugene Loring
opened: February 24, 1955
   America 93:109, Apr 23, 1955
   Catholic World 181:67, Apr 1955
   Commonweal 61:676, Apr 1, 1955
   Life 38:93-4+, Mar 21, 1955
   Look 19:66-8, Feb 8, 1955
   Mademoiselle 40:142, Nov 1954
   Nation 180:226, Mar 12, 1955
   New York Theatre Critics' Reviews 1952:354+
   New York Times page 17, Feb 25, 1955
           II, page 1, Mar 27, 1955
   New Yorker 31:68, Mar 5, 1955
   Newsweek 45:85, Mar 7, 1955
   Saturday Review 38:26, Mar 12, 1955
           39:13+, Sep 15, 1956
   Theatre Arts 39:18+, May 1955
   Time 65:92, Mar 7, 1955
   Vogue 125:124, Jan 1955

3 For Tonight (85 performances)
special
 material: Robert Wells
music: Walter Schumann
lyrics: Robert Wells
staging: Gower Champion
opened: April 6, 1955
   America 93:165, May 7, 1955
   Catholic World 181:226, Jun 1955
   Commonweal 62:105, Apr 29, 1955
   Life 38:129-30+, Apr 25, 1955
   Nation 180:354-5, Apr 23, 1955
   New York Theatre Critics' Reviews 1955:337+
   New York Times II, page 3, Apr 3, 1955
           page 23, Apr 7, 1955
           II, page 1, Apr 17, 1955
   New Yorker 31:74+, Apr 16, 1955
   Newsweek 44:90+, Dec 13, 1954
   Saturday Review 38:25, Apr 23, 1955

Theatre Arts 39:20-1, 93, Jun 1955
Time 65:72, Apr 18, 1955
Vogue 125:122, Apr 1, 1955

Season of 1955-1956

Almost Crazy (16 performances)
sketches: James Shelton, Hal Hackady, and
                   Robert A. Bernstein
music: Portia Nelson, Raymond Taylor and
                   James Shelton
lyrics: Portia Nelson, Raymond Taylor and
                   James Shelton
staging: Lew Kesler
sets: John Robert Lloyd
costumes: Stanley Simmons
choreography: William Skipper
opened: June 20, 1955
   America 93:378-9, Jul 9, 1955
   New York Theatre Critics' Reviews 1955:298+
   New York Times page 37, Jun 21, 1955
   Theatre Arts 39:16, Sep 1955

Catch A Star! (23 performances)
sketches: Danny and Neil Simon
music: Sammy Fain and Phil Charig
lyrics: Paul Webster and Ray Golden
staging: Ray Golden
sets: Ralph Alswang
costumes: Thomas Becher
choreography: Lee Sherman
opened: September 6, 1955
   America 93:629, Sep 24, 1955
   New York Theatre Critics' Reviews 1955:290+
   New York Times page 35, Sep 7, 1955
   New Yorker 31:72+, Sep 17, 1955
   Theatre Arts 39:17, Nov 1955
   Time 66:52, Sep 19, 1955

The Littlest Revue (32 performances)
conceived by: Ben Bagley
sketches: Nat Hiken, Billy Friedberg, Eudora
                   Welty, Mike Stewart, George Baxt,

212

                          Bud McCreery, Allan Manings, Bob
                          Van Scoyk
music and
  lyrics: Ogden Nash, Vernon Duke, John La-
                          touche, Sheldon Harnick, Lee Adams,
                          Charles Strouse, Sidney Shaw,
                          Sammy Cahn, Michael Brown
staging: Paul Lammers
sets: Klaus Holm
costumes: Alvin Colt
choreography: Charles Weidman
opened: May 22, 1956
   America 95:290-2, Jun 16, 1956
   Catholic World 183:311, Jul 1956
   Commonweal 64:299, Jun 22, 1956
   Nation 182:497, Jun 9, 1956
   New York Theatre Critics' Reviews 1956:297+
   New York Times page 37, May 23, 1956
   New Yorker 32:58, Jun 2, 1956
   Saturday Review 39:27, Jun 9, 1956
   Theatre Arts 40:73, Aug 1956
   Time 67:95, Jun 4, 1956

The Most Happy Fella (676 performances)
book: Frank Loesser, based on Sidney
                          Howard's play They Knew What They
                          Wanted
music: Frank Loesser
lyrics: Frank Loesser
staging: Joseph Anthony
sets: Jo Mielziner
costumes: Motley
choreography: Dania Krupska
opened: May 3, 1956
   America 95:209, May 19, 1956
            100:670, Mar 7, 1959
   Catholic World 183:309, Jul 1956
   Christian Century 73:1453, Dec 12, 1956
   Colliers 138:8, Jul 6, 1956
   Commonweal 64:226, Jun 1, 1956
   Holiday 20:75+, Oct 1956
   Life 40:68+, Apr 23, 1956
   Musical America 76:13, Jul 1956

                          213

Nation 182:439, May 19, 1956
New York Theatre Critics' Reviews 1956:308+
New York Times VI, page 62, Apr 22, 1956
II, page 1, Apr 29, 1956
page 20, May 4, 1956
II, page 1, May 13, 1956
II, page 7, Jun 10, 1956
page 50, Feb 11, 1959
page 25, Apr 22, 1960
New York Times Magazine page 62, Apr 22, 1956
New Yorker 32:84+, May 12, 1956
Newsweek 47:82, May 14, 1956
Reporter 14:34-5, Jun 28, 1956
Saturday Review 39:46, May 19, 1956
39:39, Aug 25, 1956
Theatre Arts 40:17-19, Jul 1956
43:67-8, Apr 1959
Time 67:102, May 14, 1956

Mr. Wonderful (383 performances)
book: Joseph Stein and Will Glickman
music: Jerry Bock, Larry Holofcener, George
                 Weiss
lyrics: Jerry Bock, Larry Holofcener, George
                 Weiss
staging: Jack Donohue
sets: Oliver Smith
costumes: Robert Mackintosh
choreography: Jack Donohue
opened: March 22, 1956
   America 95:42, Apr 7, 1956
   Catholic World 183:150, May 1956
   New York Theatre Critics' Reviews 1956:339+
   New York Times page 23, Mar 23, 1956
   New Yorker 32:62+, Mar 31, 1956
   Saturday Review 39:34, Apr 14, 1956
   Theatre Arts 40:14, Jun 1956
   Time 67:91, Apr 2, 1956

My Fair Lady (2,717 performances)
book: Alan Jay Lerner, based on George
                 Bernard Shaw's Pygmalion
music: Frederick Loewe

214

lyrics: Alan Jay Lerner
staging: Moss Hart
sets: Oliver Smith
costumes: Cecil Beaton
choreography: Hanya Holm
opened: March 15, 1956
   America 94:723, Mar 31, 1956
   Business World pages 28-30, Jul 28, 1956
   Catholic World 183:148, May 1956
   Colliers 137:6+, May 25, 1956
   Commonweal 64:95, Apr 27, 1956
   Coronet 41:54-63, Dec 1956
            45:16+, Apr 1959
   Dance Magazine 32:15, Apr 1958
                  38:16, Aug 1964
   Etude 74:57, Jul 1956
   Holiday 20:75+, Oct 1956
   Life 40:58-60+, Mar 26, 1956
   Look 20:47-8+, Apr 17, 1956
   Nation 182:264-5, Mar 31, 1956
   New Republic 134:29-30, Apr 9, 1956
   New York Theatre Critics' Reviews 1956:345+
   New York Times page 30, Feb 13, 1956
                     VI, pages 28-9, Mar 4, 1956
                     II, page 1, Mar 11, 1956
                     page 20, Mar 16, 1956
                     II, page 1, Mar 25, 1956
                     VI, page 24, Apr 1, 1956
                     II, page 17, Apr 29, 1956
                     II, page 1, Jun 3, 1956
                     II, page 1, Aug 12, 1956
                     VI, page 27, Sep 9, 1956
                     II, page 1, Sep 23, 1956
                     page 27, Feb 5, 1957
                     II, page 3, Mar 10, 1957
                     page 33, Mar 20, 1957
                     page 22, Jul 10, 1957
                     II, page 1, Mar 9, 1958
                     VI, page 22, Mar 9, 1958
                     page 34, May 1, 1958
                     II, page 3, May 4, 1958
                     page 26, Jan 27, 1959
                     page 24, Feb 16, 1959

215

page 25, Feb 21, 1959
VI, pages 16-17, Mar 15, 1959
page 12, Apr 4, 1959
page 24, Aug 10, 1959
page 35, Aug 12, 1959
page 52, Dec 15, 1959
page 31, Jan 9, 1961
page 24, Jul 13, 1961
page 40, Oct 26, 1961
page 22, Jan 9, 1962
II, page 3, Mar 11, 1962
VI, page 55, Mar 11, 1962
page 28, Mar 15, 1962
page 24, Jun 14, 1962
page 27, Sep 11, 1962
page 15, Sep 29, 1962
page 38, Oct 1, 1962
page 34, May 1, 1963
page 32, Jun 3, 1963
page 8, Jul 4, 1963
page 37, Aug 21, 1963
page 19, Sep 2, 1963
page 13, Sep 21, 1963
page 16, Nov 16, 1963
page 40, Dec 13, 1963
page 24, Feb 20, 1964
page 43, May 21, 1964
page 29, Oct 31, 1965
New York Times Magazine pages 28-9, Mar 4, 1956
page 27+, Sep 9, 1956
page 14+, Mar 10, 1957
pages 16-17+, Mar 15, 1959
New Yorker 32:80+, Mar 24, 1956
Newsweek 47:94, Mar 26, 1956
47:80-1, Apr 2, 1956
51:94+, May 12, 1958
Reporter 14:34, Jun 28, 1956
Saturday Evening Post 231:34-5+, May 2, 1959
Saturday Review 39:26-7, Mar 31, 1956
Senior Scholastic 85:5, Oct 21, 1964
Theatre Arts 40:14, Nov 1956
40:18-19, May 1956

```
                40:68-9, Jun 1956
                40:26-8, Dec 1956
                41:29+, Mar 1957
                41:63-4+, Oct 1957
                42:70-1, May 1958
     Time 67:89, Mar 26, 1956
          68:42-6, Jul 23, 1956
          73:44-5, Mar 2, 1959
     Vogue 127:116, Apr 1, 1956
           127:52-5, Jun 1956
           144:152-5, Nov 1, 1964
```

Pipe Dream (246 performances)
book: Oscar Hammerstein II, based on John
                Steinbeck's novel Sweet Thursday
music: Richard Rodgers
lyrics: Oscar Hammerstein II
staging: Harold Clurman
sets: Jo Mielziner
costumes: Alvin Colt
opened: November 30, 1955
     America 94:417-18, Jan 7, 1956
     Catholic World 182:388, Feb 1956
     Commonweal 63:331, Dec 30, 1955
     Nation 181:544, Dec 17, 1955
     New York Theatre Critics' Reviews 1955:198+
     New York Times II, page 1, Nov 27, 1955
                     page 44, Dec 1, 1955
                  II, page 5, Dec 11, 1955
     New Yorker 31:104+, Dec 10, 1955
     Newsweek 46:110, Dec 12, 1955
     Saturday Review 38:24, Dec 17, 1955
                     39:13, Sep 15, 1956
     Theatre Arts 40:12-13, Feb 1956
     Time 66:67, Dec 12, 1955

The Vamp (60 performances)
book: John Latouche and Sam Locke, based
                on a story by John Latouche
music: James Mundy
lyrics: John Latouche
staging: David Alexander
sets: Raoul Pene du Bois

costumes: Raoul Pene du Bois
choreography: Robert Alton
opened: November 10, 1955
  Catholic World 182:310, Jan 1956
  Commonweal 63:285, Dec 16, 1955
  Look 19:108+, Nov 29, 1955
  New York Theatre Critics' Reviews 1955:210+
  New York Times II, page 1, Nov 6, 1955
                page 30, Nov 11, 1955
  New Yorker 31:121, Nov 19, 1955
  Newsweek 46:68, Nov 21, 1955
  Saturday Review 38:26, Nov 26, 1955
  Theatre Arts 40:20-1, Jan 1956
  Time 66:110+, Nov 21, 1955

Season of 1956 - 1957

Bells Are Ringing (924 performances)
book: Betty Comden and Adolph Green
music: Jule Styne
lyrics: Betty Comden and Adolph Green
staging: Jerome Robbins
sets: Raoul Pene du Bois
costumes: Raoul Pene du Bois
choreography: Jerome Robbins and Bob Fosse
opened: November 29, 1956
  America 96:742, Mar 30, 1957
  Catholic World 184:386-7, Feb 1957
  Commonweal 65:408, Jan 18, 1957
  Life 42:69-70+, Feb 11, 1957
  Nation 183:526, Dec 15, 1956
  New York Theatre Critics' Reviews 1956:182+
  New York Times VI, page 29, Sep 16, 1956
                VI, page 29, Nov 4, 1956
                page 18, Nov 30, 1956
                II, page 3, Dec 16, 1956
                page 37, Nov 15, 1957
  New Yorker 32:88+, Dec 1956
  Newsweek 48:77, Dec 10, 1956
  Reporter 16:35, Jan 24, 1957
  Saturday Review 39:25, Dec 29, 1956
  Theatre Arts 40:76-8, Dec 1956
              41:15-16, Feb 1957

218

41:27-8+, Mar 1957
Time 68:70, Dec 10, 1956

Candide (73 performances)
book: Lillian Hellman, based on Voltaire's
             satire
music: Leonard Bernstein
lyrics: Richard Wilbur, John LaTouche,
             Dorothy Parker
staging: Tyrone Guthrie
sets: Oliver Smith
costumes: Irene Sharaff
opened: December 1, 1956
   Catholic World 184:384-5, Feb 1957
   Commonweal 65:333-4, Dec 28, 1956
   Musical America 76:26, Dec 15, 1956
   Nation 183:527, Dec 15, 1956
   New Republic 135:30-1, Dec 17, 1956
   New York Theatre Critics' Reviews 1956:176+
   New York Times VI, page 28, Nov 4, 1956
                   II, page 1, Nov 18, 1956
                   page 40, Dec 3, 1956
                   II, page 5, Dec 9, 1956
                   II, page 9, Dec 16, 1956
   New Yorker 32:52+, Dec 15, 1956
   Newsweek 48:77, Dec 10, 1956
   Reporter 16:35, Jan 24, 1957
   Saturday Review 39:34, Dec 22, 1956
   Time 68:70, Dec 10, 1956

Cranks (40 performances)
book: John Cranko
music: John Addison
lyrics: John Cranko
staging: John Cranko
opened: November 26, 1956
   Christian Century 74:172, Feb 6, 1957
   Nation 183:526, Dec 15, 1956
   New York Theatre Critics' Reviews 1956:185+
   New York Times page 23, May 14, 1956
                   page 32, Nov 27, 1956
   New Yorker 32:90-1, Dec 8, 1956
              32:25, Dec 15, 1956

219

Saturday Review 39:26, Dec 15, 1956
Theatre Arts 41:19, Feb 1957
Time 68:70, Dec 10, 1956

Follies (1957) (see Ziegfeld Follies)

Happy Hunting (412 performances)
book: Howard Lindsay and Russel Crouse
music: Harold Karr
lyrics: Matt Dubey
staging: Abe Burrows
sets: Jo Mielziner
costumes: Irene Sharaff
choreography: Alex Romero and Bob Herget
opened: December 6, 1956
   America 96:743, Mar 30, 1957
   Catholic World 184:386, Feb 1957
   New York Theatre Critics' Reviews 1956:166+
   New York Times VI, page 29, Sep 16, 1956
                 VI, page 29, Nov 4, 1956
                 page 30, Dec 7, 1956
                 II, page 3, Dec 16, 1956
   New Yorker 32:54+, Dec 22, 1956
   Newsweek 48:66, Dec 17, 1956
   Reporter 16:35, Jan 24, 1957
   Saturday Review 39:25, Dec 29, 1956
   Theatre Arts 41:20-1, Feb 1957
   Time 68:62+, Dec 17, 1956
   Vogue 128:111, Dec 1956

Li'l Abner (693 performances)
book: Norman Panama and Melvin Frank,
                 based on characters created by Al
                 Capp
music: Gene de Paul
lyrics: Johnny Mercer
staging: Michael Kidd
sets: William and Jean Eckart
costumes: Alvin Colt
choreography: Michael Kidd
opened: November 15, 1956
   America 96:398, Jan 5, 1957
   Catholic World 184:307, Jan 1957

Commonweal 65:408, Jan 18, 1957
Life 42:81-3, Jan 14, 1957
Nation 183:485, Dec 1, 1956
New York Theatre Critics' Reviews 1956:202+
New York Times VI, page 29, Sep 16, 1956
VI, page 28, Nov 4, 1956
II, page 1, Nov 11, 1956
page 24, Nov 16, 1956
II, page 1, Nov 25, 1956
II, page 3, Dec 16, 1956
New Yorker 32:114+, Dec 1, 1956
Newsweek 48:73, Nov 26, 1956
Saturday Review 39:50, Dec 1, 1956
Theatre Arts 41:28-9, Jan 1957
Time 68:58, Nov 26, 1956

Livin' the Life (25 performances)
book: Dale Wasserman and Bruce Geller,
                 based on Mark Twain's Mississippi
                 River stories
music: Jack Urbont
lyrics: Bruce Geller
staging: David Alexander
sets: William and Jean Eckart
costumes: Alvin Colt
choreography: John Butler
opened: April 27, 1957
    America 97:270, May 25, 1957
    Nation 184:427, May 11, 1957
    New York Theatre Critics' Reviews 1957:281+
    New York Times II, page 1, Apr 21, 1957
                   page 20, Apr 29, 1957
    New Yorker 33:142, May 4, 1957
    Theatre Arts 41:18, Jul 1957

New Faces of '56 (220 performances)
sketches: Paul Lynde, Richard Maury, Louis
                 Botto
music and
lyrics: June Carroll, Arthur Siegel, Marshall
                 Barer, Dean Fuller, Murray Grand,
                 Matt Dubey, Harold Karr, Irvin
                 Graham, Paul Nassau, John Rox,

Michael Brown
staging: Paul Lynde
sets: Peter Larkin
costumes: Thomas Becher
choreography: David Tihmar
opened: June 14, 1956
   America 95:332, Jun 30, 1956
   Catholic World 183:387, Aug 1956
   Commonweal 64:396, Jul 20, 1956
   New York Theatre Critics' Reviews 1956:290+
   New York Times page 32, Jun 15, 1956
   New Yorker 32:62+, Jun 23, 1956
   Saturday Review 39:22, Jun 30, 1956
   Theatre Arts 40:17-18, Aug 1956
   Time 67:86, Jun 25, 1956

New Girl in Town (431 performances)
book: George Abbott, based on Eugene
         O'Neill's play Anna Christie
music: Bob Merrill
lyrics: Bob Merrill
staging: George Abbott
sets: Helene Pons
costumes: Rouben Ter-Arutunian
choreography: Bob Fosse
opened: May 14, 1957
   America 97:311, Jun 8, 1957
   Catholic World 185:307, Jul 1957
   Life 42:109+, Jun 24, 1957
   Nation 184:486, Jun 1, 1957
   New York Theatre Critics' Reviews 1957:268+
   New York Times VI, pages 30-31, Apr 14, 1957
                    II, page 1, May 12, 1957
                    page 50, May 15, 1957
                    II, page 1, May 26, 1957
                    VI, page 25, May 26, 1957
   New York Times Magazine pages 30-1, Apr 14, 1957
                    page 25+, May 26, 1957
   New Yorker 33:82+, May 25, 1957
   Newsweek 49:70, May 27, 1957
   Saturday Review 40:22, Jun 1, 1957
   Theatre Arts 41:25-6, Jun 1957
                41:14-15, Jul 1957

Time 69:60, May 27, 1957

Shangri-La (21 performances)
book: James Hilton, Jerome Lawrence,
                Robert E. Lee, based on James
                Hilton's novel Lost Horizon
music: Harry Warren
lyrics: James Hilton, Jerome Lawrence,
                Robert E. Lee
staging: Albert Marre
costumes: Irene Sharaff
choreography: Donald Saddler
opened: June 13, 1956
   America 95:330, Jun 30, 1956
   Catholic World 183:388, Aug 1956
   New York Theatre Critics' Reviews 1956:293+
   New York Times page 40, Jun 14, 1956
   Saturday Review 39:22, Jun 30, 1956
   Theatre Arts 40:16, Aug 1956
   Time 67:86+, Jun 25, 1956

Shinbone Alley (49 performances)
book: Joe Darion and Mel Brooks, based on
                the "archy and mehitabel" stories
                of Don Marquis
music: George Kleinsinger
lyrics: Joe Darion
sets: Eldon Elder
costumes: Motley
choreography: Rod Alexander
opened: April 13, 1957
   America 97:216, May 11, 1957
   Catholic World 185:228-9, Jun 1957
   Christian Century 74:762, Jun 19, 1957
   Commonweal 66:204, May 24, 1957
   New York Theatre Critics' Reviews 1957:292+
   New York Times page 23, Apr 15, 1957
                II, page 1, Apr 28, 1957
   New Yorker 33:82+, Apr 20, 1957
   Newsweek 49:69-70, Apr 22, 1957
   Theatre Arts 41:15-16, Jun 1957
   Time 69:90, Apr 22, 1957

Ziegfeld Follies (123 performances)
sketches: Arme Rosen, Coleman Jacoby, David
                   Rogers, Alan Jeffreys, Maxwell
                   Grant
music and
 lyrics: Jack Lawrence, Richard Myers,
                   Howard Dietz, Sammy Fain, David
                   Rogers, Colin Romoff, Dean Fuller,
                   Marshall Barer, Carolyn Leigh,
                   Phillip Springer
staging: John Kennedy
sets: Raoul Pene du Bois
costumes: Raoul Pene du Bois
choreography: Frank Wagner
opened: March 1, 1957
    America 97:311, Jun 8, 1957
    Catholic World 185:147-8, May 1957
    Commonweal 66:36, Apr 12, 1957
    Life 42:89-90+, Mar 18, 1957
    Nation 184:242, Mar 16, 1957
    New York Theatre Critics' Reviews 1957:327+
    New York Times page 19, Mar 2, 1957
    New Yorker 33:64, Mar 9, 1957
    Newsweek 49:66, Mar 11, 1957
    Theatre Arts 41:18, May 1957
    Time 69:80, Mar 11, 1957

                   Season of 1957 - 1958

The Body Beautiful (60 performances)
book: Joseph Stein and Will Glickman
music: Jerry Bock
lyrics: Sheldon Harnick
staging: George Schaefer
sets: Jean and William Eckart
costumes: Noel Taylor
choreography: Herbert Ross
opened: January 23, 1958
    America 98:677, Mar 8, 1958
    Catholic World 187:70, Apr 1958
    Dance Magazine 32:15, Mar 1958
    New York Theatre Critics' Reviews 1958:386+
    New York Times page 15, Jan 24, 1958

New Yorker 33:54-6, Feb 1, 1958
Newsweek 51:55, Feb 3, 1958
Saturday Review 41:28, Feb 15, 1958
Theatre Arts 42:17-18, Apr 1958
Time 71:78, Feb 3, 1958

Copper and Brass (36 performances)
book: Ellen Violett and David Craig
music: David Baker
lyrics: David Craig
staging: Marc Daniels
sets: William and Jean Eckart
costumes: Alvin Colt
choreography: Anna Sokolow
opened: October 17, 1957
    Dance Magazine 31:13, Dec 1957
    Nation 185:310, Nov 2, 1957
    New York Theatre Critics' Reviews 1957:216+
    New York Times VI, page 20, Aug 25, 1957
                    page 19, Oct 18, 1957
    New Yorker 33:98-100, Oct 26, 1957
    Theatre Arts 41:26-7, Dec 1957
    Time 70:92, Oct 28, 1957

Jamaica (555 Performances)
book: E. Y. Harburg and Fred Saidy
music: Harold Arlen
lyrics: E. Y. Harburg
staging: Robert Lewis
sets: Oliver Smith
costumes: Miles White
choreography: Jack Cole
opened: October 31, 1957
    America 98:436, Jan 11, 1958
    Catholic World 186:304-5, Jan 1958
    Dance Magazine 31:13, Dec 1957
    Life 43:112+, Nov 18, 1957
    Nation 185:394, Nov 23, 1957
    New York Theatre Critics' Reviews 1957:196+
    New York Times VI, page 28, Aug 25, 1957
                    page 32, Nov 1, 1957
                    II, page 1, Nov 10, 1957
    New York Times Magazine pages 72-3, Oct 13, 1957

225

New Yorker 33:103, Nov 9, 1957
Newsweek 50:83, Nov 11, 1957
Saturday Review 40:48, Nov 16, 1957
Theatre Arts 41:73-4+, Oct 1957
                42:17, Jan 1958
   Time 70:93, Nov 11, 1957

Mask and Gown (39 performances)
conceived by: Leonard Sillman
continuity by: Ronny Graham and Sidney Carroll
music and
 lyrics: Ronny Graham, June Carroll, Arthur
                   Siegel, Dorothea Freitag
staging: Leonard Sillman
choreography: Jim Russell
opened: September 10, 1957
   New York Theatre Critics' Reviews 1957:259+
   New York Times page 29, Sep 11, 1957
   Theatre Arts 41:17-18, Nov 1957

The Music Man (1,375 performances)
book: Meredith Willson
music: Meredith Willson
lyrics: Meredith Willson
staging: Morton Da Costa
sets: Howard Bay
costumes: Raoul Pene du Bois
choreography: Onna White
opened: December 19, 1957
   America 98:550, Feb 8, 1958
   Catholic World 186:468, Mar 1958
   Dance Magazine 32:17, Jan 1958
                  39:24, Aug 1965
   Life 44:103-6, Jan 20, 1958
   Look 22:53-5, Mar 4, 1958
   Nation 186:126, Feb 8, 1959
   New York Theatre Critics' Reviews 1957:146+
   New York Times VI, page 128, Dec 1, 1957
                  II, page 3, Dec 15, 1957
                  page 31, Dec 20, 1957
                  II, page 16, Jan 19, 1958
                  page 22, Aug 20, 1958
                  II, page 1, Sep 28, 1958

226

page 17, Mar 18, 1961
page 32, Mar 21, 1961
page 26, Jun 17, 1965
New Yorker 33:48+, Jan 4, 1958
Newsweek 50:41, Dec 30, 1957
Saturday Review 41:21, Jan 4, 1958
Theatre Arts 42:10-11, Mar 1958
Time 70:62-4, Dec 30, 1957
72:42-6, Jul 21, 1958

Oh Captain! (192 performances)
book: Al Morgan and José Ferrer, based on
                an original screenplay by Alec Coppel
music: Jay Livingston and Ray Evans
lyrics: Jay Livingston and Ray Evans
staging: José Ferrer
sets: Jo Mielziner
costumes: Miles White
choreography: James Starbuck
opened: February 4, 1958
   America 99:26, Apr 5, 1958
   Catholic World 187:70, Apr 1958
   Dance Magazine 32:15, Mar 1958
   New Republic 138:22-3, Mar 3, 1958
   New York Theatre Critics' Reviews 1958:370+
   New York Times page 21, Feb 5, 1958
   New Yorker 33:55, Feb 15, 1958
   Newsweek 51:66, Feb 17, 1958
   Theatre Arts 42:20-1, Apr 1958
   Time 71:84, Feb 17, 1958

Portofino (3 performances)
book: Richard Ney
music: Louis Bellson and Will Irwin
lyrics: Richard Ney and Sheldon Harnick
staging: Karl Genus
sets: Wolfgang Roth
costumes: Michael Travis
choreography: Charles Weidman
opened: February 21, 1958
   New York Theatre Critics' Reviews 1958:346+
   New York Times page 8, Feb 22, 1958
   New Yorker 34:58+, Mar 1, 1958

227

Rumple (45 performances)
book: Irving Phillips
music: Ernest G. Schweikert
lyrics: Frank Reardon
staging: Jack Donohue
sets: George Jenkins
costumes: Alvin Colt
choreography: Bob Hamilton
opened: November 6, 1957
    New York Theatre Critics' Reviews 1957:188+
    New York Times page 42, Nov 7, 1957
    New Yorker 33:104+, Nov 16, 1957
    Newsweek 50:90, Nov 18, 1957
    Theatre Arts 42:22, Jan 1958
    Time 70:78, Nov 18, 1957

Say, Darling (332 performances)
book: Richard Bissell, Abe Burrows, and
               Marian Bissell, based on the novel
               by Richard Bissell
music: Jule Styne
lyrics: Betty Comden and Adolph Green
staging: Abe Burrows
sets: Oliver Smith
costumes: Alvin Colt
choreography: Matt Mattox
opened: April 3, 1958
    America 99:178, May 3, 1958
    Catholic World 187:225, Jun 1958
    Commonweal 68:351, Jul 4, 1958
    New York Theatre Critics' Reviews 1958:317+
    New York Times II, page 1, Mar 30, 1958
                   page 17, Apr 4, 1958
                   II, page 1, Apr 13, 1958
                   II, page 1, Jan 18, 1959
                   page 38, Feb 26, 1959
    New Yorker 34:67, Apr 12, 1958
    Newsweek 51:87, Apr 14, 1958
    Saturday Review 41:28, Apr 19, 1958
    Time 71:66, Apr 14, 1958

Simply Heavenly (62 performances)
book: Langston Hughes

228

music: David Martin
lyrics: Langston Hughes
staging: Joshua Shelley
sets: Raymond Sovey
opened: August 20, 1957
   Catholic World 185:388-9, Aug 1957
   Nation 185:230, Oct 5, 1957
   New York Theatre Critics' Reviews 1957:264+
   New York Times page 28, May 22, 1957
           II, page 1, Jun 2, 1957
   Saturday Review 40:24, Sep 7, 1957

West Side Story (732 performances)
book: Arthur Laurents
music: Leonard Bernstein
lyrics: Stephen Sondheim
staging: Jerome Robbins
costumes: Irene Sharaff
choreography: Jerome Robbins and Peter Gennaro
opened: September 26, 1957
   America 98:90, Oct 19, 1957
   Catholic World 186:224-5, Dec 1957
   Christian Century 75:561-2, May 7, 1958
   Dance Magazine 31:14-19, Aug 1957
             31:12-13, Nov 1957
             39:35-8, Apr 1965
             39:40-1, Nov 1965
   Good Housekeeping 145:40, Sep 1957
   Life 43:103-4+, Sep 16, 1957
   Musical America 77:11, Nov 1, 1957
   Nation 185:250-1, Oct 12, 1957
   New Republic 137:21, Sep 9, 1957
   New York Theatre Critics' Reviews 1957:252+
                      1960:275+
   New York Times VI, page 28, Aug 25, 1957
             VI, page 60, Sep 8, 1957
             page 14, Sep 27, 1957
             II, page 1, Oct 6, 1957
             II, page 9, Oct 13, 1957
             II, page 15, Oct 27, 1957
             page 31, Apr 28, 1960
             II, page 1, May 8, 1960
             II, page 5, Dec 11, 1960

page 24, Apr 9, 1964
page 50, Nov 18, 1964
New York Times Magazine pages 60-1, Sep 8, 1957
New Yorker 33:64, Oct 5, 1957
Newsweek 50:102, Oct 7, 1957
52:28, Dec 29, 1958
Reporter 17:38, Nov 14, 1957
Saturday Review 40:22, Oct 5, 1957
Theatre Arts 41:22-3, Sep 1957
41:16-17, Dec 1957
Time 70:48-9, Oct 7, 1957

Season of 1958 - 1959

Destry Rides Again (472 performances)
book: Leonard Gershe, based on a story
                 by Max Brand
music: Harold Rome
lyrics: Harold Rome
staging: Michael Kidd
sets: Oliver Smith
costumes: Alvin Colt
choreography: Michael Kidd
opened: April 23, 1959
   America 101:479, Jun 27, 1959
   Catholic World 189:320, Jul 1959
   Commonweal 70:328, Jun 26, 1959
   Dance Magazine 33:17, Jun 1959
   Life 46:49-54, May 25, 1959
   New Republic 140:20, May 11, 1959
   New York Theatre Critics' Reviews 1959:314+
   New York Times II, page 1, Apr 19, 1959
                   page 24, Apr 24, 1959
                   II, page 1, May 3, 1959
                   page 37, Jun 16, 1960
   New Yorker 35:95-7, May 2, 1959
   Newsweek 53:57, May 4, 1959
   Saturday Review 42:22, May 9, 1959
   Theatre Arts 43:22-4, Jun 1959
                43:9-10, Jul 1959
   Time 73:74, May 4, 1959

First Impressions (92 performances)

book:	Abe Burrows, based on Jane Austen's Pride and Prejudice and the play by Helen Jerome
music:	Robert Goldman, Glenn Paxton, George Weiss
lyrics:	Robert Goldman, Glenn Paxton, George Weiss
staging:	Abe Burrows
sets:	Peter Larkin
costumes:	Alvin Colt
choreography:	Jonathan Lucas
opened:	March 19, 1959

   Catholic World 189:241-2, Jun 1959
   Commonweal 70:57-8, Apr 10, 1959
   Dance Magazine 33:16, Jun 1959
   New York Theatre Critics' Reviews 1959:336+
   New York Times page 28, Mar 20, 1959
                 II, page 1, Mar 29, 1959
                 page 31, May 26, 1959
   New Yorker 35:89, Mar 28, 1959
   Saturday Review 42:28, Apr 4, 1959
   Theatre Arts 43:23-4, May 1959
   Time 73:43, Mar 30, 1959

Flower Drum Song (600 performances)

book:	Oscar Hammerstein II and Joseph Fields, based on the novel by C. Y. Lee
music:	Richard Rodgers
lyrics:	Oscar Hammerstein II
staging:	Gene Kelly
sets:	Oliver Smith
costumes:	Irene Sharaff
choreography:	Carol Haney
opened:	December 1, 1958

   America 100:438, Jan 10, 1959
   Catholic World 188:420, Feb 1959
   Commonweal 70:426-7, Apr 14, 1959
   Dance Magazine 33:16-17, Jan 1959
   Life 45:77-8+, Dec 22, 1958
   New Republic 139:23, Dec 22, 1958
   New York Theatre Critics' Reviews 1958:187+
   New York Times VI, pages 16-17, Nov 23, 1958

                    page 44, Dec 2, 1958
                    II, page 5, Dec 7, 1958
                    page 20, Mar 25, 1960
        New Yorker 34:104+, Dec 13, 1958
        Newsweek 52:53-6, Dec 1, 1958
                    52:63, Dec 15, 1958
        Saturday Review 41:33, Dec 20, 1958
        Theatre Arts 43:10, Feb 1959
        Time 72:44, Dec 15, 1958
               72:42-4+, Dec 22, 1958
        Vogue 133:95, Jan 1, 1959

Goldilocks (161 performances)
book: Walter and Jean Kerr
music: Leroy Anderson
lyrics: Joan Ford, Walter and Jean Kerr
staging: Walter Kerr
sets: Peter Larkin
costumes: Castillo
choreography: Agnes de Mille
opened: October 11, 1958
    America 100:255, Nov 22, 1958
    Catholic World 188:333, Jan 1959
    Christian Century 75:1338, Nov 19, 1958
    Dance Magazine 32:16-17, Nov 1958
    New Republic 139:22, Oct 27, 1958
    New York Theatre Critics' Reviews 1958:273+
    New York Times page 33, Oct 13, 1958
                    II, page 1, Oct 19, 1958
                    page 25, Feb 21, 1959
    New Yorker 34:55, Oct 18, 1958
    Reporter 19:37-8, Nov 13, 1958
    Theatre Arts 42:12, Dec 1958
    Time 72:100, Oct 20, 1958
    Vogue 132:104, Nov 15, 1958

Gypsy (702 performances)
book: Arthur Laurents, suggested by the
                 memoirs of Gypsy Rose Lee
music: Jule Styne
lyrics: Stephen Sondheim
staging: Jerome Robbins
sets: Jo Mielziner

costumes: Raoul Pene du Bois
choreography: Jerome Robbins
opened: May 21, 1959
   America 101:438, Jun 13, 1959
   Coronet 46:12, Oct 1959
   Dance Magazine 33:12-13, Jul 1959
   Life 47:63-4, Jul 27, 1959
   Nation 188:521, Jun 6, 1959
   New York Theatre Critics' Reviews 1959:300+
   New York Times II, page 1, May 17, 1959
                 page 31, May 22, 1959
                 II, page 1, May 31, 1959
                 VI, pages 12-13, May 31, 1959
                 II, page 1, Jun 7, 1959
   New Yorker 35:65-7, May 30, 1959
   Newsweek 53:58, Jun 1, 1959
   Saturday Review 42:29, Jun 6, 1959
   Theatre Arts 43:9+, Aug 1959
              43:18-20, May 1959
   Time 73:84+, Jun 1, 1959
   Vogue 134:60-1, Jul 1959

Juno (16 performances)
book: Joseph Stein, based on Sean O'Casey's
              play Juno and the Paycock
music: Marc Blitzstein
lyrics: Marc Blitzstein
staging: Jose Ferrer
sets: Oliver Smith
costumes: Irene Sharaff
choreography: Agnes de Mille
opened: March 9, 1959
   Dance Magazine 33:22, Apr 1959
   New Republic 140:20, Mar 30, 1959
   New York Theatre Critics' Reviews 1959:351+
   New York Times II, page 1, Mar 1, 1959
                 page 41, Mar 10, 1959
                 II, page 1, Mar 15, 1959
                 page 42, Mar 17, 1959
   New Yorker 35:97, Mar 21, 1959
   Newsweek 53:76, Mar 23, 1959
   Theatre Arts 43:65-6, May 1959
   Time 73:60, Mar 23, 1959

The Nervous Set (23 performances)
book: Jay Landesman and Theodore J.
                Flicker, based on the novel by Jay
                Landesman
music: Tommy Wolf
lyrics: Fran Landesman
staging: Theodore J. Flicker
sets: Paul Morrison
costumes: Theoni Vachlioti
opened: May 12, 1959
   Nation 188:483, May 23, 1959
   New York Theatre Critics' Reviews 1959:306+
   New York Times page 43, May 13, 1959
   New Yorker 35:72+, May 23, 1959
   Reporter 20:35-6, Jun 11, 1959
   Saturday Review 42:26, May 30, 1959
   Theatre Arts 43:10-11, Jul 1959
   Time 73:50, May 25, 1959

Once Upon A Mattress (460 performances)
book: Jay Thompson, Marshall Barer, Dean
                Fuller
music: Mary Rodgers
lyrics: Marshall Barer
staging: George Abbott
sets: William and Jean Eckart
costumes: William and Jean Eckart
choreography: Joe Layton
opened: May 11, 1959
   America 101:397-8, May 30, 1959
   Nation 188:484, May 23, 1959
   New York Theatre Critics' Reviews 1959:309+
   New York Times page 40, May 12, 1959
                II, page 1, May 17, 1959
                II, page 3, May 8, 1960
                page 14, Jul 1, 1960
                page 43, Sep 21, 1960
                page 55, Oct 11, 1960
   New Yorker 35:80-1, May 23, 1959
   Newsweek 53:78, May 25, 1959
   Saturday Review 42:26, May 30, 1959
   Time 73:50, May 25, 1959

La Plume De Ma Tante (835 performances)
book: Robert Dhery
music: Gerard Calvi
lyrics: Ross Parker
staging: Alec Shanks
sets: Charles Elson
choreography: Colette Brosset
opened: November 11, 1958
   America 100:381, Dec 20, 1958
   Christian Century 75:1435, Dec 10, 1958
   Dance Magazine 33:16, Jan 1959
   Life 45:67-8+, Dec 8, 1958
   New York Theatre Critics' Reviews 1958:206+
   New York Times page 42, Nov 12, 1958
                 page 39, Nov 13, 1958
                 II, page 1, Nov 16, 1958
                 II, page 1, Sep 13, 1959
                 II, page 3, Dec 18, 1960
   New Yorker 34:99-100, Nov 22, 1958
   Newsweek 52:78-9, Nov 24, 1958
   Saturday Review 41:24, Nov 29, 1958
   Theatre Arts 43:11+, Jan 1959
   Time 72:80+, Nov 24, 1958
   Vogue 133.94-5, Jan 1, 1959

Redhead (452 performances)
book: Herbert and Dorothy Fields, Sidney
                 Sheldon, David Shaw
music: Albert Hague
lyrics: Dorothy Fields
staging: Bob Fosse
sets: Rouben Ter-Arutunian
costumes: Rouben Ter-Arutunian
choreography: Bob Fosse
opened: February 5, 1959
   America 100:671, Mar 7, 1959
   Catholic World 189:58-9, Apr 1959
   Dance Magazine 33:40-5, May 1959
   Life 46:81-3, Feb 23, 1959
   Nation 188:234, Mar 14, 1959
   New York Theatre Critics' Reviews 1959:384+
   New York Times page 21, Feb 6, 1959
                 II, page 1, Feb 15, 1959

II, page 1, Mar 20, 1960
New Yorker 35:98+, Feb 21, 1959
Newsweek 53:94, Feb 16, 1959
Saturday Review 42:25, Feb 28, 1959
Theatre Arts 43:10-11, Apr 1959
Time 73:77, Feb 16, 1959

Whoop-Up (56 performances)
book: Cy Feuer, Ernest H. Martin, and Dan
                 Cushman, based on "Stay Away Joe"
                 by Dan Cushman
music: Moose Charlap
lyrics: Norman Gimbel
staging: Cy Feuer
sets: Jo Mielziner
costumes: Anna Hill Johnstone
choreography: Onna White
opened: December 22, 1958
   America 100:558-9, Feb 7, 1959
   Catholic World 188:506, Mar 1959
   Dance Magazine 33:18, Feb 1959
   New York Theatre Critics' Reviews 1958:161+
   New York Times page 2, Dec 23, 1958
                 II, page 1, Feb 8, 1958
   New Yorker 34:50+, Jan 3, 1959
   Saturday Review 42:67, Jan 10, 1959
   Theatre Arts 43:9, Mar 1959

Season of 1959-1960

Beg, Borrow or Steal (5 performances)
book: Bud Freeman, from a story by Marvin
                 Seiger and Bud Freeman
music: Leon Prober
lyrics: Bud Freeman
staging: Billy Matthews
sets: Carter Morningstar
costumes: Carter Morningstar
choreography: Peter Hamilton
opened: February 10, 1960
   New York Theatre Critics' Reviews 1960:370+
   New York Times page 39, Feb 11, 1960
                 page 22, Feb 12, 1960

236

New Yorker 36:101-2, Feb 20, 1960

Billy Barnes Revue (87 performances)
sketches: Bob Rodgers
dialogue: Bob Rodgers
music: Billy Barnes
lyrics: Billy Barnes
staging: Bob Rodgers
sets: Glen Holse
costumes: Peggy Morrison
opened: August 4, 1959
    Dance Magazine 33:13, Sep 1959
    New York Times page 19, Nov 25, 1959
    Saturday Review 42:33, Oct 10, 1959

Bye Bye Birdie (607 performances)
book: Michael Stewart
music: Charles Strouse
lyrics: Lee Adams
staging: Gower Champion
sets: Robert Randolph
costumes: Miles White
choreography: Gower Champion
opened: April 14, 1960
    Life 48:143+, May 23, 1960
    Nation 190:390, Apr 30, 1960
    New York Theatre Critics' Reviews 1960:296+
    New York Times VI, page 90, Mar 27, 1960
                    page 13, Apr 15, 1960
                    page 13, Jun 17, 1960
    New Yorker 36:116-18, Apr 23, 1960
    Newsweek 55:100, Apr 25, 1960
    Saturday Review 43:26, Apr 30, 1960
    Time 75:50, Apr 25, 1960

Christine (12 performances)
book: Pearl S. Buck and Charles K. Peck,
                Jr., adapted from Hilda Wernher's
                My Indian Family
music: Sammy Fain
lyrics: Paul Francis Webster
sets: Jo Mielziner
costumes: Alvin Colt

237

choreography: Hanya Holm
opened: April 28, 1960
   America 103:267, May 14, 1960
   New York Theatre Critics' Reviews 1960:272+
   New York Times page 27, Apr 29, 1960
   New Yorker 36:114+, May 7, 1960
   Saturday Review 43:28, May 14, 1960
   Time 75:56, May 9, 1960

Fiorello! (795 performances)
book: Jerome Weidman and George Abbott
music: Jerry Bock
lyrics: Sheldon Harnick
staging: George Abbott
sets: William and Jean Eckart
costumes: William and Jean Eckart
choreography: Peter Gennaro
opened: November 23, 1959
   America 102:594, Feb 13, 1960
   Christian Century 76:1506, Dec 23, 1959
   Commonweal 71:422, Jan 8, 1960
   Life 48:55-7, Jan 18, 1960
   Nation 189:475, Dec 19, 1959
   New York Theatre Critics' Reviews 1959:219+
   New York Times VI, page 18, Nov 8, 1959
                II, page 1, Nov 22, 1959
                page 45, Nov 24, 1959
                page 19, Nov 25, 1959
                II, page 1, Nov 29, 1959
                page 12, Oct 28, 1961
                page 24, Jun 14, 1962
                page 60, Oct 10, 1962
   New Yorker 35:95-7, Dec 5, 1959
   Newsweek 54:96, Dec 7, 1959
   Saturday Review 42:26-7, Dec 12, 1959
                43:75, Jan 16, 1960
   Time 74:54+, Dec 7, 1959

From A To Z (22 performances)
sketches: Woody Allen, Herbert Farjeon, Mark
               Epstein and Christopher Hewett,
               Nina Warner Hook
music and

238

lyrics: Jerry Herman, Jay Thompson, Dickson
                  Hughes and Everett Sloane, Jack
                  Holmes, Mary Rodgers and Marshall
                  Barer, Paul Klein and Fred Ebb,
                  Fred Ebb and Norma Martin, William
                  Dyer and Don Parks, Paul Klein and
                  Lee Goldsmith and Fred Ebb, Charles
                  Zwar and Alan Melville
staging: Christopher Hewett
sets: Fred Voelpel
costumes: Fred Voelpel
choreography: Ray Harrison
opened: April 20, 1960
   New York Theatre Critics' Reviews 1960:284+
   New York Times page 23, Apr 21, 1960
   New Yorker 36:84+, Apr 30, 1960

The Girls Against the Boys (16 performances)
sketches: Arnold B. Horwitt
music: Richard Lewine (additional music by
                    Albert Hague)
lyrics: Arnold B. Horwitt
staging: Aaron Ruben
sets: Ralph Alswang
costumes: Sal Anthony
choreography: Boris Runanin
opened: November 2, 1959
   New York Theatre Critics' Reviews 1959:239+
   New York Times page 26, Nov 3, 1959
                  II, page 1, Nov 8, 1959
                  page 56, Nov 10, 1959
   New Yorker 35:121-2, Nov 14, 1959
   Newsweek 54:108, Nov 16, 1959
   Time 74:57, Nov 16, 1959

Greenwillow (97 performances)
book: Lesser Samuels and Frank Loesser,
                  based on the novel by B. J. Chute
music: Frank Loesser
lyrics: Frank Loesser
staging: George Roy Hill
sets: Peter Larkin
costumes: Alvin Colt

choreography: Joe Layton
opened: March 8, 1960
    Commonweal 72:16, Apr 1, 1960
    New York Theatre Critics' Reviews 1960:325+
    New York Times II, page 3, Feb 28, 1960
                    page 38, Mar 9, 1960
                    II, page 1, Mar 20, 1960
                    page 26, May 13, 1960
    New Yorker 36:117, Mar 19, 1960
    Newsweek 55:116, Mar 21, 1960
    Time 75:74, Mar 21, 1960

Happy Town (5 performances)
book: Max Hampton
music: Gordon Duffy (additional music by Paul
                 Nassau)
lyrics: Harry M. Haldane (additional lyrics
                 by Paul Nassau)
staging: Allan A. Buckhantz
sets: Curt Nations
costumes: J. Michael Travis
choreography: Lee Scott
opened: October 7, 1959
    New York Theatre Critics' Reviews 1959:279+
    New York Times page 49, Oct 8, 1959
                    page 22, Oct 9, 1959
    New Yorker 35:134, Oct 17, 1959

Saratoga (80 performances)
book: Morton Da Costa, based on Edna
                 Ferber's Saratoga Trunk
music: Harold Arlen
lyrics: Johnny Mercer
staging: Morton Da Costa
sets: Cecil Beaton
costumes: Cecil Beaton
choreography: Ralph Beaumont
opened: December 7, 1959
    America 102:594+, Feb 13, 1960
    New York Theatre Critics' Reviews 1959:195+
    New York Times page 59, Dec 8, 1959
                    page 23, Feb 1, 1960
    New Yorker 35:81, Dec 19, 1959

Newsweek 54:83, Dec 21, 1959
Saturday Review 42:25, Dec 26, 1959
Theatre Arts 44:17-21, Jan 1960
Time 74:34, Dec 21, 1959
Vogue 135:114-15, Feb 1, 1960

The Sound of Music (1,443 performances)
book: Howard Lindsay and Russel Crouse,
               suggested by Maria Augusta Trapp's
               The Trapp Family Singers
music: Richard Rodgers
lyrics: Oscar Hammerstein II
staging: Vincent J. Donehue
sets: Oliver Smith
costumes: Lucinda Ballard
choreography: Joe Layton
opened: November 16, 1959
   America 102:402, Jan 2, 1960
   Catholic World 191:19-22, Apr 1960
   Christian Century 76:1407-8, Dec 2, 1959
   Life 47:137-46, Nov 23, 1959
   Musical America 79:15, Dec 1, 1959
   New Republic 141:25-6, Dec 28, 1959
   New York Theatre Critics' Reviews 1959:227
   New York Times VI, pages 22-23, Nov 1, 1959
                II, page 1, Nov 15, 1959
                page 40, Nov 17, 1959
                II, page 1, Nov 22, 1959
                page 22, May 19, 1961
                page 41, May 19, 1965
   New Yorker 35:106+, Nov 28, 1959
   Newsweek 54:100+, Nov 30, 1959
   Saturday Review 42:28-9, Dec 5, 1959
   Theatre Arts 44:65-9, Jan 1960
                46:57-9+, Nov 1962
   Time 74:64, Nov 30, 1959

Take Me Along (448 performances)
book: Joseph Stein and Robert Russell, based
               on Eugene O'Neill's Ah, Wilderness!
music: Robert Merrill
lyrics: Robert Merrill
staging: Peter Glenville

241

sets: Oliver Smith
costumes: Miles White
choreography: Onna White
opened: October 22, 1959
  America 102:255, Nov 21, 1959
  Commonweal 71:240, Nov 20, 1959
  Dance Magazine 33:24-5, Dec 1959
  Life 47:117-20, Nov 2, 1959
  New York Theatre Critics' Reviews 1959:244+
  New York Times page 22, Oct 23, 1959
                    II, page 1, Nov 1, 1959
                    page 50, Dec 14, 1960
  New Yorker 35:134-5, Oct 31, 1959
  Newsweek 54:94, Nov 2, 1959
  Saturday Review 42:40, Nov 14, 1959
  Theatre Arts 43:13, Dec 1959
  Time 74:30+, Nov 2, 1959

                Season of 1960-1961

Camelot (873 performances)
book: Alan Jay Lerner, based on T. H.
                White's The Once and Future King
music: Frederick Loewe
lyrics: Alan Jay Lerner
staging: Moss Hart
sets: Oliver Smith
costumes: Adrian and Tony Duquette
choreography: Hanya Holm
opened: December 3, 1960
  America 104:546, Jan 21, 1961
  Commonweal 74:379, Jul 7, 1961
  Coronet 50:15, May 1961
  Dance Magazine 35:16, Feb 1961
  Horizon 3:102-4, May 1961
  Life 49:90-3, Dec 19, 1960
  Musical America 81:264, Jan 1961
  Nation 191:510, Dec 24, 1960
  National Review 10:224-6, Apr 8, 1961
  New York Theatre Critics'Reviews 1960:154+
  New York Times VI, page 4, Oct 2, 1960
                    page 35, Oct 3, 1960
                    VI, page 68, Oct 16, 1960

II, page 1, Nov 27, 1960
page 42, Dec 5, 1960
II, page 5, Dec 11, 1960
VI, pages 26-27, Dec 11, 1960
page 20, Aug 7, 1961
VI, page 34, Dec 3, 1961
page 5, Jan 5, 1963
page 34, Aug 20, 1964
New York Times Magazine pages 18-19, Sep 18, 1960
New Yorker 36:95, Dec 10, 1960
Newsweek 56:94, Dec 12, 1960
56:104-5, Dec 5, 1960
Saturday Review 43:30, Dec 24, 1960
Theatre Arts 44:25-6, Dec 1960
45:8-9, Feb 1961
Time 76:78, Oct 17, 1960
76:64-6+, Nov 14, 1960
76:63, Dec 19, 1960
Vogue 137:116-17, Feb 15, 1961

Carnival! (719 performances)
book: Michael Stewart, based on material by
               Helen Deutsch
music: Bob Merrill
lyrics: Bob Merrill
staging: Gower Champion
sets: Will Steven Armstrong
costumes: Freddy Wittop
choreography: Gower Champion
opened: April 13, 1961
   America 105:410, Jun 3, 1961
   Catholic World 193:271-2, Jul 1961
   Commonweal 74:327-8, Jun 23, 1961
   Coronet 50:10, Aug 1961
   Dance Magazine 35:15, Jun 1961
   Life 50:85-6+, May 5, 1961
   Musical America 81:25-6, Jul 1961
   Nation 192:378, Apr 29, 1961
   New York Theatre Critics' Reviews 1961:304+
   New York Times II, page 1, Apr 9, 1961
                    page 22, Apr 14, 1961
                    II, page 1, Apr 23, 1961
                    VI, page 16, Apr 23, 1961

243

page 37, Jun 6, 1962
page 5, Jan 5, 1963
New Yorker 37:116+, Apr 22, 1961
Newsweek 57:90, Apr 24, 1961
Saturday Review 44:22, Apr 29, 1961
Theatre Arts 45:29+, Jun 1961
Time 77:60, Apr 21, 1961

The Conquering Hero (8 performances)
book: Larry Gelbart, based on Preston
                 Sturges' Hail, the Conquering Hero
music: Moose Charlap
lyrics: Norman Gimbel
sets: Jean Rosenthal and William Pitkin
costumes: Patton Campbell
opened: January 16, 1961
   New York Theatre Critics' Reviews 1961:388+
   New York Times page 40, Jan 17, 1961
                 page 29, Jan 18, 1961
   New Yorker 36:64, Jan 28, 1961

Do Re Mi (400 performances)
book: Garson Kanin
music: Jule Styne
lyrics: Betty Comden and Adolph Green
staging: Garson Kanin
sets: Boris Aronson
costumes: Irene Sharaff
choreography: Marc Breaux and Deedee Wood
opened: December 26, 1960
   America 104:549, Jan 21, 1961
   Commonweal 73:509, Feb 10, 1961
   Coronet 49:16, Apr 1961
   Dance Magazine 35:16-17, Feb 1961
   Life 50:53-4+, Feb 10, 1961
   Nation 192:39, Jan 14, 1961
   New York Theatre Critics' Reviews 1960:129+
   New York Times II, page 3, Dec 25, 1960
                 page 23, Dec 27, 1960
                 II, page 1, Jan 8, 1961
                 page 27, Oct 13, 1961
   New Yorker 36:68, Jan 14, 1961
   Newsweek 57:52, Jan 9, 1961

Saturday Review 44:28, Jan 14, 1961
Time 77:51, Jan 6, 1961

Donnybrook! (68 performances)
book: Robert E. McEnroe, based on Maurice
                 Walsh's The Quiet Man
music: Johnny Burke
lyrics: Johnny Burke
staging: Jack Cole
sets: Rouben Ter-Arutunian
costumes: Rouben Ter-Arutunian
choreography: Jack Cole
opened: May 18, 1961
   America 105:532, Jul 15, 1961
   Dance Magazine 35:20, Jul 1961
   New York Theatre Critics' Reviews 1961:292+
   New York Times II, page 1, May 14, 1961
                    page 23, May 19, 1961
                    II, page 1, May 28, 1961
                    page 26, Jul 10, 1961
                    page 13, Jul 14, 1961
   New Yorker 37:72+, May 27, 1961
   Saturday Review 44:51, Jun 17, 1961
   Theatre Arts 45:9-10, Jul 1961
   Time 77:79, May 20, 1961

The Happiest Girl in the World (96 performances)
book: Fred Saidy and Henry Myers, based
                 on Aristophanes' Lysistrata and
                 Bullfinch's stories of Greek mythology
music: Jacques Offenbach
lyrics: E. Y. Harburg
staging: Cyril Ritchard
sets: William and Jean Eckart
costumes: Robert Fletcher
choreography: Dania Krupska
opened: April 3, 1961
   America 105:410, Jun 3, 1961
   Dance Magazine 35:13-14, May 1961
   Nation 192:358, Apr 22, 1961
   New York Theatre Critics' Reviews 1961:314+
   New York Times II, page 1, Apr 2, 1961
                       page 42, Apr 4, 1961

245

Newsweek 57:69, Apr 17, 1961
New Yorker 37:76, Apr 15, 1961
Theatre Arts 45:32, Jun 1961
Time 77:106+, Apr 14, 1961

Irma La Douce (524 performances)
book: Julian More, David Hencker and Monty
                Norman, English version of the
                original book by Alexandre Breffort
music: Marguerite Monnot
lyrics: Julian More, David Heneker and Monty
                Norman, English version of the
                original lyrics by Alexandre Breffort
staging: Peter Brook
sets: Rolf Gerard
costumes: Rolf Gerard
choreography: Onna White
opened: September 29, 1960
   America 104:130+, Oct 22, 1960
   Commonweal 73:152, Nov 4, 1960
   Coronet 49:14, Jan 1961
   Dance Magazine 34:32, Dec 1960
   Life 49:53+, Nov 14, 1960
   Nation 188:462, May 16, 1959
          191:253, Oct 15, 1960
   New Republic 143: 21-2, Oct 17, 1960
   New York Theatre Critics' Reviews 1960:230+
   New York Times II, page 3, Sep 25, 1960
                     page 31, Sep 30, 1960
                     II, page 1, Oct 16, 1960
                     II, page 1, Oct 30, 1960
   New Yorker 36:95, Oct 8, 1960
   Newsweek 56:65, Oct 10, 1960
   Saturday Review 43:36, Oct 15, 1960
   Time 76:84, Oct 10, 1960

Show Girl (100 performances)
sketches: Charles Gaynor (additional sketches by
                Ernest Chambers)
music: Charles Gaynor
lyrics: Charles Gaynor
staging: Charles Gaynor
sets: Oliver Smith

costumes: Miles White
choreography: Richard D'Arcy
opened: January 12, 1961
   America 104:557, Jan 28, 1961
   New York Theatre Critics' Reviews 1961:394+
   New York Times page 37, Jan 13, 1961
                II, page 1, Jan 29, 1961
                page 27, Apr 3, 1961
   Newsweek 57:57, Jan 23, 1961
   Saturday Review 44:27, Jan 28, 1961
   Time 77:77, Jan 20, 1961

Tenderloin (216 performances)
book: George Abbott and Jerome Weidman,
               based on the novel by Samuel Hopkins
               Adams
music: Jerry Bock
lyrics: Sheldon Harnick
staging: George Abbott
sets: Cecil Beaton
costumes: Cecil Beaton
choreography: Joe Layton
opened: October 17, 1960
   America 104:354+, Dec 3, 1960
   Christian Century 77:1382, Nov 23, 1960
   Dance Magazine 34:33, Dec 1960
   Nation 191:353, Nov 5, 1960
   New York Theatre Critics' Reviews 1960:205+
   New York Times page 47, Oct 18, 1960
                page 20, Nov 4, 1900
                page 30, Apr 13, 1961
   New Yorker 36:86, Oct 29, 1960
   Newsweek 56:84, Oct 31, 1960
   Saturday Review 43:39, Nov 5, 1960
   Theatre Arts 44:12, Dec 1960
   Time 76:68, Oct 31, 1960

13 Daughters (28 performances)
book: Eaton Magoon (additional book material
               by Leon Tokatyan)
music: Eaton Magoon
lyrics: Eaton Magoon
staging: Billy Matthews

sets: George Jenkins
costumes: Alvin Colt
choreography: Rod Alexander
opened: March 2, 1961
   New York Theatre Critics' Reviews 1961:350+
   New York Times page 17, Mar 3, 1961
              page 30, Mar 23, 1961
   New Yorker 37:112, Mar 11, 1961

The Unsinkable Molly Brown (532 performances)
book: Richard Morris
music: Meredith Willson
lyrics: Meredith Willson
staging: Dore Schary
sets: Oliver Smith
costumes: Miles White
choreography: Peter Gennaro
opened: November 3, 1960
   America 104:353-4, Dec 3, 1960
   Christian Century 77:1441-2, Dec 7, 1960
   Dance Magazine 34:33, Dec 1960
   Life 49:141-3+, Dec 5, 1960
   Nation 191:421, Nov 26, 1960
   New York Theatre Critics' Reviews 1960:184+
   New York Times VI, page 41, Oct 23, 1960
              page 28, Nov 4, 1960
   New Yorker 36:103, Nov 12, 1960
   Newsweek 56:61, Nov 14, 1960
   Saturday Review 43:38, Nov 19, 1960
   Theatre Arts 45:58-9, Jan 1961
   Time 76:84, Nov 14, 1960

Vintage '60 (8 performances)
sketches: Jack Wilson, Alan Jeffreys, Maxwell
                Grant
additional
  material: David Rogers, Mickey Deems, Mark
                Bucci, Sheldon Harnick, David Baker,
                Phil Green, Tommy Garlock, Fred
                Ebb, Paul Klein, William Lanteau,
                Alice Clark, David Morton, Lee
                Goldsmith, Michael Ross, Barbara
                Heller, Fay DeWitt, Ronald Axe,

William Link, Richard Levinson
staging: Jonathan Lucas
sets: Fred Voelpel
costumes: Fred Voelpel
choreography: Jonathan Lucas
opened: September 12, 1960
   New York Theatre Critics' Reviews 1960:247+
   New York Times page 41, Sep 13, 1960
                  page 44, Sep 21, 1960
   New Yorker 36:97, Sep 24, 1960
   Newsweek 56:109, Sep 26, 1960
   Theatre Arts 44:10, Nov 1960

Wildcat (171 performances)
book: N. Richard Nash
music: Cy Coleman
lyrics: Carolyn Leigh
staging: Michael Kidd
sets: Peter Larkin
costumes: Alvin Colt
choreography: Michael Kidd
opened: December 16, 1960
   America 104:546, Jan 21, 1961
   Coronet 49:16, Apr 1961
   Nation 191:531, Dec 31, 1960
   New York Theatre Critics' Reviews 1960:134+
   New York Times page 20, Dec 17, 1960
                  page 39, Feb 7, 1961
   New Yorker 36:38, Dec 24, 1960
   Newsweek 56:53, Dec 26, 1960
   Saturday Review 43:28, Dec 31, 1960
   Theatre Arts 45:9-10, Feb 1961

Season of 1961-1962

All American (86 performances)
book: Mel Brooks, based on Robert Lewis
                 Taylor's Professor Fodorski
music: Charles Strouse
lyrics: Lee Adams
staging: Joshua Logan
sets: Jo Mielziner
costumes: Patton Campbell

                      249

choreography: Danny Daniels
opened: March 19, 1962
   America 107:278-9, May 19, 1962
   New York Theatre Critics' Reviews 1962:318+
   New York Times page 44, Mar 20, 1962
                          page 29, May 24, 1962
   New Yorker 38:104-6, Mar 31, 1962
   Newsweek 59:58, Apr 2, 1962
   Theatre Arts 46:58, May 1962
   Time 79:46, Mar 30, 1962

The Billie Barnes People (7 performances)
sketches: Bob Rodgers
music: Billy Barnes
lyrics: Billy Barnes
staging: Bob Rodgers
sets: Spencer Davies
costumes: Grady Hunt
opened: June 13, 1961
   New York Theatre Critics' Reviews 1961:276+
   New York Times page 10, Jun 14, 1961

Bravo Giovanni (76 performances)
book: A. J. Russell, adapted from Howard
                 Shaw's The Crime of Giovanni
                 Venturi
music: Milton Schafer
lyrics: Ronny Graham
staging: Stanley Prager
sets: Robert Randolph
costumes: Ed Wittstein
choreography: Carol Haney and Buzz Miller
opened: May 19, 1962
   America 107:429-30, Jun 23, 1962
   Commonweal 76:304, Jun 15, 1962
   New York Theatre Critics' Reviews 1962:276+
   New York Times page 41, May 21, 1962
                          II, page 1, May 27, 1962
                          page 34, Sep 12, 1962
   New Yorker 38:91-2, May 26, 1962
   Newsweek 59:65, Jun 4, 1962
   Saturday Review 45:24, Jun 2, 1962
   Theatre Arts 46:67-9, Jul 1962

Time 79:83, Jun 1, 1962

A Family Affair (65 performances)
book: James Goldman, John Kander, William
                Goldman
music: James Goldman, John Kander, William
                Goldman
lyrics: James Goldman, John Kander, William
                Goldman
staging: Harold Prince
sets: David Hays
costumes: Robert Fletcher
choreography: John Butler
opened: January 27, 1962
   America 106:737, Mar 3, 1962
   New York Theatre Critics' Reviews 1962:374+
   New York Times page 17, Jan 29, 1962
                page 36, Mar 26, 1962
   Theatre Arts 46:58-9, Apr 1962
   Time 79:61, Feb 9, 1962

From the Second City (87 performances)
sketches: Howard Alk, Severn Darden, Barbara
                Harris, Paul Sand, Alan Arkin,
                Andrew Duncan, Mina Kolb, Eugene
                Troobnick
music: William Mathieu
staging: Paul Sills
sets: Frederick Fox
opened: September 20, 1961
   Commonweal 75:94, Oct 20, 1961
   Nation 193:255, Oct 14, 1961
          194:127, Feb 10, 1962
   New York Theatre Critics' Reviews 1961:259+
   New York Times page 32, Sep 27, 1961
                II, page 1, Oct 8, 1961
                page 49, Dec 5, 1961
                page 47, Dec 15, 1961
                page 30, Jan 12, 1962
   New Yorker 37:129, Oct 7, 1961
   Reporter 25:44+, Nov 23, 1961
   Saturday Review 44:78, Oct 14, 1961

A Funny Thing Happened on the Way to the Forum
(964 performances)
book: Burt Shevelove and Larry Gelbart,
                 based on Plautus' plays
music: Stephen Sondheim
lyrics: Stephen Sondheim
staging: George Abbott
sets: Tony Walton
costumes: Tony Walton
choreography: Jack Cole
opened: May 8, 1962
    America 107:360-1, Jun 2, 1962
    Commonweal 76:279, Jun 8, 1962
    Dance Magazine 36:27, Jul 1962
    Life 53:93-5, Jul 20, 1962
    Nation 195:60, Aug 11, 1962
    New Republic 146:28-30, May 28, 1962
    New York Theatre Critics' Reviews 1962:290+
    New York Times page 49, May 9, 1962
                    II, page 1, May 20, 1962
                    page 22, Jul 6, 1962
                    page 83, Oct 14, 1962
                    page 14, May 11, 1963
                    page 20, Aug 6, 1964
                    page 14, Aug 7, 1964
    New Yorker 38:103, May 19, 1962
    Newsweek 59:85, May 21, 1962
    Saturday Review 45:22, May 26, 1962
    Theatre Arts 46:66-8, Jul 1962
    Time 79:76, May 18, 1962

The Gay Life (113 performances)
book: Fay and Michael Kanin, suggested by
                 Arthur Schnitzler's Anatol
music: Arthur Schwartz
lyrics: Howard Dietz
staging: Gerald Freedman
sets: Oliver Smith
costumes: Lucinda Ballard
choreography: Herbert Ross
opened: November 18, 1961
    America 106:737, Mar 3, 1962
    Dance Magazine 36:13-14, Jan 1962

252

Life 52:49-51, Jan 19, 1962
New York Theatre Critics' Reviews 1961:168+
New York Times II, page 1, Nov 12, 1961
                page 38, Nov 18, 1961
New Yorker 37:118, Dec 2, 1961
Newsweek 58:79, Dec 4, 1961
Theatre Arts 46:11-12, Feb 1962
Time 78:64, Dec 1, 1961

How to Succeed in Business Without Really Trying
  (1,417 performances)
book: Abe Burrows, Jack Weinstock, Willie
                Gilbert, based on Shepherd Mead's
                novel
music: Frank Loesser
lyrics: Frank Loesser
staging: Abe Burrows
sets: Robert Randolph
costumes: Robert Fletcher
choreography: Hugh Lambert
opened: October 14, 1961
  America 106:632, Feb 10, 1962
  Business Week pages 30-1, Oct 21, 1961
  Christian Century 79:234, Feb 21, 1962
  Commonweal 75.154, Nov 3, 1961
  Dance Magazine 35:23, Dec 1961
                 36:12-13, Jan 1962
  Life 51:192-4, Nov 17, 1961
  National Review 12:31-3, Jan 16, 1962
  Nation 193:361-2, Nov 4, 1961
  New Republic 145:23, Nov 6, 1961
  New York Theatre Critics' Reviews 1961:224+
  New York Times II, page 1, Oct 8, 1961
                    page 34, Oct 16, 1961
                    II, page 3, Sep 2, 1962
                    page 5, Mar 30, 1963
                    page 43, Oct 11, 1963
                    page 30, Feb 12, 1964
                    II, page 7, Mar 8, 1964
                    page 10, Jul 18, 1964
  New Yorker 37:129, Oct 21, 1961
  Newsweek 58:50-3, Nov 27, 1961
           58:62, Oct 23, 1961

Reporter 25:58, Nov 9, 1961
Saturday Evening Post 235:24-7, Jun 23, 1962
Saturday Review 44:33, Oct 28, 1961
Theatre Arts 45:8-9, Dec 1961
Time 78:79, Oct 27, 1961
       80:38, Dec 14, 1962

I Can Get It For You Wholesale (300 performances)
book: Jerome Weidman, based on his novel
music: Harold Rome
lyrics: Harold Rome
staging: Arthur Laurents
sets: Will Steven Armstrong
costumes: Theoni V. Aldredge
choreography: Herbert Ross
opened: March 22, 1962
  Dance Magazine 36:18, May 1962
  Life 52:103-4, May 18, 1962
  Nation 194:338, Apr 14, 1962
  New York Theatre Critics' Reviews 1962:314+
  New York Times page 29, Mar 23, 1962
  Newsweek 59:58, Apr 2, 1962
  Saturday Review 45:28, Apr 14, 1962
  Theatre Arts 46:58+, May 1962
  Time 79:46, Mar 30, 1962

Kean (92 performances)
book: Peter Stone, based on Jean Paul
               Sartre's play and Alexandre Dumas'
               play
music: Robert Wright and George Forrest
lyrics: Robert Wright and George Forrest
staging: Jack Cole
sets: Ed Wittstein
costumes: Ed Wittstein
choreography: Jack Cole
opened: November 2, 1961
  Commonweal 75:389, Jan 5, 1962
  Dance Magazine 35:23, Dec 1961
  Nation 193:438, Nov 25, 1961
  New York Theatre Critics' Reviews 1961:180+
  New York Times page 28, Nov 3, 1961
         II, page 1, Nov 12, 1961

New Yorker 37:117, Nov 11, 1961
Newsweek 58:94, Nov 13, 1961
Theatre Arts 45:17-24, Dec 1961
            46:11-12, Jan 1962
Time 78:66, Nov 10, 1961

Kwamina (32 performances)
book: Robert Alan Aurthur
music: Richard Adler
lyrics: Richard Adler
staging: Robert Lewis
sets: Will Steven Armstrong
costumes: Motley
choreography: Agnes de Mille
opened: October 23, 1961
   America 106:257, Nov 18, 1961
   Dance Magazine 35:23, Dec 1961
   New Republic 145:23, Nov 6, 1961
   New York Theatre Critics' Reviews 1961:206+
   New York Times II, page 3, Oct 22, 1961
                 page 42, Oct 24, 1961
                 II, page 1, Nov 12, 1961
   New Yorker 37:126, Nov 4, 1961
   Newsweek 58:69, Nov 6, 1961
   Saturday Review 44:39, Nov 18, 1961
   Theatre Arts 46:13-14, Jan 1962
   Time 78:44, Nov 3, 1961

Let It Ride (68 performances)
book: Abram S. Grimes, based on John
                Cecil Holm and George Abbott's
                Three Men On A Horse
music: Jay Livingston and Ray Evans
lyrics: Jay Livingston and Ray Evans
staging: Stanley Prager
sets: William and Jean Eckart
costumes: Guy Kent
choreography: Onna White
opened: October 12, 1961
   Commonweal 75:154, Nov 3, 1961
   Dance Magazine 35:22, Dec 1961
   New York Theatre Critics' Reviews 1961:230+
   New York Times page 27, Oct 13, 1961

page 49, Dec 4, 1961
New Yorker 37:129, Oct 21, 1961
Theatre Arts 45:13, Dec 1961
Time 78:64, Oct 20, 1961.

Milk and Honey (543 performances)
book: Don Appell
music: Jerry Herman
lyrics: Jerry Herman
staging: Albert Marre
sets: Howard Bay
costumes: Miles White
choreography: Donald Saddler
opened: October 10, 1961
   America 106:376+, Dec 9, 1961
   Commonweal 75:154, Nov 3, 1961
   Dance Magazine 35:28-30, Nov 1961
   Nation 193:361, Nov 4, 1961
   New York Theatre Critics' Reviews 1961:238+
   New York Times page 52, Oct 11, 1961
   New Yorker 37:130, Oct 21, 1961
   Newsweek 58:60+, Oct 23, 1961
   Saturday Review 44:32, Nov 4, 1961
   Theatre Arts 45:10-11, Dec 1961
   Time 78:64, Oct 20, 1961

New Faces of 1962 (28 performances)
conceived by: Leonard Sillman
sketches: Ronny Graham, Paul Lynde, Jean
                 Shepherd, Richard Maury, Joey
                 Carter, R. G. Brown, and others
music and
 lyrics: June Carroll, Arthur Siegel, David
                 Rogers, Mark Bucci, Jack Holmes,
                 Ronny Graham, and others
staging: Leonard Sillman and Richard Maury
sets: Marvin Reiss
costumes: Thomas Becher
choreography: James Moore and others
opened: February 1, 1962
   America 106:737, Mar 3, 1962
   New York Theatre Critics' Reviews 1962:366+
   New York Times page 25, Feb 2, 1962

256

page 22, Feb 9, 1962
page 21, Feb 22, 1962
Theatre Arts 46:63, Apr 1962

No Strings (580 performances)
book: Samuel Taylor
music: Richard Rodgers
lyrics: Richard Rodgers
staging: Joe Layton
sets: David Hays
costumes: Fred Voelpel and Donald Brooks
choreography: Joe Layton and Buddy Schwab
opened: March 15, 1962
   America 106:869, Mar 31, 1962
   Christian Century 79:493, Apr 18, 1962
   Dance Magazine 36:19-21, May 1962
   Ebony 17:40-2+, Jul 1962
   Nation 194:337-8, Apr 14, 1962
   New Republic 146:26-7+, Apr 9, 1962
   New York Theatre Critics' Reviews 1962:328+
   New York Times page 24, Mar 16, 1962
                  II, page 1, Mar 25, 1962
                  page 17, Jan 1, 1964
   New Yorker 38:100+, Mar 31, 1962
   Newsweek 59:85, Mar 26, 1962
   Saturday Review 45:27, Mar 31, 1962
   Theatre Arts 46:57-9, May 1962
   Time 79:51, Mar 23, 1962

Sail Away (167 performances)
book: Noel Coward
music: Noel Coward
lyrics: Noel Coward
staging: Noel Coward
sets: Oliver Smith
costumes: Helene Pons and Oliver Smith
choreography: Joe Layton
opened: October 3, 1961
   Commonweal 75:154, Nov 3, 1961
   Dance Magazine 35:28, Nov 1961
   Nation 193:361, Nov 4, 1961
   New Republic 145:22, Nov 6, 1961
   New York Theatre Critics' Reviews 1961:251+

New York Times page 17, Aug 10, 1961
                II, page 1, Oct 1, 1961
                page 48, Oct 4, 1961
                page 14, Jun 23, 1962
New Yorker 37:162+, Oct 14, 1961
Newsweek 58:101, Oct 16, 1961
Reporter 25:53, Oct 26, 1961
Saturday Review 44:34, Oct 21, 1961
Theatre Arts 45:10-11, Dec 1961
Time 78:58, Oct 13, 1961

Subways Are for Sleeping (205 performances)
book: Betty Comden and Adolph Green,
               suggested by Edmund G. Love's novel
music: Jule Styne
lyrics: Betty Comden and Adolph Green
staging: Michael Kidd
sets: Will Steven Armstrong
costumes: Freddy Wittop
choreography: Michael Kidd and Marc Breaux
opened: December 27, 1961
   America 106:737, Mar 3, 1962
   Dance Magazine 36:13, Mar 1962
   New York Theatre Critics' Reviews 1961:135+
   New York Times II, page 3, Dec 17, 1961
                  page 22, Dec 28, 1961
                  page 27, Jun 21, 1962
   New Yorker 37:56, Jan 6, 1962
   Newsweek 59:44, Jan 8, 1962
   Theatre Arts 46:60, Mar 1962
   Time 79:52, Jan 5, 1962

Season of 1962-1963

The Beast in Me (4 performances)
conceived by: Haila Stoddard, based on James
                 Thurber's Fables for our Time
book: adapted by James Costigan
music: Don Elliott
lyrics: James Costigan
staging: John Lehne
sets: Jean Rosenthal
costumes: Leo Van Witsen

choreography: John Butler
opened: May 16, 1963
   New York Theatre Critics' Reviews 1963:324+
   New York Times II, page 1, May 12, 1963
                  page 29, May 17, 1963
   New Yorker 39:57, May 25, 1963
   Newsweek 61:93, May 27, 1963

Hot Spot (43 performances)
book: Jack Weinstock and Willie Gilbert
music: Mary Rodgers
lyrics: Martin Charnin
sets: Rouben Ter-Arutunian
costumes: Rouben Ter-Arutunian
opened: April 19, 1963
   Commonweal 78:225, May 17, 1963
   New York Theatre Critics' Reviews 1963:336+
   New York Times II, page 1, Apr 14, 1963
                  page 17, Apr 20, 1963
                  page 26, May 21, 1963
   New Yorker 39:82, Apr 27, 1963
   Newsweek 61:54, Apr 29, 1963
   Theatre Arts 47:66, Jun 1963
   Time 81:50, Apr 26, 1963

Little Me (257 performances)
book: Neil Simon, based on the novel by
                  Patrick Dennis
music: Cy Coleman
lyrics: Carolyn Leigh
staging: Cy Feuer and Bob Fosse
sets: Robert Randolph
costumes: Robert Fletcher
choreography: Bob Fosse
opened: November 17, 1962
   America 107:1258, Dec 15, 1962
   Commonweal 77:280, Dec 7, 1962
   Dance Magazine 37:24+, Jan 1963
   Life 53:113-15, Nov 30, 1962
   Nation 195:411, Dec 8, 1962
   New York Theatre Critics' Reviews 1962:196+
   New York Times page 58, Oct 10, 1962
                page 41, Nov 19, 1962

II, page 1, Dec 2, 1962
New York Times Magazine pages 75-6, Nov 4, 1962
New Yorker 38:118+, Dec 1, 1962
Newsweek 60:51-4, Nov 26, 1962
Reporter 27:43-4, Dec 20, 1962
Saturday Review 45:51, Dec 8, 1962
Theatre Arts 46:17-19+, Nov 1962
   47:12, Jan 1963
Time 80:53, Nov 30, 1962

Mr. President (265 performances)
book: Howard Lindsay and Russel Crouse
music: Irving Berlin
lyrics: Irving Berlin
staging: Joshua Logan
sets: Jo Mielziner
costumes: Theoni V. Aldredge
choreography: Peter Gennaro
opened: October 20, 1962
 America 107:1230, Dec 8, 1962
 Business Week page 31, Sep 29, 1962
 Commonweal 77:279, Dec 7, 1962
 Dance Magazine 36:98, Dec 1962
 National Review 14:78-9, Jan 29, 1963
 New York Theatre Critics' Reviews 1962:238+
 New York Times page 18, Aug 29, 1962
     page 36, Sep 26, 1962
     II, page 1, Oct 14, 1962
     page 34, Oct 22, 1962
     page 38, May 29, 1963
 New Yorker 38:147, Oct 27, 1962
 Newsweek 60:74, Nov 5, 1962
 Reporter 27:43, Dec 20, 1962
 Saturday Review 45:40, Nov 3, 1962
 Theatre Arts 46:14-16, Nov 1962
     46:14, Dec 1962
 Time 80:62, Sep 7, 1962
   80:82, Nov 2, 1962
 Vogue 140:144-7+, Nov 1, 1962

Nowhere to Go But Up (9 performances)
book: James Lipton
music: Sil Berkowitz

lyrics: James Lipton
staging: Sidney Lumet
sets: Peter Larkin
costumes: Robert Fletcher
choreography: Ronald Field
opened: November 10, 1962
   Dance Magazine 37:24, Jan 1963
               37:28-9, Feb 1963
   New York Theatre Critics' Reviews 1962:209+
   New York Times page 46, Oct 9, 1962
               page 36, Nov 12, 1962
               page 46, Nov 15, 1962
   New Yorker 38:147, Nov 17, 1962
   Theatre Arts 46:15, Dec 1962

Oliver! (774 performances)
book: Lionel Bart, adapted from Charles
               Dickens' Oliver Twist
music: Lionel Bart
lyrics: Lionel Bart
staging: Peter Coe
sets: Sean Kenny
costumes: Sean Kenny
opened: January 6, 1963
   Commonweal 77:493, Feb 1, 1963
   Life 54:75-7, Jan 18, 1963
   New York Theatre Critics' Reviews 1963:397+
   New York Times page 34, Aug 8, 1962
               page 32, Sep 27, 1962
               page 27, Nov 2, 1962
               VI, page 60, Dec 9, 1962
               page 5, Jan 8, 1963
               page 35, Aug 3, 1965
               page 85, Nov 21, 1965
   New York Times Magazine page 60, Dec 9, 1962
   New Yorker 36:145, Oct 8, 1960
            38:85-6, Jun 2, 1962
            38:60, Jan 19, 1963
   Newsweek 60:87, Aug 20, 1962
            61:65, Jan 14, 1963
   Saturday Review 46:26, Jan 19, 1963
   Theatre Arts 46:19-20, Dec 1962
            47:10-11+, Feb 1963

Time 81:52, Jan 11, 1963

She Loves Me (301 performances)
book: Joe Masteroff, based on Miklos
                 Laszlo's play Parfumerie
music: Jerry Bock
lyrics: Sheldon Harnick
staging: Harold Prince
sets: William and Jean Eckart
costumes: Patricia Zipprodt
choreography: Carol Haney
opened: April 23, 1963
    Commonweal 78:225, May 17, 1963
    Life 55:49-50+, Jul 12, 1963
    New York Theatre Critics' Reviews 1963:330+
    New York Times page 39, Apr 24, 1963
                    II, page 1, May 5, 1963
                    page 20, Jan 10, 1964
    New Yorker 39:90, May 4, 1963
    Newsweek 61:83, May 6, 1963
    Saturday Review 46:26, May 11, 1963
    Theatre Arts 47:12-13, Jun 1963
    Time 81:76, May 3, 1963

Sophie (8 performances)
book: Phillip Pruneau
music: Steve Allen
lyrics: Steve Allen
staging: Jack Sydow
sets: Robert Randolph
costumes: Fred Voelpel
choreography: Donald Saddler
opened: April 15, 1963
    New York Theatre Critics' Reviews 1963:344+
    New York Times page 32, Apr 16, 1963
                    page 28, Apr 19, 1963
    Newsweek 61:54, Apr 29, 1963
    Theatre Arts 47:66, Jun 1963

Stop the World - I Want to Get Off (555 performances)
book: Leslie Bricusse and Anthony Newley
music: Leslie Bricusse and Anthony Newley
lyrics: Leslie Bricusse and Anthony Newley

```
staging:          Anthony Newley
sets:             Sean Kenny
choreography: John Broome and Virginia Mason
opened:           October 3, 1962
   America 107:1231, Dec 8, 1962
   Catholic World 196:200, Dec 1962
   Commonweal 77:201, Nov 16, 1962
   Dance Magazine 36:24-5+, Dec 1962
   Life 53:117, Nov 30, 1962
   Nation 195:246-7, Oct 20, 1962
   New York Theatre Critics' Reviews 1962:260+
   New York Times page 39, Sep 17, 1962
                  page 45, Oct 4, 1962
                  VI, page 36, Oct 7, 1962
                  II, page 1, Oct 14, 1962
   New York Times Magazine page 36, Oct 7, 1962
   New Yorker 38:180, Oct 13, 1962
   Newsweek 60:68, Oct 15, 1962
   Reporter 27:42, Dec 20, 1962
   Saturday Review 45:37, Oct 20, 1962
   Theatre Arts 46:11, Nov 1962
   Time 80:67, Oct 12, 1962
```

Tovarich (264 performances)
```
book:             David Shaw, based on the play by
                  Robert E. Sherwood and Jacques
                  Deval
music:            Lee Pockiss
lyrics:           Anne Crosswell
staging:          Peter Glenville
sets:             Rolf Gerard
costumes:         Motley
choreography: Herbert Ross
opened:           March 18, 1963
   America 108:651, May 4, 1963
   Commonweal 78:224, May 17, 1963
   National Review 14:535-7, Jul 2, 1963
   Nation 196:334, Apr 20, 1963
   New York Theatre Critics' Reviews 1963:308+
   New York Times page 5, Jan 23, 1963
                  page 5, Mar 20, 1963
                  page 40, Nov 11, 1963
   New Yorker 39:108+, Mar 30, 1963
```

Newsweek 61:78, Apr 1, 1963
Saturday Review 46:40, Apr 6, 1963
Theatre Arts 47:14-15+, May 1963
Time 81:46, Mar 29, 1963

Season of 1963-1964

Anyone Can Whistle (9 performances)
book: Arthur Laurents
music: Stephen Sondheim
lyrics: Stephen Sondheim
staging: Arthur Laurents
sets: William and Jean Eckart
costumes: Theoni V. Aldredge
choreography: Herbert Ross
opened: April 4, 1964
    New York Theatre Critics' Reviews 1964:301+
    New York Times page 36, Apr 6, 1964
                 page 17, Apr 11, 1964

Cafe Crown (3 performances)
book: Hy Kraft, based on his play
music: Albert Hague
lyrics: Marty Brill
staging: Jerome Eskow
sets: Sam Leve
costumes: Ruth Morley
choreography: Ronald Field
opened: April 17, 1964
    Dance Magazine 38:26-7, May 1964
    New York Theatre Critics' Reviews 1964:284+
    New York Times page 32, Apr 18, 1964
                 page 83, Apr 19, 1964
    New Yorker 40:130, Apr 25, 1964

Fade Out -- Fade In (271 performances)
book: Betty Comden and Adolph Green
music: Jule Styne
lyrics: Betty Comden and Adolph Green
staging: George Abbott
sets: William and Jean Eckart
costumes: Donald Brooks
choreography: Ernest Flatt

opened: May 26, 1964
   America 111:114-15, Aug 1, 1964
   Dance Magazine 38:17, Aug 1964
   Life 57:30, Sep 25, 1964
   Nation 198:611, Jun 15, 1964
   New York Theatre Critics' Reviews 1964:248+
   New York Times page 45, May 27, 1964
               page 42, May 28, 1964
               II, page 1, Jun 7, 1964
               page 56, Nov 10, 1964
               page 34, Apr 14, 1965
   Newsweek 63:69, Jun 8, 1964
   Saturday Review 47:28, Jun 20, 1964
   Time 83:75, Jun 5, 1964

Foxy (72 performances)
book: Ian McLellan Hunter and Ring Lardner,
               Jr., suggested by Ben Jonson's
               Volpone
music: Robert Emmett Dolan
lyrics: Johnny Mercer
staging: Robert Lewis
sets: Robert Randolph
costumes: Robert Fletcher
choreography: Jack Cole
opened: February 16, 1964
   America 110:465, Mar 28, 1964
   Commonweal 79:723, Mar 13, 1964
   New York Theatre Critics' Reviews 1964:349+
   New York Times page 26, Feb 17, 1964
               page 30, Mar 20, 1964
               page 33, Apr 14, 1964
   New Yorker 40:106, Feb 29, 1964
   Newsweek 63:56, Mar 2, 1964
   Saturday Review 47:23, Mar 7, 1964
   Time 83:61, Feb 28, 1964

Funny Girl (885 performances*)
book: Isobel Lennart
music: Jule Styne
lyrics: Bob Merrill
staging: Garson Kanin
sets: Robert Randolph

costumes: Irene Sharaff
choreography: Carol Haney
opened: March 26, 1964
   America 111:114, Aug 1, 1964
   Commonweal 80:147, Apr 24, 1964
   Life 56:10, Apr 17, 1964
   Nation 198:384, Apr 13, 1964
   New York Theatre Critics' Reviews 1964:314+
   New York Times II, page 3, Mar 22, 1964
                 page 15, Mar 27, 1964
                 II, page 3, Apr 5, 1964
                 page 24, Dec 11, 1965
   New Yorker 40:76, Apr 4, 1964
   Newsweek 63:76-7, Apr 6, 1964
   Saturday Review 47:34, Apr 11, 1964
   Time 83:54, Apr 3, 1964

The Girl Who Came to Supper (112 performances)
book: Harry Kurnitz, based on Terence
                Rattigan's play The Sleeping Prince
music: Noel Coward
lyrics: Noel Coward
staging: Joe Layton
sets: Oliver Smith
costumes: Irene Sharaff
opened: December 8, 1963
   America 110:26, Jan 4, 1964
   New York Theatre Critics' Reviews 1963:178+
   New York Times VI, pages 64, 67, Nov 24, 1963
                 II, page 5, Dec 8, 1963
                 page 49, Dec 9, 1963
                 page 54, Dec 10, 1963
   New Yorker 39:62, Dec 21, 1963
   Saturday Review 47:52, Jan 11, 1964
   Time 82:81, Dec 20, 1963
   Vogue 143:62, Feb 1, 1964

Hello Dolly! (989 performances*)
book: Michael Stewart, suggested by Thornton
                Wilder's The Matchmaker
music: Jerry Herman
lyrics: Jerry Herman
staging: Gower Champion

sets: Oliver Smith
costumes: Freddy Wittop
choreography: Gower Champion
opened: January 16, 1964
   America 110:552, Apr 18, 1964
   Life 56:107-9, Apr 3, 1964
   Mademoiselle 59:56, May 1964
   New York Theatre Critics' Reviews 1964:384+
   New York Times II, page 1, Jan 12, 1964
                    page 22, Jan 17, 1964
                    II, page 1, Jan 26, 1964
                    page 28, Feb 5, 1964
                    II, page 1, Jan 10, 1965
                    II, page 8, Aug 8, 1965
                    page 17, Aug 10, 1965
                    page 43, Dec 3, 1965
                    II, page 7, Dec 12, 1965
   New Yorker 39:72, Jan 25, 1964
   Newsweek 63:59, Jan 27, 1964
   Saturday Review 47:22, Feb 8, 1964
   Time 83:44, Jan 24, 1964

Here's Love (334 performances)
book: Meredith Willson, based on Valentine
                     Davies and George Seaton's screen
                     play Miracle on 34th Street
music: Meredith Willson
lyrics: Meredith Willson
staging: Stuart Ostrow
sets: William and Jean Eckart
costumes: Alvin Colt
choreography: Michael Kidd
opened: October 3, 1963
   America 109:642-3, Nov 16, 1963
   New York Theatre Critics' Reviews 1963:258+
   New York Times page 24, Aug 6, 1963
                   page 28, Sep 20, 1963
                   VI, page 51, Sep 22, 1963
                   II, page 3, Sep 29, 1963
                   page 28, Oct 4, 1963
                   page 28, Jul 2, 1964
   Newsweek 62:72, Oct 14, 1963
   Saturday Review 46:18, Nov 2, 1963

Theatre Arts 48:11, Jan 1964
Time 82:72, Oct 11, 1963

High Spirits (375 performances)
book: Hugh Martin and Timothy Gray, based
                 on Noel Coward's play Blithe Spirit
music: Hugh Martin
lyrics: Timothy Gray
staging: Noel Coward
sets: Robert Fletcher
costumes: Robert Fletcher and Valentina Rasch
choreography: Danny Daniels
opened: April 7, 1964
    America 111:114, Aug 1, 1964
    Life 56:9, May 1, 1964
        56:125-7, May 15, 1964
    Look 28:87-91, Mar 10, 1964
    National Review 16:546-7, Jun 30, 1964
    New York Theatre Critics' Reviews 1964:292+
    New York Times page 34, Apr 8, 1964
                 page 46, Nov 4, 1964
    New Yorker 40:108, Apr 18, 1964
    Time 83:65, Apr 17, 1964

110 in the Shade (330 performances)
book: N. Richard Nash, based on his play
                 The Rainmaker
music: Harvey Schmidt
lyrics: Tom Jones
staging: Joseph Anthony,
sets: Oliver Smith
costumes: Motley
choreography: Agnes deMille
opened: October 24, 1963
    America 109:644, Nov 16, 1963
    New York Theatre Critics' Reviews 1963:218+
    New York Times page 33, Sep 12, 1963
                 page 37, Oct 25, 1963
    New Yorker 39:93, Nov 2, 1963
    Newsweek 62:63, Nov 4, 1963
    Saturday Review 46:32, Nov 9, 1963
    Theatre Arts 48:68, Jan 1964
    Time 82:74, Nov 1, 1963

Jennie (82 performances)
book: Arnold Schulman, suggested by
               Marguerite Courtney's biography
               Laurette
music: Arthur Schwartz
lyrics: Howard Dietz
staging: Vincent J. Donehue
sets: George Jenkins
costumes: Irene Sharaff
choreography: Matt Mattox
opened: October 17, 1963
   America 109:644, Nov 16, 1963
   New York Theatre Critics' Reviews 1963:234+
   New York Times II, page 1, Oct 13, 1963
                 page 35, Oct 18, 1963
                 page 21, Dec 20, 1963
   New Yorker 39:113, Oct 26, 1963
   Newsweek 62:91, Oct 28, 1963
   Saturday Review 46:18, Nov 2, 1963
   Theatre Arts 48:67, Jan 1964
   Time 82:75, Oct 25, 1963

Rugantino (28 performances)
book: Pietro Garinei and Sandro Giovannini,
               with Festa Campanile and Franciosa;
               English version by Alfred Drake
music: Armando Trovaioli
lyrics: Pietro Garinei and Sandro Giovannini;
               English version by Edward Eager
staging: Pietro Garinei and Sandro Giovannini
sets: Giulio Coltellacci
costumes: Giulio Coltellacci
choreography: Dánia Krupska
opened: February 6, 1964
   Nation 198:204, Feb 24, 1964
   New York Theatre Critics' Reviews 1964:362+
   New York Times page 25, Jan 17, 1964
                 II, page 1, Feb 2, 1964
                 page 24, Feb 20, 1964
   New Yorker 39:113, Feb 15, 1964
   Newsweek 63:90-1, Feb 17, 1964
   Time 83:69, Feb 14, 1964

The Student Gypsy or The Prince of Liederkranz
(16 performances)
book: Rick Besoyan
music: Rick Besoyan
lyrics: Rick Besoyan
staging: Rick Besoyan
sets: Raoul Pene du Bois
costumes: Raoul Pene du Bois
choreography: Ray Harrison
opened: September 30, 1963
    New York Theatre Critics' Reviews 1963:266+
    New York Times page 34, Oct 1, 1963
                   page 51, Oct 10, 1963
    Newsweek 62:77, Oct 14, 1963
    Theatre Arts 47:13, Dec 1963

Tambourines to Glory (24 performances)
book: Langston Hughes, adapted from his
                   novel
music: Jobe Huntley
lyrics: Langston Hughes
staging: Nikos Psacharapoulos
sets: John Conklin
costumes: John Conklin
opened: November 2, 1963
    New York Theatre Critics' Reviews 1963:207+
    New York Times page 47, Nov 4, 1963
                   page 46, Nov 12, 1963
                   page 28, Nov 15, 1963
                   page 43, Nov 22, 1963

What Makes Sammy Run? (540 performances)
book: Budd and Stuart Schulberg, based on
                   the novel by Budd Schulberg
music: Ervin Drake
lyrics: Ervin Drake
staging: Abe Burrows
sets: Herbert Senn and Helene Pons
costumes: Noel Taylor
choreography: Matt Mattox
opened: February 27, 1964
    America 110:465, Mar 28, 1964
    Life 57:30, Sep 25, 1964

New York Theatre Critics' Reviews 1964:328+
New York Times II, page 3, Feb 9, 1964
                        page 19, Feb 28, 1964
Saturday Review 47:34, Apr 11, 1964
Time 83:50, Mar 6, 1964

Season of 1964-1965

Baker Street (311 performances)
book: Jerome Coopersmith, adapted from
                    Sir Arthur Conan Doyle's stories
music: Marion Grudeff and Raymond Jessel
lyrics: Marion Grudeff and Raymond Jessel
staging: Harold Prince
sets: Oliver Smith
costumes: Motley
choreography: Lee Becker Theodore
opened: February 16, 1965
    America 112:589, Apr 17, 1965
    Commonweal 82:21-2, Mar 26, 1965
    Dance Magazine 39:18-19, Apr 1965
    Life 58:133-4, Apr 2, 1965
    National Review 17:561, Jun 29, 1965
    New York Theatre Critics' Reviews 1965:374+
    New York Times page 36, Feb 17, 1965
                        II, page 1, Feb 28, 1965
    New Yorker 41:94+, Feb 27, 1965
    Newsweek 65:84, Mar 1, 1965
    Saturday Review 48:22, Mar 6, 1965
    Time 85:78, Feb 26, 1965
    Vogue 145:100, Apr 1, 1965

Bajour (232 performances)
book: Ernest Kinoy, based on Joseph
                    Mitchell's New Yorker stories
music: Walter Marks
lyrics: Ernest Kinoy
staging: Lawrence Kasha
sets: Oliver Smith
costumes: Freddy Wittop
choreography: Peter Gennaro and Wally Seibert
opened: November 23, 1964
    America 112:25, Jan 2, 1965

271

Commonweal 81:422-3, Dec 18, 1964
Dance Magazine 39:19-20, Jan 1965
New York Theatre Critics' Reviews 1964:132+
New York Times page 42, Nov 24, 1964
New Yorker 40:88, Dec 5, 1964
Newsweek 64:94, Dec 7, 1964
Time 84:88, Dec 4, 1964

Ben Franklin in Paris (215 performances)
book: Sidney Michaels
music: Mark Sandrich, Jr.
lyrics: Sidney Michaels
staging: Michael Kidd
sets: Oliver Smith
costumes: Motley
choreography: Michael Kidd
opened: October 27, 1964
   America 111:758, Dec 5, 1964
   Commonweal 81:423, Dec 18, 1964
   Dance Magazine 38:16, Dec 1964
   New York Theatre Critics' Reviews 1964:181+
   New York Times page 52, Oct 28, 1964
   Newsweek 64:92, Nov 9, 1964
   Saturday Review 47:53, Nov 14, 1964
   Senior Scholastic 86:21, Mar 4, 1965
   Time 84:52, Nov 6, 1964

Cambridge Circus (23 performances)
sketches: Tim Brooke-Taylor, Graham Chapman,
               John Cleese, David Hatch, Jo Kendall,
               Jonathan Lynn, Bill Oddie, and others.
music: Bill Oddie, Hugh MacDonald, David
               Palmer
staging: Humphrey Barclay
sets: Stephen Mullin
costumes: Judy Birdwood
opened: October 6, 1964
   Dance Magazine 38:16-17, Dec 1964
   Nation 199:286, Oct 26, 1964
   New York Theatre Critics' Reviews 1964:201+
   New York Times page 53, Oct 7, 1964
                page 44, Oct 27, 1964
   Time 84:77, Oct 16, 1964

Do I Hear A Waltz? (220 performances)
book: Arthur Laurents, based on his play
                The Time of the Cuckoo
music: Richard Rodgers
lyrics: Stephen Sondheim
staging: John Dexter
sets: Beni Montresor
costumes: Beni Montresor
choreography: Herbert Ross
opened: March 18, 1965
    America 112:590-1, Apr 17, 1965
    Commonweal 82:85-6, Apr 9, 1965
    Dance Magazine 39:28-9, May 1965
    New York Theatre Critics' Reviews 1965:357+
    New York Times page 29, Nov 6, 1964
                   page 40, Feb 16, 1965
                   page 28, Mar 19, 1965
                   II, page 1, Mar 28, 1965
    New Yorker 41:144, Mar 27, 1965
    Newsweek 65:82, Mar 29, 1965
    Saturday Review 48:36, Apr 3, 1965
    Time 85:60, Mar 26, 1965

Fiddler On the Roof (702 performances*)
book: Joseph Stein, based on the stories of
                Sholom Aleichem
music: Jerry Bock
lyrics: Sheldon Harnick
staging: Jerome Robbins
sets: Boris Aronson
costumes: Patricia Zipprodt
choreography: Jerome Robbins
opened: September 22, 1964
    America 112:25, Jan 2, 1965
    Commentary 38:73-5, Nov 1964
                39:12+, Apr 1965
    Commonweal 81:100, Oct 16, 1964
    Dance Magazine 38:24-5+, Nov 1964
    Life 57:104-5+, Dec 4, 1964
    Nation 199:229-30, Oct 12, 1964
    New Republic 151:31+, Oct 17, 1964
    New York Theatre Critics' Reviews 1964:214+
    New York Times page 10, Aug 8, 1964

273

                    page 56, Sep 23, 1964
                    page 47, Sep 24, 1964
                    II, page 1, Oct 4, 1964
                    page 36, Oct 6, 1964
                    page 14, Jan 23, 1965
                    page 40, Jun 9, 1965
                    II, page 2, Aug 15, 1965
New Yorker 40:96, Oct 3, 1964
Newsweek 64:106, Oct 5, 1964
Saturday Review 47:33, Oct 10, 1964
Time 84:82, Oct 2, 1964
Vogue 144:66, Nov 1, 1964

Flora, the Red Menace (87 performances)
book: George Abbott and Robert Russell,
                   based on Lester Atwell's Love Is
                   Just Around the Corner
music: John Kander
lyrics: Fred Ebb
staging: George Abbott
sets: William and Jean Eckart
costumes: Donald Brooks
choreography: Lee Theodore
opened: May 11, 1965
    America 113:121-2, Jul 31, 1965
    Dance Magazine 39:23, Jul 1965
    National Review 17:561-2, Jun 29, 1965
    New York Theatre Critics' Reviews 1965:330+
    New York Times page 31, Mar 2, 1965
                  page 41, May 12, 1965
    New Yorker 41:114, May 22, 1965
    Newsweek 65:99, May 24, 1965
    Saturday Review 48:50, May 8, 1965
    Time 85:69, May 21, 1965
    Vogue 146:38, Jul 1965

Folies Bergère (191 performances)
book: Paul Derval
music: Henri Betti, additional music by
                   Phillippe Gerard
staging: Michel Gyarmathy
sets: Michel Gyarmathy
costumes: Michel Gyarmathy

274

choreography: George Reich
opened: June 2, 1964
   New York Theatre Critics' Reviews 1964:242+
   New York Times page 52, May 13, 1964
                   II, page 1, May 31, 1964
                   page 36, Jun 3, 1964
                   II, page 1, Jun 21, 1964
                   page 53, Sep 17, 1964
                   page 18, Sep 19, 1964

Golden Boy (568 performances)
book: Clifford Odets and William Gibson,
                   based on Odets' play
music: Charles Strouse
lyrics: Lee Adams
staging: Arthur Penn
sets,   Tony Walton
costumes: Tony Walton
choreography: Donald McKayle, Jaime Rogers
opened: October 20, 1964
   America 111:639, Nov 14, 1964
   Commonweal 81:287-9, Nov 20, 1964
   Dance Magazine 38:16, Dec 1964
   Life 57:84A-85+, Nov 13, 1964
   Nation 199:340-1, Nov 9, 1964
   New York Theatre Critics' Reviews 1964:185+
   New York Times II, page 3, Oct 18, 1964
                   page 56, Oct 21, 1964
                   II, page 1, Nov 1, 1964
   Newsweek 64:94-5, Nov 2, 1964
   New Yorker 40:129, Oct 31, 1964
   Saturday Review 47:29, Nov 7, 1964
   Time 84:79, Oct 30, 1964

Half a Sixpence (458 performances*)
book: Beverly Cross, based on H. G. Wells's
                   Kipps
music: David Heneker
lyrics: David Heneker
staging: Gene Saks
sets: Loudon Sainthill
costumes: Loudon Sainthill
choreography: Onna White and Tom Panko

opened: April 25, 1965
    America 113:63, Jul 10, 1965
    Commonweal 82:383-4, Jun 11, 1965
    Dance Magazine 39:22-3, Jul 1965
    New York Theatre Critics' Reviews 1965:346+
    New York Times page 38, Apr 26, 1965
                    II, page 12, Aug 29, 1965
    New Yorker 41:120, May 8, 1965
    Newsweek 65:100, May 10, 1965
    Saturday Review 48:24, May 15, 1965
    Time 85:88, May 7, 1965

I Had A Ball (199 performances)
book: Jerome Chodorov
music: Jack Lawrence and Stan Freeman
lyrics: Jack Lawrence and Stan Freeman
staging: Lloyd Richards
sets: Will Steven Armstrong
costumes: Ann Roth
choreography: Onna White and Tom Panko
opened: December 15, 1964
    America 112:335-6, Mar 6, 1965
    New York Theatre Critics' Reviews 1964:107+
    New York Times page 50, Dec 16, 1964
    New Yorker 40:50, Dec 26, 1964
    Newsweek 64:57, Dec 28, 1964
    Saturday Review 48:32, Jan 2, 1965
    Time 84:62, Dec 25, 1964

Kelly (1 performance)
book: Eddie Lawrence
music: Moose Charlap
lyrics: Eddie Lawrence
staging: Herbert Ross
sets: Oliver Smith
costumes: Freddy Wittop
choreography: Herbert Ross
opened: February 6, 1965
    New York Theatre Critics' Reviews 1965:382+
    New York Times page 28, Feb 8, 1965
                    page 42, Feb 9, 1965
    New Yorker 40:76, Feb 13, 1965
    Saturday Evening Post 238:32-4+, Apr 24, 1965

Oh What A Lovely War (125 performances)

book:	The Theatre Workshop, Charles Chilton, and members of the cast
music:	The Theatre Workshop, Charles Chilton, and members of the cast
lyrics:	The Theatre Workshop, Charles Chilton, and members of the cast
staging:	Joan Littlewood
sets:	John Bury
costumes:	Una Collins
choreography:	Bob Stevenson
opened:	September 30, 1964

America 111:497-8, Oct 24, 1964
Catholic World 200:131-2, Nov 1964
Commonweal 81:134, Oct 23, 1964
Dance Magazine 38:56-7, Nov 1964
Esquire 60:34+, Dec 1963
Nation 196:450+, May 25, 1963
      199:256, Oct 19, 1964
New Republic 151:26, Oct 24, 1964
New York Theatre Critics' Reviews 1964:209+
New Yorker 30:76 7, Jun 20, 1963
      39:98, Sep 7, 1963
      40:95, Oct 10, 1964
Newsweek 64:104, Oct 12, 1964
Saturday Review 47:29, Oct 17, 1964
Theatre Arts 47:31-2+, Jun 1963
Time 84:92, Oct 9, 1964
Vogue 144:64, Nov 15, 1964

The Roar of the Greasepaint - The Smell of the Crowd (231 performances)

book:	Leslie Bricusse and Anthony Newley
music:	Leslie Bricusse and Anthony Newley
lyrics:	Leslie Bricusse and Anthony Newley
staging:	Anthony Newley
sets:	Sean Kenny
costumes:	Freddy Wittop
choreography:	Gillian Lynne
opened:	May 16, 1965

America 112:867-8, Jun 12, 1965

Catholic World 201:151-2, May 1965
Dance Magazine 39:22-3, Jul 1965
New York Theatre Critics' Reviews 1965:326+
New York Times page 46, May 17, 1965
New Yorker 41:56, May 29, 1965
Newsweek 65:76, May 31, 1965
Reporter 32:45-6, Apr 8, 1965
Saturday Review 48:38, Jun 5, 1965
Time 85:83, May 28, 1965

Something More! (15 performances)
book: Nate Monaster, based on Gerald
                 Green's Portofino P.T.A.
music: Sammy Fain
lyrics: Marilyn and Alan Bergman
staging: Jule Styne
sets: Robert Randolph
costumes: Alvin Colt
choreography: Bob Herget
opened: November 10, 1964
    Dance Magazine 39:18-19, Jan 1965
    New York Theatre Critics' Reviews 1964:159+
    New York Times II, page 3, Oct 4, 1964
                    page 36, Nov 11, 1964
                    page 52, Nov 18, 1964
    Time 84:81, Nov 20, 1964

*Denotes play still running.   Performances are
those through May 31, 1966.

Long Run Musicals*

Performances	Show	Season
2,717	My Fair Lady	1955-1956
2,248	Oklahoma	1942-1943
1,925	South Pacific	1948-1949
1,443	The Sound of Music	1959-1960
1,417	How to Succeed in Business Without Really Trying	1961-1962
1,404	Hellzapoppin	1938-1939
1,375	The Music Man	1957-1958
1,246	The King and I	1950-1951
1,200	Guys and Dolls	1950-1951
1,147	Annie Get Your Gun	1945-1946
1,108	Pins and Needles	1937-1938
1,063	The Pajama Game	1953-1954
1,070	Kiss Me, Kate	1948-1949
1,019	Damn Yankees	1954-1955
989	Hello Dolly!*	1963-1964
964	A Funny Thing Happened on the Way to the Forum	1961-1962
924	Bells Are Ringing	1956-1957
892	Can-Can	1952-1953
890	Carousel	1944-1945
888	Fanny	1954-1955
885	Funny Girl*	1963-1964
882	Follow the Girls	1943-1944
873	Camelot	1960-1961
835	La Plume De Ma Tante	1958-1959
795	Fiorello!	1959-1960
792	Where's Charley?	1948-1949
774	Oliver!	1962-1963
742	Sons O' Fun	1941-1942
740	Gentlemen Prefer Blondes	1949-1950
734	Call Me Mister	1945-1946

279

732	West Side Story	1957-1958
727	High Button Shoes	1947-1948
725	Finian's Rainbow	1946-1947
719	Carnival!	1960-1961
702	Fiddler On the Roof*	1964-1965
702	Gypsy	1958-1959
693	Li'l Abner	1956-1957
676	The Most Happy Fella	1955-1956
654	Bloomer Girl	1944-1945
644	Call Me Madam	1950-1951
609	Star and Garter	1942-1943
607	Bye Bye Birdie	1959-1960
600	Flower Drum Song	1958-1959
598	Wish You Were Here	1952-1953
592	Blossom Time	1921-1922
583	Kismet	1953-1954
581	Brigadoon	1946-1947
580	No Strings	1961-1962
572	Show Boat	1927-1928
570	Sally	1920-1921
568	Golden Boy	1964-1965
567	One Touch of Venus	1943-1944
559	Wonderful Town	1952-1953
555	Jamaica	1957-1958
555	Stop the World--I Want to Get Off	1962-1963
553	Ziegfeld Follies (1943)	1942-1943
547	Let's Face It	1941-1942
543	Milk and Honey	1961-1962
540	What Makes Sammy Run?	1963-1964
532	The Unsinkable Molly Brown	1960-1961
531	The Red Mill	1945-1946
524	Irma La Douce	1960-1961
517	Sunny	1925-1926
509	The New Moon	1928-1929
504	Up in Central Park	1944-1945
503	Carmen Jones	1943-1944
501	Panama Hattie	1940-1941
485	The Boy Friend	1954-1955
481	Mexican Hayride	1943-1944
478	Silk Stockings·	1954-1955
477	Wildflower	1922-1923

472	Destry Rides Again	1958-1959
463	On the Town	1944-1945
461	Plain and Fancy	1954-1955
460	Lend An Ear	1948-1949
460	Once Upon A Mattress	1958-1959
458	Half a Sixpence*	1964-1965
452	Redhead	1958-1959
448	Take Me Along	1959-1960
444	Louisiana Purchase	1939-1940
441	Of Thee I Sing	1931-1932
440	Music Box Revue (1921)	1921-1922
431	New Girl in Town	1956-1957
429	Make Mine Manhattan	1947-1948
427	By Jupiter	1941-1942
424	George White's Scandals (1926)	1925-1926
422	Something for the Boys	1942-1943
420	Anything Goes	1934-1935
420	As the Girls Go	1948-1949
418	A Connecticut Yankee	1927-1928
413	Hold Everything	1928-1929
412	Happy Hunting	1956-1957
409	The Girl Friend	1925-1926
408	DuBarry Was A Lady	1939-1940
403	Follow Thru	1928-1929
400	As Thousands Cheer	1933-1934
400	Do Re Mi	1960-1961
400	Earl Carroll's Sketch Book (1929)	1929-1930
399	Inside U.S.A.	1947-1948
395	The Cat and the Fiddle	1931-1932
383	Mr. Wonderful	1955-1956
382	Early to Bed	1943-1944
379	Whoopee	1928-1929
377	The Cocoanuts	1925-1926
375	High Spirits	1963-1964
374	Pal Joey	1940-1941
365	New Faces of 1952	1951-1952
358	Me and Juliet	1952-1953
357	Flying High	1929-1930
352	Hit the Deck	1926-1927
350	Top Banana	1951-1952
342	Music in the Air	1932-1933

338	I Married An Angel	1937-1938
335	Rosalie	1927-1928
334	Here's Love	1963-1964
333	Peggy-Ann	1926-1927
332	Say Darling	1957-1958
330	110 in the Shade	1963-1964
330	Lady Be Good	1924-1925
327	Three to Make Ready	1945-1946
326	Best Foot Forward	1941-1942
321	The Little Show (1929)	1928-1929
321	No! No! Nanette!	1925-1926
319	Louie the 14th	1924-1925
315	Allegro	1947-1948
315	On Your Toes	1935-1936
312	My Maryland	1927-1928
311	Baker Street	1964-1965
311	Rose-Marie	1924-1925
308	Miss Liberty	1949-1950
307	Leave It to Me	1938-1939
301	She Loves Me	1962-1963
300	Angel in the Wings	1947-1948
300	I Can Get It For You Wholesale	1961-1962
298	The Great Waltz	1934-1935
295	Roberta	1933-1934
295	Sons O'Guns	1929-1930
290	I'd Rather Be Right	1937-1938
289	Babes in Arms	1936-1937
289	Paint Your Wagon	1951-1952
286	Dearest Enemy	1925-1926
281	Two On the Aisle	1951-1952
278	Earl Carroll's Vanities (1931)	1931-1932
278	Michael Todd's Peep Show	1950-1951
274	Streets of Paris	1939-1940
273	Lost in the Stars	1949-1950
273	Music Box Revue (1922)	1922-1923
273	Music Box Revue (1923)	1923-1924
272	Girl Crazy	1930-1931
272	Three's A Crowd	1930-1931
271	Fade Out--Fade In	1963-1964
270	By the Beautiful Sea	1953-1954

219	Hot Chocolates	1929-1930
216	Tenderloin	1960-1961
215	Ben Franklin in Paris	1964-1965
215	Earl Carroll's Vanities (1930)	1930-1931
213	May Wine	1935-1936
211	Garrick Gaieties (1925)	1924-1925
210	Three Cheers	1928-1929
208	Yokel Boy	1939-1940
207	Earl Carroll Sketch Book (1935)	1934-1935
207	Murder at the Vanities	1933-1934
207	Tickle Me	1920-1921
206	Criss Cross	1926-1927
205	Subways Are for Sleeping	1961-1962
204	The Fireman's Flame	1937-1938
203	Vanities (1928)	1928-1929
202	George White's Scandals (1931)	1931-1932
200	Horray for What!	1937-1938

*Denotes show still running. Performances given are those through May 31, 1966.

284

New York Drama Critics' Circle Award Musicals

First award for "Best Musical Production" granted in 1945-1946.

1945-1946	Carousel
1946-1947	Brigadoon
1947-1948	no award
1948-1949	South Pacific
1949-1950	The Consul
1950-1951	Guys and Dolls
1951-1952	Pal Joey
1952-1953	Wonderful Town
1953-1954	The Golden Apple
1954-1955	The Saint of Bleecker Street
1955-1956	My Fair Lady
1956-1957	The Most Happy Fella
1957-1958	The Music Man
1958-1959	La Plume de Ma Tante
1959-1960	Fiorello!
1960-1961	Carnival
1961-1962	How to Succeed in Business Without Really Trying
1962-1963	no award
1963-1964	Hello Dolly!
1964-1965	Fiddler on the Roof

Pulitzer Prize Musicals

1931-1932	Of Thee I Sing
1949-1950	South Pacific
1959=1960	Fiorello!
1961-1962	How to Succeed in Business Without Really Trying

Index of Authors, Composers, Lyricists

Farjeon, Herbert 201, 238
Farkas, Karl 150
Faulkner, Virginia 114
Fay, Frank 73
Ferrer, José 227
Fetter, Ted 59, 91, 93, 95
Feuer, Cy 236
Fields, Dorothy 38, 48, 59, 66, 106, 123, 128, 134, 143, 144, 173, 189, 199, 235
Fields, Herbert 25, 26, 28, 29, 30, 31, 38, 45, 53, 57, 72, 107, 119, 123, 128, 134, 143, 144, 173, 199, 235
Fields, Joseph 175, 198, 200, 231
Fields, Lew 12, 35, 59
Fields, W. C. 13, 17
Fine, Sylvia 111
Finletter, Gretchen Damrosch 16
Flick, Pat C. 115
Flicker, Theodore J. 234
Fogarty, Alexander 45, 85
Fomeen, Basil 46
Ford, Carey 75
Ford, Hugh 16
Ford, Joan 232
Forrest, George 168, 202, 254
Foster, Ray 177
Foster, Stephen 106
Francis, Arthur (see Gershwin, Ira)
Frank, Melvin 220
Franklin, Eva 108
Fray, Jacques 60
Freedman, David 27, 58, 78, 81, 90, 92, 93, 94
Freeman, Bud 236
Freeman, Stan 276
Freitag, Dorthea 226
Friedberg, William 193, 212
Friedlander, William B. 129, 130
Friedman, Charles 98, 105, 196
Friend, Cliff 47
Friml, Rudolf 11, 14, 16, 21, 24, 29, 30, 34, 56, 81
Fuller, Dean 221, 224, 234

Gabrielson, Frank 80, 81

Gannon, Kim 191
Garlock, Tommy 248
Gaskill, Clarence 48
Gaynor, Charles 167, 246
Gelbart, Larry 244, 252
Geller, Bruce 221
Genovese, Gen 193
Gensler, Lewis 18, 43, 55, 68
Gerard, Phillippe 274
Gerber, Alex 12, 24
Gershe, Leonard 173, 230
Gershwin, Arthur 139
Gershwin, George 15, 17, 18, 19, 21, 23, 25, 27,
    29, 30, 32, 42, 49, 50, 55, 65, 72, 76, 87, 90,
    94, 117, 138, 157
Gershwin, Ira 13, 23, 25, 27, 29, 30, 32, 42, 46,
    49, 51, 55, 65, 66, 72, 76, 81, 87, 90, 94, 117,
    138, 157
Gibson, William 275
Gilbert and Sullivan 103
Gilbert, Billy 193
Gilbert, Edwin 85
Gilbert, Jean 65
Gilbert, John 50
Gilbert, Willie 253, 259
Gimbel, Norman 236, 244
Glazer, Benjamin F. 137
Glickman, Will 167, 173, 209, 214, 224
Goetz, Ray 17, 19, 40
Goldberg, Rube 48
Golden, Ernie 44
Golden, Ray 118, 130, 173, 212
Goldman, Harold 46
Goldman, James 251
Goldman, Robert 231
Goldman, William 251
Goldsmith, Lee 239, 248
Goode, Herbert 66
Goodman, Alfred 17
Goodman, Lee 175
Gordon, Irving 128
Gordon, Mack 62, 65, 68, 72
Gorney, Jay 45, 66, 68, 118, 165, 181

Hanley, James 29, 48, 83
Harbach, Otto 11, 13, 14, 19, 24, 26, 27, 28, 29,
30, 31, 37, 57, 61, 77, 91
Harburg, E. Y. 45, 46, 54, 60, 66, 68, 74, 78, 81,
96, 116, 136, 155, 183, 225, 245
Harnick, Sheldon 190, 213, 224, 227, 238, 247, 248,
262, 273
Harris, Barbara 251
Harris, Howard 166
Hart, Lorenz 12, 22, 25, 26, 27, 29, 30, 31, 32, 35,
42, 47, 50, 53, 84, 86, 90, 92, 96, 97, 100, 109,
112, 118, 121, 122
Hart, Moss 48, 62, 74, 80, 84, 92, 97, 117, 142,
161
Hartman, Grace 159
Hartman, Paul 159
Harvey, Roslyn 125
Hatch, David 272
Hauff, Hugo 108
Hayes, Alfred 120
Hazzard, Jack 66
Heagney, William 67
Hecht, Ben 84, 142, 194
Hecht, Harold 105
Hecht, Marie 51
Helburn, Theresa 96
Heller, Barbara 248
Hellinger, Mark 64, 68
Hellman, Lillian 219
Henderson, Charles 177
Henderson, Ray 26, 36, 38, 46, 63, 64, 72, 82, 83,
130
Heneker, David 246, 275
Henning, Magnus 91
Henry, Grace 59
Herbert, Victor 11, 12, 13, 16, 18, 21, 22, 151
Herendeen, Fred 57, 74, 89, 91
Herman, Jerry 239, 256, 266
Hermann, Harry 180
Herold, Don 116
Herrick, Landon 46
Herzig, Sig 59, 66, 136
Hewett, Christopher 238

303

Reisenfeld, Hugo 68
Revel, Harry 62, 65, 68, 72, 145
Revil, Rudi 116
Rice, Andy 17
Rice, Edmund 180
Rice, Elmer 157
Rich, Max 80
Rickman, Carol 54
Roberts, Alan 128, 164
Roberts, Ben 133, 134
Robin, Leo 28, 29, 38, 73, 175, 200
Robinson, A. 66
Robinson, Bertrand 60
Robinson, Earl 125
Robison, Willard 46, 73
Roche, Jack 180
Rodgers, Bob 237, 250
Rodgers, Mary 234, 239, 259
Rodgers, Richard 12, 22, 25, 26, 27, 29, 30, 31,
    32, 35, 42, 47, 50, 53, 84, 86, 90, 93, 96, 97,
    100, 109, 112, 118, 121, 122, 126, 158, 170, 185,
    196, 217, 231, 241, 257, 273
Rogers, David 224, 248, 256
Rogers, Howard Emmett 56
Rollo, Walter 19
Romberg, Sigmund 12, 13, 14, 15, 17, 18, 19, 21, 22,
    23, 24, 28, 31, 32, 40, 57, 61, 70, 85, 91, 124,
    143, 169, 200
Rome, Harold J. 98, 105, 111, 125, 128, 130, 147,
    173, 182, 187, 197, 206, 230, 254
Romilli, G. 36
Romoff, Colin 224
Ronell, Ann 125
Roos, William 165, 187, 189
Root, Lynn 115
Rose, Billy 54, 58, 142
Rose, Vincent 45
Rose, William 47
Rosen, Arme 224
Rosenberg, J. B. 125, 126
Rosendahl, Henry 89
Rosener, George 81
Rosoff, Charles 107

307

Violett, Ellen 225
Violinsky 48

Waggoner, George 73
Wainer, Lee 105
Walker, Don 131, 140, 189
Wallach, Ira 208
Waller, Jack 73
Waller, Thomas 48, 133
Wallop, Douglass 205
Walsh, William 73
Walter, Serge 37, 69
Walters, Lou 131
Ward, Edward 73
Warnick, Clay 133, 140, 180
Warren, Harry 54, 64, 223
Washington, Ned 75, 76
Wasserman, Dale 221
Waters, Marianne Brown 98, 99
Wayburn, Ned 39
Weatherly, Tom 84
Webb, Kenneth 60, 70
Webster, Paul Francis 75, 173, 212, 237
Weidman, Jerome 238, 247, 254
Weill, Kurt 103, 117, 135, 138, 157, 168, 177
Weinberg, Charles 67
Weinstock, Jack 253, 259
Weiss, George 214, 231
Welch, Eddie 61
Welles, Orson 145
Wells, Eleanor 124
Wells, John 47
Wells, Robert 211
Wells, William K. 23, 25, 26, 36, 47, 70, 83, 124,
    130, 187, 201
Welty, Eudora 212
Wenrich, Percy 60
Werris, Sam E. 116
Weston, R. P. 73
Whedon, John 180
Whipper, Leigh 67
White, Dan 130
White, E. B. 66

311

White, George 15, 17, 19, 23, 26, 36, 47, 63, 70, 83, 108
White, Les 130
Whiting, Richard 43, 63, 73
Wilbur, Richard 210
Wilk, Max 170
Wilkinson, Dudley 18
Williams, Alexander 66
Willson, Meredith 246, 248, 267
Wilner, Sis 128
Wilson, Al 67
Wilson, Jack 248
Wilson, Sandy 204
Wiman, Dwight Deere 58, 59
Wimperis, Arthur 23
Wodehouse, P. G. 20, 29, 32, 78
Wolf, Tommy 234
Wolfe, Jaques 109
Wolfson, Victor 210
Wood, Cyrus 14, 19, 50, 52
Woodward, Matthew 19
Woolf, Edgar Allen 12
Wright, Robert 168, 202, 254
Wylie, Lauri 201
Wynn, Ed 49, 50, 64, 115

Yellen, Jack 49, 60, 83, 108, 115, 123, 130
Youmans, Vincent 13, 19, 20, 26, 28, 29, 41, 47, 58, 67, 73
Young, Harry 130
Young, Joseph 64, 75
Young, Rida Johnson 22
Young, Victor 75, 76, 188, 210

Zaret, Hy 125
Zelinka, Sidney 166
Zeno, Norman 79
Ziegfeld, Florenz 68
Zwar, Charles 239

Index of Directors, Designers, Choreographers

313

du Bois, Raoul Pene 83, 84, 96, 104, 105, 107, 112, 113, 116, 119, 120, 123, 132, 139, 145, 165, 167, 173, 183, 186, 190, 195, 198, 202, 209, 217, 218, 224, 226, 233, 270
Dunham, Katherine 147
Dunkel, Eugene 91, 95
Du Pont, Paul 125, 130, 135
Duquette, Adrian and Tony 242

Eagle, Oscar 19, 25
Eckart, William and Jean 201, 205, 220, 221, 224, 225, 234, 238, 245, 255, 262, 264, 267, 274
Eckley, Dan 125, 131
Eisele, Lou 134, 140, 149, 160, 169
Elder, Eldon 200, 208, 223
Elson, Charles 235
Errol, Leon 14
Eskow, Jerome 264
Eyck, Ten 91

Fay, Frank 73
Feist, Frances 104, 114
Felix, Seymour 28, 32, 44, 50, 72
Ferrer, José 227, 233
Feuer, Cy 211, 236, 259
Ffolkes, David 154, 165, 169, 172, 184, 191
Field, Ronald 261, 264
Fielding, Marjery 85, 99, 114
Fields, Herbert 22, 26
Fields, Lew 26, 28
Finklehoffe, Fred F. 204
Fischer, Nelle 188
Flatt, Ernest 264
Fletcher, Robert 245, 251, 253, 259, 261, 265, 268
Fletcher, Ron 192
Florell, Walter 150, 154
Florenz, Paul 89
Flicker, Theodore J. 234
Forrest, Sam 35
Fosse, Bob 203, 205, 218, 222, 235, 259
Foster, Allan K. 85
Fox, Frederick 91, 163, 251
Frazee, H. H. 26

Freedman, Gerald 252
French, Bert 13
Friedlander, William B. 48, 65, 130
Friedman, Charles 98, 105, 109, 157, 196

Garinei, Pietro 269
Garnegie, Hattie 117
Gaynor, Charles 246
Gennaro, Peter 210, 229, 238, 248, 260, 271
Gensler, Lewis E. 68
Genus, Karl 227
Gerard, Rolf 246, 263
Giehse, Therese 92
Gilbert, Billy 151
Gilbert, Edward 111, 114, 156, 158, 161, 164
Gillespie, Frank M. 47
Gilmore, W. H. 18, 40
Giovannini, Sandro 269
Glenville, Peter 241, 263
Godfrey, Vaughn 80
Golden, Ray 212
Goldsmith, Eleanor 155, 161, 180
Goldwasser, Lawrence 111
Gordon, Michael 195
Gordon, Robert H. 125, 131, 136, 147, 173
Gosler, Lotte 111
Gould, Dave 37, 55, 58, 105
Graham, H. Gordon 105
Graham, June 195
Graham, Ronny 250
Grant, Mary 135, 150, 151
Green, Morris 55, 73
Greene, H. C. 38
Grona, Van 76, 149
Guthrie, Tyrone 219
Gyarmathy, Michel 274

Haack, Morton 163
Haakon, Paul 135
Hale, Chester 65, 99, 124
Hale, George 47, 51, 55, 57, 72, 92
Hambleton, John 97, 105, 106, 109
Hamilton, Bob 228

321

322

323

Russell, Jim 226

Saddler, Donald 198, 202, 223, 256, 262
Saidy, Fred 183
Sainthill, Loudon 275
Saks, Gene 275
Samrock, Victor 161
Sanford, Robert 91
Santiago, Emile 152
Sapero, Lillian 128
Saron, Alexander 96
Saulpaugh, Edwin 82
Savage, Steele 75
Schaefer, George 224
Schary, Dore 248
Scheck, Max 42, 67, 69
Schenck, Mary Percy 139
Schraps, Ernest 118, 143
Schwab, Buddy 257
Scott, Lee 240
Seabury, William 17
Seibert, Wally 271
Selwyn, Edgar 14
Senn, Herbert 270
Shanks, Alex 235
Sharaff, Irene 84, 86, 93, 97, 100, 108, 111, 114,
    115, 117, 120, 122, 124, 125, 128, 146, 168, 175,
    185, 187, 196, 199, 219, 220, 223, 229, 231, 233,
    244, 266, 269
Shaw, Mary 142
Shelley, Joshua 229
Shelton, James 175
Sherman, Lee 151, 163, 212
Shevelove, Burt 170
Short, Hassard 16, 17, 20, 28, 29, 53, 59, 62, 74,
    77, 80, 84, 94, 99, 117, 120, 128, 132, 134, 142,
    150, 163, 187, 191
Shubert, J. J. 22, 31, 43, 52, 57
Sidney, Carl 84
Sidney, Robert 129, 153, 158, 165, 175
Sillman, Leonard 85, 100, 114, 126, 226, 256
Sills, Paul 251
Silvernail, Clarke 38

Index of Original Works and Authors

333

Index of Titles

338

339

344